Stannary Law

Stannary Law

A HISTORY OF THE MINING LAW OF
CORNWALL AND DEVON

ROBERT R. PENNINGTON, LLD
PROFESSOR OF COMMERCIAL LAW
UNIVERSITY OF BIRMINGHAM

DAVID & CHARLES
NEWTON ABBOT

0 7153 5783 2

SET IN ELEVEN POINT LECTURA TWO POINTS LEADED
AND PRINTED IN GREAT BRITAIN
BY CLARKE DOBLE & BRENDON LIMITED PLYMOUTH
FOR DAVID & CHARLES (HOLDINGS) LIMITED
SOUTH DEVON HOUSE NEWTON ABBOT DEVON

Contents

Preface

THE SYSTEM OF LAW WHICH GOVERNED metalliferous mining in Cornwall and Devon was unique in two ways. In the first place the tin mining and smelting industries were subject to comprehensive regulation by laws different in origin and content from the common law of England, which governed all other industries; these special laws were enforced by specialised local courts, whose jurisdiction was confined at first to tin mining and miners, but was extended in 1836 to metalliferous mining and miners generally. Secondly, the system of law governing tin mining and smelting was universal in that it related not only to operations and transactions necessarily occurring in the industries (such as mining leases and smelting contracts), but also extended to all aspects of the lives of those who were engaged in tin affairs. Three instances of this universality may illustrate the pervasive reach of the law with which this book is concerned.

The tin miners and adventurers had their own Parliament or Convocation in each county, and the Convocations had legislative powers in respect of mining, smelting and dealing in tin which equalled those of the national Parliament at Westminster; newly smelted tin was subject to a special tax called coinage-duty, which in the Middle Ages was counterbalanced by the tinners' total immunity from other forms of taxation; the local mining courts in Cornwall and Devon heard cases in which tin miners were involved, whether relating to mining matters or not, and whether the other party to the litigation was a miner or not. Mining for other metals than tin in Cornwall and Devon was not governed by a similar comprehensive code, but some of the law relating to tin mining rubbed off on other forms of mining, and they, too, were subject in certain respects to peculiar local rules. For example, the interpretation of mining leases by the local mining courts was based on the rules governing tin mining, whether the lease authorised the lessee to work for tin or for other metals as well; again, the special form of company which evolved for carrying on tin mining, the cost book company, was based on principles quite different from English common law, and these principles were applied to all mining partnerships and companies, whether they worked for tin, copper, lead or any other metal.

Because the body of law that governed metalliferous mines and miners in Cornwall and Devon was so individual and comprehensive, it is appropriate to give it a distinctive name, and the name which springs most readily to mind is that by which the special law relating to tin mining was known—stannary law. Hence the title of this book. It is true that the title is not wholly accurate because this book is concerned with the law governing mining for other metals as well as tin, but since the rules relating to other forms of mining were mostly extensions or adaptations of those governing tin mining, none but the purist should object. Today stannary law has to be referred to in the past tense, because the specialised local mining courts of Devon and Cornwall have long ceased to exist, and most of the substantive law of the stannaries has now become obsolete. Nevertheless, except where the Parliament at Westminster has legislated to abolish stannary institutions (as it did in 1838 in respect of the tin coinage duty and in 1896 in respect of the last surviving stannary court), stannary law is still formally a part of the law of England. It is, moreover, one of the oldest parts of the law, for its origins predate the Norman Conquest, possibly even the Anglo-Saxon conquest of Cornwall in the tenth century.

A detailed knowledge of the history of mining and smelting is not necessary for an understanding of this book, and where special points of mining or smelting technique are relevant to an explanation of the law, a short account of them is given. Equally, a knowledge of English law in general on the reader's part is not essential. Where rules of English common or statute law are relevant because stannary law departed from them or added to them, a brief explanation of the underlying law is included. In short, this book is intended for the general reader and not only the mining or legal specialist.

Citations of Acts of Parliament and the reports of cases decided by the national courts at Westminister are given in the standard form familiar to lawyers on the assumption that only persons who already use such materials in other connections will resort to the originals. Enactments of the two Convocations or Parliaments of Tinners are referred to as Convocation Acts, with the county for which the Convocation sat and the year of the enactment added. Thus, the legislation enacted by the Convocation of Cornwall in 1636 is referred to as Convocation Act (Cornwall), 1636, and the number of the section cited follows. All the Convocation enactments (with the exception of those for Devon of 1494 and those for Cornwall of 1588 and 1752) were gathered together by Thomas Pearce in his *Laws and Customs of the Stannaries in the Counties of Cornwall and Devon* published in 1725, and the Cornish enactments from 1624 to 1752 were published in Joseph Tregoning's *The Laws of the Stannaries of Cornwall*, the first edition of which appeared in 1820 and the second in 1824. Copies of these collections are still available in a few public and university libraries. Judgements of the stannary courts are cited in this book by reference to the date of the decision; copies of the petitions and decrees of the court of the Vice-Warden of

Cornwall between 1764 and 1767 and between 1780 and 1834 are contained in bound volumes deposited at the Cornwall County Record Office, Truro, and may be inspected there. From 1833 until the Vice-Warden's court was abolished at the end of 1896, reports of cases before the court appeared regularly in the *Royal Cornwall Gazette*, the only surviving complete series of which is at the Royal Institute of Cornwall Museum, Truro. Such cases are cited in this book by the abbreviation *RCG* and the date of the issue of the *Gazette* in which the report of the case appears.

Writing this book and carrying out the necessary preliminary research has been an enjoyable task extending over several years, and has been made all the easier by the unstinting help I have received from many quarters in Cornwall and elsewhere. In particular my thanks are due to Mr P. J. Hull, MA, the County Archivist of Cornwall, Mr H. L. Douch, BA, the Curator of the Royal Institute of Cornwall Museum, Truro, and to Mr S. Opie, BA, the Librarian of the Duchy of Cornwall Office, London, all of whom directed my attention to valuable records which might otherwise have been overlooked. It is perhaps needless to add that all blemishes in my presentation of the materials I have investigated are exclusively my own.

ROBERT R. PENNINGTON

University of Birmingham
March 1972

CHAPTER I

The Stannary Institutions

THE MINING LAW OF CORNWALL AND DEVON was, and to some extent still is, different from the common law governing mining throughout the rest of England and Wales. It is therefore not surprising that specialised institutions should have been set up to enforce this local mining law, and the existence of these institutions from an early time has undoubtedly influenced the form and development of the local law. All but one of the stannary institutions have now been abolished by legislation, and the legal existence of the one remaining, the Convocation or Parliament of Tinners, is only a tenuous shadow. The Convocation for Cornwall last met in 1752–3, when it enacted the most recent official restatement of stannary law; the Convocation for Devon last enacted legislation in 1600, but it met subsequently to accept proposals for the exercise of the royal right pre-emption of tin, and during the late eighteenth and early nineteenth centuries formal meetings were held though no business was transacted. There is now no possibility of either Convocation being convened again.

The history of the stannary institutions begins with the tin coinage, the tax payable to the King on smelted tin, the incidence and details of which are dealt with in Chapter 4. The coinage duty was probably first imposed in the late eleventh or early twelfth centuries, but by that time there was already in existence a body of customary mining law, and some account must therefore be given, even if it is largely speculative, of the pre-coinage organisation of mining.

No documentary or literary evidence remains of the organisation of mining in Cornwall and Devon during the pre-Roman, Roman, Celtic and Anglo-Saxon periods, and no firm conclusions can be reached from the few archaeological remains that have been discovered. Apart from the Roman period there was in all probability little law, even of a customary character, until a century or so before the Norman Conquest, and the disintegration of the two counties into a multitude of small sub-kingdoms and tribal districts after the end of the Roman occupation would have made the enforcement of any law, other than that of the strong arm, almost impossible. The absence of any clear law after the Roman period may account for the origins of the vague custom of bounding tin streamworks, which is examined in detail in the next chapter. This custom was well established by the time the tin coinage came into being in the late eleventh or early twelfth centuries, but suffered then, as it has ever since, from a lack of precision that suggests it originated at a period when government was primitive.

If there was a hiatus in mining in Cornwall and Devon after the end of the Roman occupation, one would expect that when mining was resumed on a considerable scale in the late eleventh or early twelfth centuries it would be governed by Norman or Anglo-Norman law. There is in fact no mention of an indigenous mining law in any of the collections of customary laws issued by the Norman kings, and the known contents of mining law at the end of the twelfth century would in any case have fitted badly with the Norman law of land tenure. It would not have been inconsistent with Anglo-Saxon land law, although it was different in many important respects from the Anglo-Saxon mining law in operation in other parts of the country, such as the Wirksworth and High Peak districts of Derbyshire. The only direct evidence of Anglo-Saxon influence on mining in Cornwall is the prevalence of mining terms which may be of Anglo-Saxon origin, and even these may be attributable to the influence of German miners who were imported later (1). However, even if this is considered to be evidence at all, it is counterbalanced by the fact that there are far more Cornish mining terms of Celtic origin (2).

The law probably developed therefore from all three sources—Cornish, Anglo-Saxon and Norman. Cornish customary law may have contributed the vague rules as to bounding streamworks, these rules being kept alive from generation to generation by the small amount of mining that may have continued for a domestic market. Anglo-Saxon customs may have added the formal requirements as to setting up corner bounds on streamworks and as to the free status of the miner, a custom which came into collision with Norman feudal concepts in the reign of King John. If this is so, Norman law tolerated and absorbed the existing law instead of giving birth to it, and this absorption was undoubtedly coincidental to the establishment of the coinage system.

THE TIN COINAGE AND THE CHARTERS

The earliest surviving records of the tin coinage show that the coinage duty was collected from 1156 to 1160 by Richard de Tracy (3) and from 1161 to 1165 by Hugh de Ralega (4), both sheriffs of Devon. From 1170 to the end of Henry II's reign the coinage was farmed to persons other than the sheriff, the coinage of Cornwall being farmed separately for the first time in 1177 (5). In 1194, 1196 and 1199 Richard Revel, sheriff of Devon, accounted for the coinage of Devon (other than the additional duty of 1 mark per thousandweight imposed in 1198), and he also accounted for the coinage of Cornwall in 1194 (6). This shows that before the reforms of 1198 the coinage duty was treated like all other public revenues of the Crown, and was collected by the sheriff unless granted to someone else. It is true that the sheriff compounded for the duty he had collected by paying a fixed sum into the Exchequer, and that his payment was said to be in respect of the farm of tin (*firma minarie stagni*) just like the rent paid by a private grantee. But the fact that he accounted in his capacity as sheriff shows that he was acting as the public official charged with the supervision of the stannaries.

The fact that no special administrative arrangements were made for the stannaries before 1198 also meant that litigation in respect of mines must have been brought in the ordinary hundred and shire courts of Cornwall and Devon under their general jurisdiction to try all matters, civil and criminal, not expressly reserved to the King's judges. Similarly, since the distinction between legislation and adjudication was unknown in the twelfth century, the shire courts and the hundred courts undoubtedly declared the extent and content of the mining customs, and when Hubert Walter, the justiciar and chief minister of Richard I, issued a writ convening juries of miners before William de Wrotham at Exeter and Launceston in January 1198 to declare the law and practice relating to the coinage, they undoubtedly sat too as courts. It was from these sessions of twelve jurymen 'who are better informed about the truth of the matter' sitting under a royal official that the Convocations or Parliaments of Tinners originated.

The reforms initiated by Hubert Walter's writ of 1198 went farther than adding 1 mark to the existing coinage duty of 30d per thousandweight in Devon and 60d per thousandweight in Cornwall. De Wrotham, who had already been appointed in November 1197 to act in all matters concerning the King in the stannaries, was appointed to be the first chief warden of the stannaries, and the writ also confirmed the 'just and ancient customs and liberties' of miners, smelters and merchants of tin, and prohibited the sale of uncoined tin and the transport of any tin outside Devon and Cornwall without the licence of the chief warden. In effect the writ of 1198 and de Wrotham's action upon it set up the administrative machinery of the stannaries. Three years later a controversial charter of King John (7) granted free status to tin miners in Devon and Cornwall, and made them subject only to the jurisdiction of the chief warden. While they were working for tin, miners were freed from all pleas of villeinage, which meant that they could not be claimed by the lords of the manors to which they belonged. This was an open invitation to villeins to obtain their freedom by absconding and becoming miners. The reason given for this emancipation by the charter was that the working of tin benefited the king by way of the coinage duty, to which was added the provocatively vague *quia stannariae sunt nostra dominica* (because the stannaries are our demesne). This may have been either an innocuous statement of the king's obvious financial interest in mining, or an assertion of proprietary rights over land where tin was mined, which would be accompanied, under feudal law, by a corresponding territorial jurisdiction. This seems to have been in the king's mind, for a later part of the charter went on to confer power on the chief warden and his stewards (*ballivi*) to do justice and right in respect of tinners (*ad eos justificandos et ad rectum producendos*), to imprison them in the stannary gaol and to seize the chattels of those of them who were outlawed.

During the course of the thirteenth century stewards' courts with a common law jurisdiction over tin miners and tin affairs were established in the eight mining districts of Cornwall and Devon. Each such district was itself known as a stannary, and the jurisdiction of the steward was confined to it, though the boundaries between the stannaries were never defined, probably because each was separated from the others by a band of country which was not tin-bearing. From west to east, the four stannaries of Cornwall were Penwith and Kerrier (corresponding to the Land's End and Lizard peninsulas and the area between Hayle, Redruth and Helston), Tywarnhaile (stretching from Truro to Penryn in the east to St Agnes in the west), Blackmore (corresponding to the Hensbarrow granite boss) and Foweymore (covering Bodmin Moor). The four stannaries of Devon were centred on Chagford, Ashburton, Tavistock and Plympton, but the parts of Dartmoor assigned to them respectively were never satisfactorily defined.

The next important event of which there is documentary evidence was the grant by Edward I of the two great Charters of 1305, which defined the privileges of the miners of Cornwall and Devon respectively in the same terms (8). These charters were frequently confirmed by succeeding monarchs, and both charters were approved by Parliament in 1305 and 1343 (9), but it would not appear that this gave them the force and effect of Acts of Parliament.

Each of the two Charters of 1305 begins by reciting that it was granted 'for the emendation of the stannaries and for the tranquility and benefit of our tinners of the same', and each goes on to grant immunity from the jurisdiction of all manorial and royal courts to 'all the said tinners working in the stannaries which are our demesne so long as they are working in the said stannaries'. Instead they are subjected to the jurisdiction of the warden of the stannaries 'for all pleas and suits arising within the said stannaries except pleas of land, life and limb'. Defining the extent of this immunity and special jurisdiction was to provide lawyers with work for centuries to come. At the time the Charters were granted the stewards' courts did not seem to be ambitious to extend their jurisdiction, and the tinners' complaint was that the special mining jurisdiction was encroached upon by the feudal courts and the shire and hundred courts (10). But before long the inhabitants of Devon were complaining to Parliament that 'the said tinners and the ministers of the said stannary take cognisance of all manner of suits at the instance of the said tinners and of other persons who claim to be tinners, whether arising within or outside the stannary, and they arrest and distrain persons outrageously outside as well as within the stannary' (11). Matters came to a head with petitions in identical terms presented to Parliament by the commonalty of Devon and Cornwall in 1376. This resulted in a Parliamentary interpretation of the category of persons who were entitled to the privileges of tinners and to the extent of the jurisdiction of the stannary courts (12), but in so imprecise a form that the original uncertainty continued as great as before.

The purpose of the 1305 Charters is, nevertheless, reasonably clear. Working tinners were not to be hailed before the ordinary courts except upon charges of serious crime (murder, manslaughter and mayhem) or in cases where the title of land was in question. In all other suits, whether relating to tin mining or not, tinners were to sue and be sued in their franchise court, namely the court of the warden of the stannaries. A later part of the Charters spoiled this simple idea, however, by trying to underline it. They provided that 'our warden or his deputy [the Vice-Warden] shall hear all pleas arising between the said tinners and also [all pleas] between them and others foreign [to the stannary] concerning all trespasses, disputes and contracts made in the places where they work if such pleas similarly arise within the stannaries', and that the warden should do justice between the parties 'as it has hitherto been customary in the stannaries'. It looks as though the first of the provisions quoted in the last sentence limited the warden's jurisdiction when non-tinners were parties to litigation before him, and it becomes difficult to reconcile these limitations as to subject matter and place with the general prohibition at the beginning of the Charters against other courts trying cases to which tinners were parties.

In addition to dealing with the jurisdiction of the stannary court and the related matters of the imprisonment and outlawry of tinners, the Charters also provided that in any litigation before the stannary courts in which any facts were in issue which did 'not touch the stannaries', half the jury should consist of tinners and the other half of foreigners (non-tinners), but if only facts 'touching the stannaries' were in issue, the whole jury should be composed of tinners. This was a matter of considerable practical importance, for, as Richard Carew, writing at the beginning of the seventeenth century, relates (13), the quality of justice a non-tinner got before a stannary court depended on the extent to which it was dominated by tinners. The Charters contained no limitation of this provision for a mixed jury to cases where the other party to the litigation was a non-tinner, but in practice when both or all parties were tinners, the jury, too, was wholly composed of tinners, irrespective of the issues to be tried. The provision for mixed juries applied only to the stannary courts, and so if a tinner sued or was properly sued in another court, the jury was constituted in accordance with its own rules, and the fact that the plaintiff or defendant was a tinner was irrelevant.

Mixed up with its provisions about the jurisdiction and procedure of the stannary courts, the Charters also conferred certain privileges on tinners to mine for tin and to dig turves for smelting tin 'in our lands, moors and wastes and in those of all other persons whatsoever in the said county'. Read literally, such a grant, if valid, would go far beyond the bounding custom previously in force, and also far beyond anything which the tinners subsequently claimed in Cornwall. The discrepancies between the bounding custom and the Charters will be examined more fully in the next chapter. The Charters also made more specific provision for the coinage of tin at the appointed towns (14), and empowered the tinners to sell their coined tin to whomsoever they wished, subject only to the royal right of pre-emption.

Finally, the Charters exempted tinners from certain royal, feudal and local taxes and imposts, namely, tallages (or arbitrary taxes imposed by the king on the tenants of his demesne lands and on boroughs holding royal charters, or by a feudal lord on his tenants (15)), tolls (or charges for the use of markets, roads, bridges and other facilities), stallages (or charges for the use of a particular place in a market town for the sale of goods, a valuable privilege since tin was usually sold in the town where it was coined), and aids (or feudal imposts exacted by the king or a feudal lord from his tenants to assist him with occasional heavy expenditure). To ensure that exemption from local taxation and imposts was complete, the Charters also granted the tinners immunity from 'all other customary duties whatsoever in towns, ports, fairs and markets held within the said county' of Cornwall or Devon (16). Despite the width of the fiscal privileges conferred on the tinners, the Charters of 1305 did not exempt them from paying the lay subsidy, that is the tax of one-tenth or one-fifteenth of the value of the taxpayer's possessions periodically voted to the king by Parliament. But the confirmation of the Devon Charter made by Edward III in 1327 (17) extended the exemption from imposts to all 'taxes and contributions whatsoever', apparently including the lay subsidies, which the Cornish tinners still had to pay.

The Cornish Charter of 1305 was confirmed and supplemented in one minor respect by a charter of Edward IV granted in 1466, which gave the Cornish tinners the right already enjoyed by the tinners of Devon to take turves and to make charcoal in the royal forest of Dartmoor for the purpose of smelting their tin (18). But the next important charter, and the last one of the series, was granted to the Cornish tinners in 1508 by Henry VII (19). It was in form a Charter of Pardon, relieving forty named landowners, nine proprietors and merchants and 'all other tinners, bounders or possessors of tinworks . . . proprietors of blowing houses . . . buyers of black or white tin and dealers in white tin . . . [and] fabricators of tin' from the penalties they had incurred for infringing the laws governing the stannaries, and, in particular, for infringing ordinances made in the name of the king's eldest son, Arthur, Prince of Wales and Duke of Cornwall, in 1496. These ordinances had been widely disregarded by the Cornish tinners, in part through inertia, but no doubt also in part deliberately, because they introduced stricter rules governing the recording of tin bounds and smelting houses and the marking of tin blocks with the smelters' house marks and with symbols showing the quality of the tin; and such rules appealed little to the conservative and independent Cornish spirit. The

Charter of Pardon was granted in no royal mood of charity; it cost the petitioners £1,000 (20), which was raised by a general levy on all the tinners.

The most interesting feature of the Charter of 1508 was its provisions for the self-government of the stannaries. All ordinances previously made by the king or former kings and the ordinances made in the name of Prince Arthur were restrospectively repealed, and the king conceded for the future:

> that no statutes, acts, ordinances . . . or proclamations shall take effect in the said county [of Cornwall] or elsewhere to the prejudice or in exoneration of the said tinners, bounders, possessors of tinworks . . . proprietors of blowing houses . . . buyers of black or white tin or dealers in white tin or the heirs or successors of any of them, unless there has previously been convened twenty-four good and lawful men of the four stannaries of the county of Cornwall, namely, six men from each of the stannaries elected and appointed from time to time as occasion requires . . . whenever, howsoever and wheresoever such statutes, ordinances . . . or proclamations are made by us or our council or by our heirs or successors or by the Prince of Wales and Duke of Cornwall by his council . . . ; so that no statutes, ordinances . . . or proclamations to be made in future by us, our heirs and successors, or by the said Prince and Duke of Cornwall for the time being shall be made except with the consent of the said twenty-four men so elected and appointed. . . .

Herein lay the constitution of the Stannary Convocations of Cornwall of the sixteenth, seventeenth and eighteenth centuries. The only power given by the Charter to the twenty-four stannators who were to be elected by mayor and governing bodies of the four boroughs of Truro, Lostwithiel, Launceston and Helston, was to veto legislation enacted by the king or the Duke of Cornwall, not to enact legislation themselves. However, the dividing line between veto and initiative in legislating was one which Convocation was not too concerned to observe, and in the course of the seventeenth century the power to legislate was exercised by the Convocation of Cornwall, as it had been by the Convocation of Devon without the benefit of any charter provision from the beginning of the sixteenth century. Henry VII was obviously concerned about the legality of the power he had conferred on the Convocation of Cornwall, for he promised in the Charter to have it ratified by Act of Parliament as soon as possible; but no Parliament met before his death in 1509, and the Charter was not ratified by any succeeding Parliament. Had the Charter been formally incorporated in an Act of Parliament, a nice constitutional question would have arisen as to whether the Convocation of Cornwall had a power of veto over Acts of Parliament concerning the stannaries. The Charter of 1508 extended this power to statutes, which was sufficient to comprehend Acts of Parliament as well as enactments by the king alone. The fact that Parliament did not ratify the Charter left this question in abeyance, however, and no doubt has ever been expressed about Parliament's power to enact legislation for the stannaries without the need to obtain the consent of Convocation.

THE STANNARY CONVOCATIONS

At the beginning of the sixteenth century the independence of the stannaries was seriously threatened by the centripetal effect of strong Tudor government. The Cornish tinners' petition for the inclusion in the Charter of 1508 of a right for them to veto statutes and royal ordinances affecting the stannaries was a recognition of this threat, and it was for this, rather than the formal pardon, that they paid the king £1,000.

The history of the stannary institutions of the sixteenth to the eighteenth centuries shows how the influence of the central government over the tinners gradually diminished, until by the eighteenth century the mine proprietors and smelters were completely independent. The stannary convocations ceased to be of any importance as vehicles of central-government power after the last exercise of the royal right of pre-emption of tin in 1703, and the existing law governing property in mines and tin was calculated to preserve the interests of the proprietors and smelters and leave them free to pursue their interests without restriction. The administration of the law was almost wholly in their own hands, for the Vice-Warden and the stewards of the stannary courts were appointed from among their own ranks. The eighteenth century was a period of legal and institutional stability in the stannaries simply because the people whose opinions counted were happy, out of self-interest, to leave things just as they were. The draught of institutional and legal reform was not to come until the nineteenth century was well under way.

The Stannary Convocation of Devon, officially called the Great Court or Parliament of Tinners, met in September 1510 under the presidency of Thomas Deneys, the Vice-Warden of Devon. Twenty-four jurates represented each of the stannary courts of Chagford, Ashburton, Plympton and Tavistock, and from their description as jurates it seems that their function was still seen to be confined to declaring and clarifying the existing stannary law, just as the juries called to attend before William de Wrotham had done three centuries previously. Nevertheless their enactments did contain new provisions, and in particular they repeated the substance of the ordinance of Prince Arthur for Cornwall as to the marking of tin blocks with a symbol denoting their quality and the house mark of the blowing house which smelted them (21). A further Convocation was held in October 1532 under Sir Philip Champernown, the Vice-Warden, and each stannary court was again represented by twenty-four jurates (except Chagford, which sent only twenty-two). Once more Convocation added new provisions to the existing law, especially a requirement, corresponding to that in Prince Arthur's ordinance, that the bounding of tinworks should be recorded in the local stannary court (22).

Towards the end of the sixteenth century, royal influence over the Devon Convocation diminished, although the Privy Council still kept as close a watch over civil disorders among the working tinners as the Court of Star Chamber had done earlier in the century. The Crown's financial interest in the stannaries was adequately looked after by the law administered by the Lord Warden and his officers. The role of Convocation was now seen to be the improvement of stannary law in general, and the central government considered that this function could safely be left in the hands of the wealthy class of landowners and merchants which had grown up during Elizabeth's reign and whose members arranged that they or their nominees should be chosen as jurates. It is noticeable that not one of the jurates at the Convocations of 1510, 1532, 1533 or 1552 was a knight or a gentleman, but at the Convocation of 1574 the jurates included one knight and twelve gentlemen, and that of 1600 was attended by six esquires and forty-seven gentlemen, all of whom were given appropriate precedence in the records. Another noticeable feature of the enactments of the Convocations of 1552, 1574 and 1600 is the absence of any radical new ideas. The provisions of the earlier legislation of 1510 and 1532 were amplified and made more explicit, the procedure in the stannary courts was regulated in some detail (particularly in regard to fees), but the only new law that was introduced related to the protection of proprietary interest in tinworks or mines.

The later Convocations of 1688 and 1703 were concerned primarily with settling the terms for the exercise of the royal right of pre-emption, and they made only slight alterations to the existing stannary law. The landowning class had by now gained complete control of Convocation. Of the ninety-six jurates at the 1688 Convocation, three were baronets, two were knights, and all the remainder except nine were esquires or gentlemen. At the 1703 Convocation there were only two baronets and one knight, and the number of jurates not entitled to courtesy titles, and who may therefore have included working tinners, rose to fourteen, but even so it is not difficult to see that the landowning interest still predominated.

The Stannary Convocation of Cornwall was far less active and ambitious than its Devon counterpart in the sixteenth century, and it only realised its full powers in the seventeenth. In fact no Convocation for Cornwall was held after the grant of the Charter of Pardon in 1508 until 1588. The Charter left the mining law of Cornwall in an uncertain state, for it repealed the ordinances made in the name of Prince Arthur in 1496 without replacing them by new regulations, and it was unclear to what extent the rules set out in the repealed ordinances were part of the customary law of mining and so survived the repeal in that form. For example, it was uncertain whether the compulsory recording of tin bounds in the stewards' courts was part of the customary law as well as expressly required by the ordinances (23), and so out of caution or habit the Cornish tinners continued to have their pitching of bounds proclaimed and registered by the stewards' courts. This state of affairs continued until 1525 when Henry VIII, through the Lord Warden of the Stannaries of Cornwall and Devon, the Marquis of Exeter, issued a commission to five persons, one of whom was William Godolphin, the Vice-Warden for Cornwall, directing them to determine the customary law of the stannaries of Cornwall exactly (24). The five commissioners sat during September 1525 at Lostwithiel, taking evidence from tinners and other interested persons, and in the same month reported their findings to the King (25). The report repeated much of the law found in the Charter of 1305 and the accepted customary law, but it also accepted without question that tin bounds were valid only if recorded and proclaimed, and expressly set out the requirements of the ordinance of 1496 that blowing-house keepers must be registered in the stewards' court and must be sworn not to corrupt the tin they smelted. In other words, the ordinances, although repealed, remained part of the mining law of Cornwall without interruption, because by thirty years after their enactment they had become accepted as customary law.

The commissioners of 1525 were only concerned with the existing law, not with making new law. When the next Cornwall Convocation was held at Lostwithiel sixty-three years later in 1588 its members (who called themselves stannators, not jurates) were struck with doubts about their power to go further than the commissioners had done. The convocation had been called by a warrant addressed by the Lord Warden, Sir Walter Raleigh, to the mayors of Truro, Lostwithiel, Launceston and Helston requiring them each to send six good and lawful men in accordance with the Charter of 1508. From this one would imagine that new royal legislation was to be laid before the stannators and they were to be asked to waive their right of veto under the Charter. But this did not happen. The convocation met for only one day, 18 January 1588, and undoubtedly it had a prepared document laid before it for adoption, but the Act of Convocation it passed purported merely to be a declaration of existing stannary law. Each clause begins with the words 'We find' or 'We find and affirm', and in no part of the Act are there enacting or ordaining words showing that the convocation considered that it was legislating or approving legislation. Some of the clauses of the Act did contemplate future measures, such as the fixing of the boundaries of each of the four stannaries, the safeguarding of the seal of the tinners, the prescription of the fees chargeable by the stewards' courts and the reform of the stannary gaol at Lostwithiel. But these aspirations are expressed in terms of what ought to be done, not what the convocation ordains shall be done.

Most revealing however, is an early part of the Act of 1588, which, after reciting the Charter of 1508, continues (26):

> . . . but finding that neither we now assembled, nor any other twenty-four in like manner chosen, may make laws nor ordinances of ourselves . . . by intendment of . . . the said charter of pardon, and also accounting it almost an impossibility to find and set down all that needeth reformation amongst tinners, or to conclude that which shall be necessary, seeing nothing may be established as a statute, act or ordinance, unless the whole number of twenty-four do thereunto agree and assent. We therefore humbly desire that . . . there may be moreover sufficient authority granted to enable six more good and lawful men out of every stannary, besides the six to be returned by the several mayors of the four towns . . . and that the major part of the said number may have authority to establish and make statutes, acts etc. . . . as now and of a long time hath been thought fit and by a greater

> number used in the four stannaries of Devon; which number of six more . . . may be chosen at any open tin court within each of the four stannaries by the most part of the tinners there assembled. . . .

These words may have been used as the result of the stannators making any one of the following suppositions: (1) that the abolition of the stannary convocation of Cornwall had been implicit in the Charter of 1508, and the body of twenty-four stannators that replaced it had not inherited its power to legislate; (2) that the stannary convocation of Cornwall, unlike that of Devon, had never had power to legislate; or (3) that the Charter of 1508, in giving the stannators a power of veto over royal ordinances, did not also give them an implied power to legislate, because the stannators were not elected by, and did not represent, the tinners collectively. We shall never know which of these suppositions moved the stannators to express their humble desire for the constitution of a stannary legislature. We do know, however, that nothing was done to give effect to their wish, and the convocations of the next century remedied the situation simply by asserting and exercising the power to legislate; and to enable convocation to act more effectively in this respect, they also asserted the power of the stannators to act by a two-thirds majority vote and to appoint twenty-four assistants to advise them expertly on proposed legislation.

There were five Convocations held in Cornwall in the seventeenth and eighteenth centuries to enact legislation, as well as Convocations held in 1662, 1674, 1686–8, 1703 and 1710 to settle the terms for the exercise of the royal right of pre-emption of tin. The legislative convocations of Cornwall were held in 1624 and 1636 under the Vice-Warden, William Coryton; in 1686 to 1688 under the Lord Warden, the Earl of Bath; in 1750 under the Lord Warden, Thomas Pitt; and in 1752 to 1753 under the Vice-Warden, John Hearle. The Acts of these Convocations consist in part of declarations of the existing law, introduced by the words 'We find and present', and in part of new enactments, introduced by the words 'We agree, constitute and ordain'. The stannators quite clearly understood the difference between restating the existing law and making new law.

The composition of the Convocations of Cornwall from 1588 onwards shows the increasing dominance of the landed gentry and the wealthy merchants, and the reactionary legislation of the last convocation of 1752–3 evidences their ability to exercise their powers in their own favour without regard to the interests of the working tinners or the small proprietors of streamworks. The stannators in 1588 comprised two knights, nine gentlemen, eight yeomen (probably proprietors of tin streamworks) and five whose positions are unspecified but who may have been working tinners. In 1624 there were no knights, but all the stannators were either esquires or gentlemen, though none of them were big landowners. In 1636 there was one knight, and he and the esquires outnumbered the gentlemen by nineteen to five; the Blackmore stannators included Hugh Boscawen and Jonathan Rashleigh, the Penwith and Kerrier stannators numbered no less than three Godolphins, and Tywarnhaile was represented among others, by Jacob Daniell, the founder of the mercantile family of Truro that was to flourish in the next century. The Convocation of 1686–8 was attended by three baronets, two knights, (one of them was Sir John Molesworth, the founder of the Copper Miners Company), eighteen esquires and one gentleman. In 1752–3 there were two baronets (one of whom was Sir John St Aubyn, a member of Parliament and an extensive landowner in the Penzance district), twenty-one esquires and one clerk in holy orders, Thomas Herle, brother of the Vice-Warden. Convocation was now a club of the rich men of Cornwall, and for the moment it and the classes to which its members belonged held unchallenged power.

In 1677 an enterprising attempt was made to deal with the problem of the composition of Convocation and the election of stannators by a Government bill which passed the House of Lords and got as far as second reading and committal to a select committee in the House of Commons (27). It was re-introduced in Parliament the following session and this time reached the committee stage in the Commons before Parliament was prorogued (28), whereupon it was dropped. The bill provided that upon the Lord Warden receiving the King's or Duke of Cornwall's commission to convene a Convocation, he should send writs or warrants to the mayors of the four stannary towns for the election of stannators forty days before the date on which Convocation was to assemble, and the mayors were to post up a copy of the writ or warrant in a public place in their respective towns and have the election proclaimed on market days in two successive weeks (29). According to the original bill each stannary town was to return six stannators, but this number was increased to eight in committee of the House of Lords. Candidates for election had to hold freehold, copyhold, or leasehold land in Cornwall worth at least £400 per annum, or to be tinners, adventurers or in receipt of toll or farm tin and hold freehold, copyhold or leasehold land in Cornwall worth at least £200 per annum (30). The electorate was to consist of all persons who had resided in the stannary in question for six months and were either adventurers, or in possession of tin bounds, or entitled to freehold land in right of which they received toll or farm tin, but day labourers and persons in receipt of wages were not entitled to vote (31). Elected stannators were to be immune from arrest during the time Convocation was sitting and for six days before and afterwards (32). Before acting as stannators they were to take an oath to be administered by the Lord Warden that they would use their best skill and wisdom in Convocation to do what was in the interest of the King's revenues and for the good of the stannaries; refusal to take this oath made their election void (32).

The original bill provided that the Lord Warden should determine all disputed elections and should have power to fine the mayors and any officers of the towns concerned in elections up to £20 for misconduct in connection with an election, but in committee of the House of Lords these powers were transferred to the stannators, to be exercised by a simple majority vote (33). The Stannaries Convocation Bill was undoubtedly a distinct improvement on the existing system. In particular, although it restricted the membership of Convocation to the wealthy landowners who had come to dominate it during the seventeenth century, the franchise for electing stannators was far wider than the current forty-shilling freeholder franchise for electing members of Parliament and would have given voting rights to the people who were concerned with tin mining.

THE ORIGIN OF THE STANNARY COURTS

The stewards' courts of the eight stannaries of Cornwall and Devon came into being in the thirteenth century. Throughout their existence, until they were abolished by the Stannaries Courts Act, 1836, they were purely courts of common law. This meant that they were tied to administering the system of law laid down by the common law courts at Westminster, except so far as it was expressly varied by stannary custom or Acts of Convocation. The common law became rigid during the fourteenth century, particularly in respect of the remedies it provided for civil wrongs, and there grew up complicated forms of action or formulas, within the limits of which claims had to be brought if they were to succeed. The stewards' courts had to adhere to these forms, too, and so their court rolls were almost entirely taken up with civil claims for debt, trespasses to streamworks, trespasses to and misappropriations of tin ore and actions for nuisances, such as flooding or silting up another tinner's streamworks. In the sixteenth century the common-law courts became more flexible, recognising a new form of action known as *assumpsit* for breaches of contract, and at the beginning of the seventeenth century a special form of this action called *indebitatus assumpsit* became the standard remedy for recovering debts. These actions, too, were taken over by the stewards' courts, and for the remainder of their active lives they were primarily courts for the collection of small debts.

The stewards' courts could trace their jurisdiction back to the charter of 1201, but during the fourteenth century there grew up a second stannary jurisdiction which had no foundation in a charter or statute, namely the equitable jurisdiction of the Vice-Warden of the Stannaries. The Charter of 1305 had made the tinners subject to the jurisdiction of the Lord Warden or his *locum tenens* (meaning the Vice-Warden), but by the beginning of the sixteenth century, if not earlier, this was understood to mean a common-law jurisdiction by way of appeal from the judgments of the stewards' courts (34). This interpretation of the Charter was confirmed by a judgment of the Court of Star Chamber in 1564 (35), by a resolution of the common-law judges at Westminster in 1608 and twice by the stannary convocation of Cornwall, in 1588 and 1624 (36). The Vice-Warden's equitable jurisdiction must therefore be traced to some other source.

Historically the stannary equitable jurisdiction originated in the same way and at the same time as the equitable jurisdiction of the Chancellor of England and the court he established to exercise it, the Court of Chancery. It had been common from the earliest times for persons who could not get justice in the regular courts, either because of the special features of their case, or because of the influence of the wrongdoer over the court, or because of the delay or expense of litigation in the ordinary way, to appeal direct to the king or his council. When Parliament began to meet regularly in the last quarter of the thirteenth century, such petitions were often addressed to it, and in this process of petition and grant of special relief by Parliament began the private bill procedure for local or personal enactments we know today. The remedies which the petitioners to the king or Parliament sought were, of course, not confined to those available at common law. Indeed, with the growing inflexibitity of the common law in the fourteenth century, the commonest reason for petitioning the king or Parliament was that there was no remedy available at common law because the petitioner's complaint did not fall within one of the recognised common-law forms of action. Nevertheless, the petitioner humbly submitted that relief should be given to him in fairness and justice and in accordance with that vague and malleable moral code which the Church taught was superior to human law. The more important of such petitions were dealt with by the king, his council or by Parliament. The remainder were referred to individual ministers to do what they thought fitting, and the principal recipient of such petitions was the Chancellor, who at that time was always an ecclesiastic. The formula of reference endorsed on the petition varied, but Parliament habitually used a standard form when it referred a petition to the Chancellor, namely that he should hear the interested parties and dispose of the petition according to *droit et reson*, which may be translated as according to right and fairness.

The Duchy Council of the Duke of Cornwall was a microcosm of the king's council, and the Black Prince's Register shows that a similar practice existed in Cornwall of petitioning the Duke for relief against injustices in respect of tin mining as obtained on a national scale at Westminster. The Duke referred such petitions to the Lord Warden or sometimes to the sheriff of Cornwall, and they made the final decision. In most cases the form of the reference was the same as was used by Parliament, that the referee should hear the parties and do *droit et reson*.

There are five such petitions recorded in the Register. The first was presented in July 1353 by one John Coulyng, complaining of his eviction from his tin streamworks and the burning of his house by the retainers of Sir John Beaupré, who was lord of Ladock; the petition was referred to Sir John Dabernon, the Lord Warden, with directions to hear it and to take security from Beaupré for keeping the peace (37). The second petition was presented in February 1357 by Abraham, a tinner, who complained that he had been imprisoned by the mayor of Fowey for allowing the tailings or waste from his streamworks to silt up Fowey harbour; this was a simple matter to resolve, and so the petition was referred to William de Spridlington, the Prince's auditor, to enquire and report (38). The third petitioner was Stephen de Treveygnoun (or Trevanion), the parson of Ladock, who in July 1357 complained that tinners were digging for tin in his churchyard;

the Prince sent the petition to Robert de Elford, the Lord Warden and sheriff of Cornwall, with instructions to summon the parties, and, after hearing them, to do them right and justice (*leur facez droit et reson*) in accordance with his findings; if he was in doubt he was instructed to refer the matter to the Prince's Council (39). The fourth petition was presented in 1359 by Henry Nanfan, who complained that local tinners had interfered with his stream-works on Lamorna Moor in contravention of the stannary customs; the Prince referred the petition to Sir John Dabernon, now again Lord Warden, with instructions to give redress to Nanfan and to ensure that all tinners enjoyed the franchises granted to them by the Prince's progenitors (40). The last petitioner, John de Treeures, asked for an unusual remedy. He complained that sixty tinners had entered his demesne lands and destroyed his corn, barley, oats, beans and peas in digging for tin, and he asked that he should be awarded an increase in the normal rate of toll tin to compensate him for the damage. The Prince sent his petition to the sheriff of Cornwall to fix the proper rate of toll tin and to do *droit et reson* (41).

Unfortunately no records of petitions to the King or the Duke of Cornwall in respect of mining matters survive from the period between the death of the Black Prince (1376) and the end of the sixteenth century. Undoubtedly such petitions continued to be presented, and with the adoption of the practice of appointing a peer of the realm or a landed magnate to be the Lord Warden of the Stannaries, which began in the middle of the fifteenth century and became invariable in the next century, it is probable that petitions were referred to the Lord Warden's deputy, the Vice-Warden, for trial, and that the petitions came eventually to be addressed direct to the Vice-Warden, and not to the Duke or the Lord Warden. At the beginning of the seventeenth century Carew described the structure of the stannary courts in words that would seem to confirm this suggestion (42):

> . . . there is assigned a Warden of the Stannaries, who supplieth the place both of a judge for law and of a chancellor for conscience. . . .

> He substituteth some gentleman of the shire of good calling and discretion to be his Vice-Warden, from whom either party, complainant and defendant, may appeal to him; as from his (a case of rare experience) to the Lords of the [Duchy Council]; and from their Honours to her Majesty's person. . . . To each of [the stannaries of Foweymore, Blackmore, Tywarnhaile and Penwith and Kerrier] is assigned by the Lord Warden a steward, who keepeth his court once in every three weeks; they are termed stannary courts . . . and hold plea of whatsoever action of debt or trespass, whereto anyone dealing with black or white tin, either as plaintiff or defendant, is a party.

The system of appeals in common-law cases, from steward to Vice-Warden, to Lord Warden, to the Duchy Council was already in existence at the beginning of the sixteenth century, and it is probable that the parallel course of appeal in equity cases tried by the Vice-Warden at first instance was originated at about that time.

The earliest record we have of an equity case tried by the Vice-Warden is *Glanville* v *Courtney*, which was heard on appeal by the Lord Warden, Sir Walter Raleigh, between 1591 and 1593 (43). The proceedings began with a petition to Christopher Harris, the Vice-Warden, for a declaration that the complainant, Glanville, and certain other persons were entitled to tin bounds in the stannary of Blackmore, and that one of their number, Richard Rescassoe, had fraudulently conspired with one of the defendants, John Dallamayne, that the latter should bound the tinwork anew for the benefit of himself and the other defendants and that Rescassoe had acquiesced in this action in order to deprive the complainant of his rights. The remedy the complainant sought was a perpetual injunction restraining the defendants from interfering with his rights, itself an equitable remedy. The Vice-Warden referred the question of fact for trial by a jury of the stannary, and according to the complainant the defendants suborned the jurymen, who 'were simple tinners', and induced them to find that there was no fraud or conspiracy, and that the complainant's bounds were void for non-renewal when Dallamayne rebounded the tinwork on the defendant's behalf. The

Vice-Warden apparently accepted the verdict, and the complainant appealed to the Lord Warden. Raleigh heard the parties first on 21 May 1591, when he ordered that four commissioners in Cornwall should take evidence locally, and that pending a further hearing all tin broken from the tinwork should be sequestered (ie taken into the custody of a nominee of the court) at the mine. After delaying applications to the Privy Council by the defendants, Raleigh held a final hearing to consider the evidence and issue a decree on 20 January 1593, and upon the defendants failing to appear on that day, he found for the complainant.

The case presents a number of interesting jurisdictional features. The first point to notice is that the proceedings were definitely not brought at common law, despite the use made of a jury. It would, of course, have been possible for the complainant to bring an action for the recovery of the tin bounds in the court of the steward of the stannary of Blackmore, and the questions of fact would then have been considered by a jury of six tinners, just as happened in the actual proceedings. But if the complainant had been successful in such a common-law action, he would have been awarded damages for dispossession of the bounds. In the equity proceedings he brought before the Vice-Warden and the Lord Warden, however, he sought and obtained the peculiar equitable remedies of a declaration and an injunction, the latter being enforced by the threat of committal of the defendants to prison if they failed to relinquish possession of the tinwork to the complainant or if they interfered with him again.

The remedy of an injunction may be considered to have been more efficacious than a judgment for damages, but it is unlikely that a sixteenth-century court of equity would have considered this a sufficient reason for asserting jurisdiction in the matter. The two possible grounds for the assertion of an equity jurisdiction by the Vice-Warden and Lord Warden in a case like *Glanville* v *Courtney* were the presence of fraud and conspiracy (moral elements which always spurred the Chancery Court into action) and the need to establish the validity of the title to property of one out of several claimants.

Custom and legislation by the Convocations of Devon and Cornwall (44) dealt with the problem of fraudulent avoidance of bounds and rebounding for the benefit of a third person, but only by punishing the partner in the original group whose bounds were lost; they gave no remedy at law for the establishment of the title of the original group and the setting aside of the fraudulent rebounding. Equity was therefore free to give this additional remedy in cases of fraud. But wholly apart from the element of fraud, Raleigh's decree may be read as an assertion of an equitable jurisdiction to settle disputed titles to bounds in all cases. The Chancery Court established such a jurisdiction in respect of disputed titles to land in the late sixteenth century (45), and Raleigh may well have been following its lead by extending the jurisdiction to the peculiar species of property with which the stannary courts were concerned, namely tin bounds. Later Vice-Wardens certainly assumed this to be so, and dealt with such disputes about the title to bounds without requiring that inequitable conduct on the part of the defendant should be alleged or proved by the plaintiff.

THE DELIMITATION OF THE STANNARY JURISDICTION DURING THE SIXTEENTH AND SEVENTEENTH CENTURIES

During the sixteenth and early seventeenth centuries the stannary courts extended their scope by interpreting widely the category of tinners over whom the Charters of 1305 gave them jurisdiction. They paid little attention to the status of the litigants before them, but concentrated on the question whether the transaction in dispute was in some way connected with tin or tin mining. Thus they entertained actions between sellers and buyers of tin blocks already coined or presented for coining (46), between sellers and purchasers of shares in tinworks or tin mines (47) and between rival claimants to tin bounds worked by employed hands (48). In the light of such cases the Cornwall Convocation of 1588 declared that 'there are two sorts of tinners, viz. the tin worker, spalliard or pyoner . . . [who] is not to sue or to be sued out of the courts of the stannary . . . except [for] matters touching land, life or mayhem' (49); and 'the second sort of tinners [who] are such as have some part or portion of tinworks, or receive toll tin either as lords or farmers thereof, or do convert black tin into white tin, or are necessary for getting or obtaining tin, as colliers, blowers, carpenters, smiths, tin merchants and such like intermeddling with traffic of tin . . . [they] *may* sue and implead (or) be sued or impleaded in the stannary courts' (50).

This declaration extended the category of tinner by treating working tinners as exclusively within the jurisdiction of the stannary courts, and other persons concerned with tin or tin mining as subject to that jurisdiction if the plaintiff (whether the person so concerned or the other party) chose to sue in a stannary court. This, of course, went further than the Charter of 1305, which simply conferred or confirmed an exclusive jurisdiction over tinners on the stannary courts. The Convocation declaration treated the Charter as applying only to working tinners 'for whose case the charters were first granted' (49), and it was therefore forced to admit by implication that the stannary courts' jurisdiction over the second sort of tinners (adventurers, bounders, etc) was an accretion that had come about since the Charter of 1305.

In 1603 the tinners of Cornwall petitioned the Lord Warden, the Earl of Pembroke, complaining that 'divers foreigners have lately sued and arrested some of us tinners and the officers of the stannary courts with writs of false imprisonment for executing stannary process and for suing them in the stannary courts', and that in such proceedings in the common-law courts at Westminster the judges had held that only working tinners had the right to sue and be sued in the stannary courts (51). The petition described working tinners as 'the least and meanest part of us', which shows clearly that the petitioners were adventurers, bounders and recipients of toll tin. Such people were anxious to maintain the jurisdiction of the local stannary courts because of their power to influence the judgments given. The jurisdiction in fact exercised by the stannary couts had by now been stretched to take in litigation to which tinners of the second sort were parties, even though the subject matter of the dispute had no connection with tin mining. Examples of this were the slander suit brought by Sir John St Leger (a recipient of toll tin) in the stewards' court of Blackmore against Thomas Hilling a landowner who had no interest in mining (52); actions brought in the stewards' courts of Chagford by the Lord of the manor of Tiverton (also a recipient of toll tin) for the recovery of rent from his agricultural tenants (53); and a suit brought before the Vice-Warden of Cornwall by an adventurer in a tinwork for the recovery of a copyhold tenement in the manor of Calstock (54). If the declaration of the Cornwall Convocation of 1588 were accepted as correct, such actions were within the stannary jurisdiction, for that jurisdiction depended on the status of the plaintiff or defendant as a tinner, even of the second sort, and the subject matter of the dispute was immaterial. The common-law courts were obviously uneasy at the wide jurisdiction exercised by the stannary courts, and had gone to the other extreme of restricting the stannary jurisdiction to disputes between labouring tinners and disputes between a labouring tinner and a stranger concerning tin matters.

The Lord Warden referred the tinners' petition to the Chief Justices of the Courts of King's Bench and Common Pleas for their opinion, but received no reply. The common-law courts continued to award damages for the enforcement of stannary judgments, and so in February 1606 the Lord Warden asked the Privy Council to intervene, which it did by putting the question of jurisdiction to the common-law judges. The result was an opinion in November 1608 signed by the two Chief Justices, Coke and Fleming, in which all the common-law judges ruled unanimously and exhaustively upon the matter (55).

They held that workers in blowing houses as well as working tinners enjoyed the privilege of suing and being sued in the stannary courts; secondly that all matters concerning the stannaries (ie tin mining and smelting and the coinage) were exclusively within the stannary jurisdiction; thirdly, that all personal actions between tinner and tinner not concerning tin mining and smelting could be brought in the stannary courts or the common-law courts at the plaintiff's choice, 'but if the one party only be a tinner or worker and the cause of action being transitory [ie personal] and collateral to the stannary [ie not concerned with tin mining and smelting] do arise out of the stannary', the defendant could refuse to have the action tried by a stannary court, and if that court persisted in hearing the action, the King's Bench would restrain it from doing so by issuing a writ of prohibition; fourthly, if in such an action between a tinner and a non-tinner the defendant did not deny the stannary courts' jurisdiction by his pleadings, he was bound by a judgment given against him and could not bring a common-law action for damages if the judgment was enforced, but this was not so if the plaintiff's pleadings showed that the contract which was the subject of the action was made outside the stannary in question or that the cause of action otherwise arose outside the stannary; finally, the stannary courts could not entertain local actions (ie for trespass to, or dispossession of, land, or the enforcement of obligations connected with land, such as the payment of rent) unless the land was within the stannary in question.

The common-law judges' opinion provided a fair, if complex, solution to the problem of jurisdiction, and very sensibly confided all litigation about tin mining and smelting and the coinage to the stannary courts. Its weakness lay in the narrowness of its definition of tinners as working tinners and workers in blowing houses. This was not stated to be an exhaustive definition, and from its form it seemed to do nothing more than remove doubts about one category of ancillary workers, namely, workers in blowing houses, by including them among privileged tinners. The Convocation of 1624 seized on this weakness to re-assert the extensive stannary jurisdiction as it had been exercised in the late sixteenth and early seventeenth centuries, as a matter of right. Tinners were widely defined as including owners of blowing houses, adventurers, smiths, colliers and tin workers and makers of mining utensils as well as working tinners and blowers; all such persons were declared to be entitled to have all personal actions arising in the stannaries to which they were parties tried in the stannary courts, and to ensure that this was done the Vice-Warden was empowered to restrain the other parties by injunctions from suing tinners in any other court and to fine and imprison them if they persisted in doing so (56).

The Lord Warden, Pembroke, again requested the opinion of the common-law judges, and they unanimously ruled in November 1627, by way of interpretation of the judges' opinion of 1608, that the category of tinners was confined to workers and labourers, whether employed in tinworks, blowing houses or activities ancilliary to tin mining, and that 'although many persons may be styled tinners, as the jurates of the several stannary courts, owners, adventurers, undertakers in tin mines and such like', these persons were not entitled to the personal privilege of suit in the stannary courts (57). The judges added that to determine whether a place was within the stannaries so that a transaction there between a tinner and a non-tinner was within the jurisdiction of the stannary court, the criterion should be whether any tinwork was being exploited in it at the time of the transaction.

The tin mining interest of Cornwall and Devon was not satisfied with this, and so the Lord Warden raised the matter in the Privy Council, which after taking the opinion of the common-law judges and the Attorney-General, declared in February 1632 at a session attended by the King that, in effect, the ruling of the judges in 1608 should stand subject to one modification—that the category of tinners should be taken to include 'tinners that do no handwork as are the owners of the soil, owners of the bounds, owners of the blowing houses, and their partners, buyers and sellers of black tin, or white tin before the deliverance' by the receiver of the coinage after the coinage duty had been paid, and that this second category of tinners *might* sue one of their number or a non-tinner in the stannary courts either 'for any matter concerning tin or tinworks' or for other personal causes of action, but if the defendant was a non-tinner, the personal cause of action must have arisen in the stannary to which the tinner belonged. The Privy Council declaration adopted a position more favourable to the stannary jurisdiction than the judges' opinions of 1608 and 1627, and it differed only in one minor respect from the claims of the Cornwall Convocation of 1588. The important feature of its declaration was the recognition of the right of non-working tinners to resort to the stannary courts and thereby exclude any other court from adjudicating on a dispute. The non-working tinners were the litigants from whom the stannary courts received most of their fees, and they were certainly the people who brought the most important questions of mining law before them for adjudication.

But the battle of jurisdiction was not yet over. The Cornwall Convocation of 1636 accepted the declaration of the stannary jurisdiction made by the judges in 1608 (58), presumably including the modification made by the Privy Council in 1632, and by so doing implicitly abandoned the far wider jurisdiction that it had itself claimed for the stannary courts in 1624. Nevertheless the stannary courts continued to hear cases outside their jurisdiction under the judges' ruling, and were encouraged to do so by the example of the Vice-Warden of Cornwall, William Coryton, who seemed to be campaigning for a general jurisdiction over all personal actions arising anywhere in the county, whether connected with tin mining or not. This time it was the House of Commons that intervened to keep the stannary jurisdiction within its proper bounds by passing the bill which became the Stannaries Act, 1641.

This Act began by reciting the Parliamentary declaration of 1376 as to the definition of tinners and the geographical limits within which a transaction had to take place, or a cause of action had to arise, for the stannary courts to have jurisdiction. It then stated that in recent years inhabitants of Cornwall and Devon had fraudulently assumed the status of tinners by acquiring 'decayed tinworks and small inconsiderable parts [shares] in the same and other tinworks [so as to be able to] vex and sue their neighbours in the stannary courts', and that the stannary courts had attempted to extend their jurisdiction geographically throughout Cornwall and Devon (59). The Act then confirmed the Parliamentary declaration of 1376, and restricted the stannary courts' jurisdiction over disputes between tinners and non-tinners to those where the contract was made or the cause of action arose in 'a vill, tithing [or] hamlet where some tinwork in work is situate' (60). So that a non-tinner might challenge the jurisdiction of a stannary court in which he was sued, the Act adopted the practice of the Devon courts (61) by allowing him to testify on oath that he was not a tinner, whereupon the action against him was to be dismissed unless the plaintiff replied on oath that 'the said plaintiff is . . . [a] true and working tinner, without fraud or deceit, and that the cause of his . . . suit arose within the said stannaries or concerneth tin or tinworks' (62). The truth of the plaintiff's oath was tried by the jury of the stannary court in which he sued, but the defendant could challenge its findings in favour of the plaintiff by suing him in a common-law court for a penalty of £10 and the damages and costs sustained or incurred by the defendant as a result of the stannary action, and the verdict of an ordinary jury in the common-law court was then substituted for that of the stannary jury (63). The Act concluded with a declaration that tinners could sue non-tinners in the common-law courts if they wished notwithstanding anything in the Charter of 1305 (64), and this was followed by a few procedural rules.

The Stannaries Act, 1641, was a vain attempt to set the clock back three centuries and to re-establish what was imagined to be the pure law laid down by the Charters of 1305. If the attempt had succeeded, the distinctive stannary law relating to mine creditors' suits and the rateable satisfaction of mining debts, and the whole complex of the rules governing cost book companies, would never have developed. Fortunately the stannary courts disregarded the statutory restriction of their jurisdiction to actions to which a working tinner was a party, and the few references to the Stannaries Act, 1641, in the judgments of the Vice-Wardens in the second half of the seventeenth century and during the two following centuries always construed it as though it had confirmed not the views of the common-law courts at Westminster but the far more liberal judges' opinion of 1608 as interpreted by the Convocation of 1624. Convocation acted in the same way. In 1686 it enacted that the grand jury for the stewards' courts should comprise 'the best and most sufficient stannators [tinners] to wit, owners of tin lands, owners of bounds, adventurers for tin . . .' (65) in total disregard of the fact that under the Act of 1641 these persons were not tinners at all. The Convocation of 1752 likewise enacted that several kinds of dispute between landowners, bounders and adventurers should be settled in the stannary courts—suits for the inspection of the defendant's underground workings which the plaintiff believed infringed his boundaries (66), suits by pursers of mining companies against adventurers for their unpaid shares of the companies' operating costs (67), and suits between adventurers for the recovery of their proper shares of black tin broken from the mine (68).

THE WORK OF SIR JOSEPH TREDENHAM AS VICE-WARDEN

Like the jurisdiction of the Court of Chancery, the equity jurisdiction of the Vice-Wardens' court survived both the attacks of the common-law courts at Westminster and the purges of the Commonwealth governments in the middle of the seventeenth century. The next important period in the history of stannary equity, during which the gains of the sixteenth century were consolidated rather than developed, was the tenure of office of Sir Joseph Tredenham as Vice-Warden of Cornwall from 1681 to 1689.

Tredenham was born in 1641, and like his immediate predecessor, Sir Jonathan Trelawny, who died in 1680, was a professionally qualified lawyer. The notes he left of his decisions as Vice-Warden (69) show a keen and careful mind, and the fact that he left any record of the proceedings in his court, unlike most of the other Vice-Wardens of the sixteenth and seventeenth centuries, reveals in itself a striving for regularity and system which was not the outstanding feature of courts of equity at the time. Tredenham performed for the equity administered by the Vice-Warden's court the same service as was done for the equity of the Court of Chancery by Heneage Finch, the Earl of Nottingham, who was Lord Chancellor from 1675 to 1682 and so Tredenham's contemporary. Both of them found that the jurisprudence of their respective courts consisted of a tangled mass of often conflicting decisions given by their predecessors. Sixteenth- and seventeenth-century Lord Chancellors and Vice-Wardens had not attempted to follow or establish precedents but had dealt with each case *ad hoc.* At the end of their tenure of office, on the other hand, Nottingham and Tredenham left the substantive rules of equity administered by their courts as an organised and coherent, though not a complete, body of principles. The substantive rules of equity of the Vice-Warden's Court were not finally settled until the third quarter of the eighteenth century; the Court of Chancery took somewhat longer. Without the groundwork laid by Tredenham, however, the equity of the Vice-Warden's Court would probably have never crystallised into a comprehensive system, or at least would have taken much longer to do so.

Tredenham showed a clear appreciation of the distinction between the common-law jurisdiction of the stewards' courts and his own original equitable jurisdiction. Petitions for the recovery of debts or damages which should have come before the stewards' courts were summarily dismissed, 'there being no matter of equity in the plaintiff's petition'. At the same time he accepted the jurisdiction of his court in suits in which the title to tinworks was in question, even though an action involving the same question could have been brought in the steward's court. In this he followed the precedent set by Raleigh as Lord Warden in *Glanville* v *Courtney* ninety years before. Nevertheless, Tredenham was careful to refer the questions of fact in such cases to a jury of the steward's court, and he devised a form of order for this purpose which neatly limited the function of the steward to trying the questions of fact while reserving the judgment of the suit to the Vice-Warden (70). This order in a debased form was used throughout the eighteenth and early nineteenth centuries until made unnecessary by the reform measures of 1836.

In two other respects Tredenham expanded his own original equity jurisdiction at the expense of the stewards' courts, and opened up a gap which in the course of the eighteenth century was widened so as to attract all actions of debt to the Vice-Warden's Court. In both cases, however, Tredenham was fully justified in intervening, for the remedies available at common law were inadequate, and this has always been a ground for the exercise of an equitable jurisdiction. The first of these cases were where the wages of working tinners were unpaid, and were likely to remain unpaid for some time because of a dispute as to whom was liable to pay them, or because the defendant partner in a mining adventure objected that if he were to pay the wages in full, he would contribute more than his fair share of the costs of the mine. In such situations Tredenham would order that the treasurer or purser of the mine (if there was one) should pay the wages out of cash in his hands, or should sell sufficient tin broken from the mine for the purpose, and, if necessary, hold a meeting of the adventurers so that calls might be made on them for any further sum required (71). If there were no purser, Tredenham would direct such a meeting of adventurers to be called under the supervision of the court, or, if the defendant partner admitted his membership of the adventure, would direct him to pay the whole of the wages and seek a proper contribution from his fellow partners (72). The variety of devices used by Tredenham to ensure that the miners were paid was due to the fact that in his day the office of purser was new, and only a few mines had one. But where a purser had been appointed Tredenham realised his usefulness, and used him to represent the mine and the partners in the mine collectively, either as plaintiff when the unpaid miners were not parties to the suit, or as a sort of agent of the court when the miners sued one or more of the partners. Here lay the origins of the purser's suit for calls against the partners and the creditor's suit against the purser for debts of the mine, both of which were to reach their full development in the eighteenth century.

The second field in which Tredenham enlarged the Vice-Warden's equity jurisdiction was in respect of debts claimed by persons other than mine-workers. Here he gave equitable remedies to those people who had supplied goods or services for the benefit of the mine, but not so extensively as for the payment of mine labourers' wages. The only two remedies he appears to have employed were to direct the purser of the mine to call a meeting of the partners so that a call on them to contribute sufficient to pay the debt in question might be made (73), and, secondly to direct the purser or some other person (if there were no purser) to retain sufficient tinstuff broken from the mine as security for the debt (74). These remedies fell far short of those accorded to creditors in the eighteenth century when the creditor's suit was fully developed, but the germ of this form of suit was nevertheless inherent in Tredenham's decrees.

The striking feature of many of Tredenham's decisions is the facility with which he devised an appropriate remedy, yet at the same time related that remedy to general principles, so that he was not merely treating the particular plaintiff more charitably than the common law would have done. An example of this is the last opportunity he always gave to a partner in a mining adventure who was threatened with forfeiture of his share for failure to make his due contribution toward the cost of the adventure. Tredenham always ensured that the partner was shown the accounts of the mine from which his contribution was calculated if he alleged that they had not been previously shown to him (75), and he then set a time limit by which the contribution must be paid or the share forfeited (76). No doubt he was following the practice that had just been established in the Court of Chancery of giving a mortgagor a last opportunity to redeem his property before extinguishing his right to do so, thus making the mortgagee beneficial owner of the property. The relief in both cases stems from the equitable doctrine that penalties and forfeitures should not be enforced unless the person liable to them is clearly unable to fulfil his obligations. The fact that such relief was not given by later Vice-Wardens against forfeitures of shares or of mining leases in no way argues against the soundness in equity of what Tredenham did.

In contrast to his ingenuity in finding appropriate equitable remedies, his contribution in working out new equitable principles and in devising new concepts was small, which is not surprising when one considers the conservative age in which he lived, especially in an industry and a part of the country where innovation was regarded with extreme suspicion. He did, however, introduce or clarify one important principle—that a partner in a mining adventure who voluntarily relinquishes his share ceases to be liable to his co-partners or to creditors of the mine for the share he has hitherto borne of the debts and expenses of the mine (77). This principle, when later combined with the privilege of transferring shares in a mining adventure, formed the foundation for that peculiar kind of mining partnership, the cost book company, which dominated the mining industry of south-west England in the following two centuries. But even in his most perceptive moments Tredenham could not have foreseen the future economic importance of this form of association. Had he lived two centuries later, however, there can be no doubt that he would have worked out the detailed consequences of the cost book principle as fully and as sensibly as the great Vice-Wardens of the nineteenth century, John Lucius Dampier and Edward Smirke.

THE STANNARY COURTS IN THE EIGHTEENTH AND EARLY NINETEENTH CENTURIES

After Sir Joseph Tredenham's tenure of office as Vice-Warden of Cornwall the Vice-Warden's court entered a long period during which little development took place in the law it administered. The main development, probably during the first half of the eighteenth century, was the general extension of the jurisdiction of the Vice-Warden's court over cases that could have been brought before the stewards' courts. This was particularly important in the case of claims for debts, which the Vice-Wardens tried without the aid of a jury, acting as judges of fact as well as of law. The only use of the jury system which survived was in connection with petitions for the recovery of tin or tinstuff or of mines, when it remained the Vice-Wardens' practice right until the abolition of the stewards' courts in 1836 to send questions of fact to the stewards for determination by the verdict of a jury specially summoned by them.

The reason why litigants preferred to present petitions in the Vice-Warden's court instead of suing in the stewards' courts was the cheapness and speed of justice in the former court as compared with the latter. Both courts were held at three-weekly intervals, but whereas it was possible for a petitioner in the Vice-Warden's court to have his petition heard at the next court after it was presented, this was never possible in the stewards' courts. In the Vice-Warden's court the date for the hearing was specified in the summons served on the defendant with a copy of the petition, and, since there were no pleadings, the defendant simply attended before the Vice-Warden on the hearing date and defended himself orally. If he did not attend, the case was adjourned for two successive sessions by appropriate orders, and then a final decree was made giving the petitioner the relief he sought or committing the defendant to the stannary gaol. In other words, the maximum interval between the issue of the petition and the final decree was nine weeks. In the stewards' courts any action took at least eighteen weeks from the issue of the summons until judgement, and if the defendant filed a plea or demurrer (as he often did) the delay could be much longer (78). Also the complexity of the common-law system of pleading employed in the stewards' courts entailed much greater expense for the parties.

It is impossible to discover when the general appropriation of the jurisdiction of the stewards' court by the Vice-Wardens' occurred, because no continuous records of proceedings in the Vice-Warden's court before 1764 have survived. In his evidence given to Sir George Harrison in 1827, in connection with a Duchy Council enquiry into the stannary jurisdiction, John Edwards of Truro, an attorney who practised in the Vice-Warden's court, thought that Henry Rosewarne, who was Vice-Warden from 1776 to 1783, was the first Vice-Warden to entertain common-law claims (79). This is clearly too late a date for the beginning of the practice, because cases of claims for debts and damages are to be found among the earliest surviving records of orders made by the Rev Walter Borlase, who was Vice-Warden in 1764 (80), and in all probability he merely continued a long established tradition. All that is known with certainty is that the erosion of the stewards' jurisdiction began after Tredenham's day. He was most punctilious in rejecting petitions which disclosed no equitable grounds for relief, but none of his eleven immediate successors were lawyers, and during the period of office of any one of them the boundaries between the common-law and equity jurisdictions may have become sufficiently blurred for the Vice-Warden to have taken over the stewards' jurisdiction, probably as the result of ignorance rather than design.

The result of the concurrent exercise of the stewards' jurisdiction by the Vice-Wardens was that the stewards' courts rapidly became obsolete. In 1809 Arthur Preckey, the steward of Foweymore, declared that he had never heard a case between his appointment in 1780 and his supersession in 1799 (79). The stewards themselves offered no resistance to the attrition of their functions, for they were all attorneys with busy practices, and the fees they earned as stewards, never exceeding £25 a year, were not sufficient to induce them to resist (81). In 1800, as an economy measure, John James, a Truro attorney, was appointed steward of all four Cornish stannaries, and Edward Bray of Tavistock was at the same time appointed steward of all four Devon stannaries (82). This ensured an income for James of about £70 a year, but a further decline in the volume of cases brought in the steward's court during the early years of the nineteenth century led to the conferment of an annual salary of £300 on the steward of the Cornish stannaries, John Borlase, in 1828 to induce him to continue in office (83). It was hoped that in the current state of uncertainty about the legality of the Vice-Warden's jurisdiction an improvement in the status of the steward would lead to a revival of litigation in his court, but the experiment proved a failure, and the stewards' courts were formally abolished in 1836.

The two most important developments in the equity jurisdiction exercised by the Vice-Wardens of Cornwall in the eighteenth century were the evolution of the creditor's and the purser's suits. Although both these forms of proceedings had their origin in the seventeenth century, neither reached its final form until well into the eighteenth century. The establishment of the creditor's suit in its fully developed form is usually attributed to Vice-Warden the Rev Walter Borlase, and is dated from his judgment in *Rawle v Usticke* in 1759, which was confirmed by the Lord Warden on appeal (84). It seems probable that this was the first case in which the rights of a mine creditor against the purser, the adventurers and the ores and equipment at the mine were fully explored. The fullness of Borlase's reasoning in his report to the Lord Warden, and the fact that he cited only one precedent in it, indicate that there was little previous judicial authority defining creditor's rights. The purser's suit was developed earlier than the creditor's, which is not surprising in view of the obvious need to give legal powers to pursers to collect calls from recalcitrant adventurers so that the mines could be kept working. In 1752 the Cornwall Convocation 'declared and enacted' that the purser or clerk of a mining adventure might petition the Vice-Warden for a decree ordering an adventurer to pay his share of costs in arrear (85), but this was probably merely a restatement of the existing practice, and the real purpose of the legislation was to confer a power on the Vice-Warden to order the sale of the adventurer's share if the costs remained unpaid despite the decree. The surviving records of the Vice-Warden's court from 1764 show that the purser's suit was then well established, and the Vice-Warden readily ordered adventurers to pay their share of the mining costs without any reflection as to the juridical basis of the purser's claim to sue as representative of the mine and of the other adventurers (86).

Little is known about the characters and personalities of the eighteenth-century Vice-Wardens. Only one of them was a professionally qualified lawyer—John Thomas, who was Vice-Warden of Cornwall from 1783 to 1817. Even Walter Borlase, who held the degree of Doctor of Laws of Oxford University, was not a lawyer but a theologian, and a mundane one at that, for besides being Vice-Warden of Cornwall from 1756 until his death in 1776, he was also the pluralist incumbent of two parishes, Madron and Kenwyn, during the whole of his adult life, and in later life also enjoyed the income of the office of prebendary of Exeter Cathedral. With the exception of John Thomas, the Bodmin attorney, the Vice-Wardens were appointed from the same social class as the members of the stannary convocations, namely that of the wealthy landowners and mine adventurers. John Hearle, who was Vice-Warden of Cornwall from 1740 to 1754, held shares in nineteen mines, including Poldice Mine (St Day). Borlase himself was an adventurer in no less than ninety-two mines, many of them streamworks, though some, such as Ding Dong (Madron) and Boscaswell and Botallack (Pendeen), were deep and profitable mines. John Vivian, who became Vice-Warden of Cornwall in 1817 at the advanced age of 68 years, was a shareholder in most of the prosperous Cornish mines, but his most extensive interests were in the Welsh copper-smelting industry. Henry Rosewarne seems to have been the only Vice-Warden who realised that his judicial functions were incompatible with holding shares in Cornish mines. On his appointment in 1776 he had all his shares in nineteen mines sold by public auction (87); this was a courageous step, for, unlike his predecessors, he had inherited no landed estates from his father, Walter Rosewarne, who was a self-made mine proprietor, and his mining shares were his only sources of income.

If many of the Vice-Wardens of Cornwall during the eighteenth century are but shadowy figures for us now, the Vice-Wardens of Devon at the same period are no more than ghosts. They were appointed only intermittently, and when contemporary lists were prepared of stannary office-holders, the Vice-Wardenship of Devon was often shown as being vacant. This was so between 1760 and 1763 and from 1780 to 1784. Furthermore, none of the court records of the Vice-Wardens of Devon have survived, unlike the corresponding Cornish records, which, with a few breaks, are complete from 1780 onwards and include Vice-Warden Borlase's records from 1764 to 1767. In fact the records of only one case from Devon remain to give us an idea of the working of its Vice-Warden's court in the eighteenth century. This is the *Dartmoor Appeal Case* (88), which was heard on appeal by the Lord Warden, Viscount Lewisham, and the survival of the record is due entirely to the fact that after the appeal was decided it was deposited in the Duchy of Cornwall Office.

REFORM, GLORY AND DECLINE OF THE VICE-WARDEN'S COURT

The first quarter of the nineteenth century passed without any perceptible change in the stannary institutions. As time elapsed, it became increasingly unlikely that another stannary Convocation would ever be called, though in the 1830s, when the abolition of the stannary system by Act of Parliament was a distinct possibility, there was some local support in Cornwall for calling a Convocation to forestall abolition by reform. The catalyst which eventually brought about radical changes was the intervention in Cornish mining of investors from outside Cornwall and Devon, particularly London shareholders. These investors were understandably dissatisfied with the stannary system; the coinage duty was to them an imposition which discriminated against tin mining without any economic justification, and they considered the stannary courts to be no more than strongholds of prejudice and incompetence. Many of these outside investors pressed the Government of the day for legislation to dismantle the stannaries, but the majority of them, along with local mine owners and adventurers, were content with measures of reform, particularly the reorganisation of the stannary courts, and it was the majority who eventually won the day. There can be no doubt, however, that had there not been agitation for abolition of the stannary courts and the coinage, no effective steps would ever have been taken toward reform by the predominantly conservative local interests.

The reform of the stannaries was sparked off by a piece of litigation which, although it obviously involved important questions, did not at first seem to contain the seeds of reform. In April 1822 William Heath and Simon Robins presented a petition in the court of the Vice-Warden, John Vivian, against Frederick Hall, the purser of and an adventurer in Baldhu Mine (near Truro). The petition was an ordinary creditor's petition, and, after hearing the parties, Vivian made a decree on 28 May 1822 for payment of the debt claimed. When this was ignored, he made a further decree for the sale by auction of the ores and machinery of the mine. Hall anticipated this last decree, which was made on 1 October 1822, by applying to the Court of Chancery for an injunction to restrain Vivian from making or enforcing it (89). The ground for Hall's application was that the Vice-Warden had no jurisdiction in equity or otherwise to hear cases at first instance, but only an appellate jurisdiction from the stewards' courts. This was not the first time such an argument had been voiced, and there was some judicial support for it. However, the Lord Chancellor, Eldon, was more impressed by the fact that the Vice-Warden had in fact exercised an original jurisdiction for over 400 years, and he dismissed Hall's application.

Hall then resorted to the common-law courts, where he expected to find a less tolerant judicial attitude towards the local stannary equity jurisdiction. In Easter term 1823 he commenced proceedings in the Court of King's Bench for damages (90) against Vivian, his secretary John Edwards (who had acted as advocate for the creditors, Heath and Robins, on the hearing before Vivian) and the auctioneer who had carried out Vivian's decree for the sale of the Baldhu ores and machinery. Vivian, as a layman, had to depend entirely on the advice he received from his own and the Duchy lawyers. The three counsel briefed by the Duchy Council were all common lawyers, Gaselee, QC, Carter and Verrall, and they disagreed as to the prospects of success of a defence by Vivian that he was exercising a lawful jurisdiction when he made the decree for sale. Verrall drew up a plea based on Gaselee's opinion that Vivian had such a defence in law, and it was entered on the record, but Gaselee was then appointed a judge and the papers were passed to William Tidd, QC.

Tidd was a black-letter lawyer with an excessive respect for formalities, and the notion that such flexibile proceedings as creditors' suits could have a lawful foundation was anathema to him. In the opinion he wrote he relied on the incompatibility of creditors' suits with the common-law rules as to parties and pleading as the principal ground for his advice that Vivian should not defend Hall's action. Vivian reluctantly accepted this advice, and judgment was entered against him and the other two defendants. There then followed a hearing before a jury in Middlesex to fix the amount of damages to be awarded to Hall. Vivian optimistically expected these to be light, but the jury were swayed by the oratory of Hall's counsel, Brougham, QC, who luridly painted his client as the victim of fraudulent scheming by a gang of self-interested Cornishmen, and by this means obtained a verdict for £900 damages. Two of Brougham's observations (91) on the working of the Vice-Warden's court are worth citing as illustrating the jaundiced view that contemporary Londoners could be expected to take of the stannary system. Brougham described Vivian, the Vice-Warden, as

> . . . a very respectable country gentleman [who] knew no more of law than did the lead ore which he had all his life been working into gold.

Despite Vivian's respectability, villainy was perpetrated by him and his adjutants in asserting a jurisdiction over Hall's rights:

> The [Vice-Warden's] court nevertheless decided questions of law. Whenever one of these arose, Mr. Edwards [the Vice-Warden's secretary], who was a sharp man, said such and such is law and nodded his head; Mr. Vivian responded with a nod of his head, and forth came the injunction, the decree, the order of sale and all other machinery for the speedy destruction of property.

As far as clarifying the law was concerned, *Hall* v *Vivian* was a fruitless action. The King's Bench court gave no ruling about the correctness of Hall's contention that the Vice-Warden had no original jurisdiction at common law or in equity. The practical problem therefore remained whether Vivian should continue to hold courts in view of the obvious possibility that actions for damages might be brought against him by parties who did not submit to trial in the Vice-Warden's court. While the action was pending, Vivian wrote to the Lord Warden, the Marquis of Hertford, stating that '. . . to avoid getting deeper into difficulties I have given notice that until this question of jurisdiction is decided, I shall decline to try any cause but such over which jurisdiction is given by some Act of Convocation'. This was written on 12 September 1824, and Vivian had held his last court on the previous 6 September, at which he heard four cases. The number of cases set down for trial in his court had declined remarkably since Hall commenced his action in March 1823: until then the number for each three-weekly sitting had averaged a little over twenty, but between then and September 1823 the average fell to seven, and during the following twelve months only twenty-one new petitions were presented. After September 1824 no sittings of the Vice-

Warden's court were held until September 1828, when the new Vice-Warden, John Wallis, a Helston attorney, sat for the first time.

Wallis had been appointed on Vivian's death in December 1826, but he no doubt at first refrained from exercising his jurisdiction for the same reason as Vivian. When the Vice-Warden's court re-opened, litigation quickly returned to it, but it was not until 1832 that business reached the level of early 1823. It is also noticeable that until 1831 no creditors' petitions were presented, although pursers' petitions and actions for the recovery of toll and farm tin were quite common. In February 1831, however, the former full jurisdiction was revived when Wallis tried a creditor's suit brought by Turner and Magor, the Truro bankers, against the adventurers of Wheal Foster (Camborne) for the recovery of the amount overdrawn on the adventurers' bank account (92). A decree for payment was made by Wallis in June 1832, but the case was not finally disposed of until Wallis had been superseded by the first of the Vice-Wardens of the reformed stannary court, John Lucius Dampier. Dampier a Chancery barrister of fifteen years standing, was appointed Vice-Warden of Cornwall in August 1834 on Wallis's voluntary retirement. Wallis was now 73 years old, and his qualifications as an attorney did not seem adequate to those who sought to preserve the Vice-Warden's court by reforming it. In the words of the royal warrant that awarded Wallis a life pension of £200 a year on his retirement, the current thinking was that 'it would tend to the dignity and advantage of our Stannaries and the administration of justice in the same if the office of Vice-Warden of the Stannaries in the County of Cornwall were held by a barrister practising in our superior courts of law and unconnected with the county of Cornwall' (93). The age of reform had at last arrived.

Judgment was entered in *Hall* v *Vivian* in March 1825. Almost immediately three of the members of Parliament for Cornwall, Sir Richard Vyvyan, Davies Gilbert and Edward Pendarves, took up the task of introducing a bill in Parliament to re-establish the jurisdiction of the stannary courts unequivocally. At first the Lord Warden, the Marquis of Hertford, showed little interest in the matter, but at an interview with him in February 1827 the three members, accompanied by Lord Falmouth, an extensive landowner in Cornwall, persuaded him to support their bill, drafted by Davies Gilbert (94). The bill consisted of a single clause confirming the jurisdiction that the Vice-Warden had hitherto exercised in fact, and extending it to copper as well as tin mines (95). Gilbert submitted it to the Duchy Council for approval, but the Council was not happy about proceeding until an enquiry had been made into the existing state of the law governing the Vice-Warden's jurisdiction. The bill was therefore laid aside, and the Council commissioned Sir George Harrison, the Duchy Auditor, to prepare a report, which he completed in 1829. The report was the most thorough that had yet appeared on the subject, and was fully reinforced by precedents, citations of practices and an historical survey of the growth of the Vice-Warden's jurisdiction.

After Harrison's report there was a delay of several years before any further action was taken. By 1834 Sir Richard Vyvyan and his two colleagues had given up the struggle to get a comprehensive reform measure, and even the mild bill drafted by Gilbert in 1827 was dropped in the face of apathy by the Duchy Council; and it was Sir George Harrison, now Duchy Attorney-General, who took the initiative in April 1835 by submitting a bill he had drafted to the members of Parliament for Cornwall and to the influential merchant and mining investor, Sir Charles Lemon (96). This bill merely confirmed all decrees, orders and acts of the Vice-Warden and his predecessors, and conferred power on him and his successors to make like degrees, etc, in future (97). The question of defining the scope of the Vice-Warden's jurisdiction was still left open, but at least the bill was a beginning. Lemon induced the Earl of Falmouth to call a meeting of the mining interests at Truro in November 1835, and this meeting took the first significant step of appointing a committee chaired by Falmouth to draft a comprehensive bill which the Cornish members would introduce in Parliament (98).

This bill was drafted by the following March, and, apart from its provision for the transfer of the stewards' courts' jurisdiction to the Vice-Warden, which was opposed by Falmouth (99) and John Basset, an influential committee member (100), the bill was an agreed measure. The bill enabled the Duke of Cornwall to apoint a Vice-Warden, who would hold office for life but who would be removed on the demand of five members of the Duchy Council; vested the existing equity jurisdiction exercised by previous Vice-Wardens in the new office holder, and extended the jurisdiction of his court to cover all metalliferous minerals as well as tin; transferred the jurisdiction of the stewards' to the Vice-Warden's court, and enabled him to try questions of fact in both common-law and equity cases by the verdict of a jury; empowered the Vice-Warden to order the sale of the shares of adventurers who failed to pay their calls; enabled appeals to be taken against the Vice-Warden's decisions to the Lord Warden sitting with three members of the Judicial Committee of the Privy Council (101); prohibited the Vice-Warden and his Registrar from engaging in private practice, so as to ensure that they would devote their full time and attention to stannary litigation; and, finally, provided for a levy of ¼d in each £ of the sale price of all metallic ores other than tin to assist towards the cost of the new court.

The bill was introduced in the House of Commons on 27 June 1836, not by one of the Cornish members but by Alexander Baring, the merchant banker, who was at that time President of the Board of Trade. It completed its passage through the Commons on 29 July, and was returned by the House of Lords with amendments on 17 August. These amendments were agreed to by the Commons on 19 August, and the Royal Assent was given on the following day.

The Stannaries Courts Act, 1836, was in many ways an unsatisfactory measure. It is true that it brought the moribund stewards' courts to an end, and economised in judicial manpower by having the Vice-Warden try common-law as well as equity cases (102). The combined administration of law and equity turned out, because of the quality of the nineteenth century Vice-Wardens, to be extremely successful, though right until the end the rules governing common-law and equity proceedings were quite different. It is true also that the Act put the Vice-Warden's court on a sound financial footing by half its net expenses (including salaries) being provided out of Duchy revenues, and the other half out of a levy on sales of ore (other than tin) by the mines plus two-thirds of the court fees received by the court (103). But the great defect of the Act was its imprecision and insufficiency in respect of the Vice-Warden's jurisdiction. After reciting that the Vice-Warden's court had hitherto exercised an original jurisdiction in respect of tin matters, the Act tamely provided that 'the original equity jurisdiction heretofore *lawfully* exercised by the Vice-Warden for the time being shall and may be henceforth exercised by the present and every future Vice-Warden', and that this jurisdiction should also extend to matters relating to 'the working, managing, conducting or carrying on any mine worked for any lead, copper or other metal or metallic mineral . . . or the searching for, working, smelting or purifying' such minerals in the same way as it hitherto had existed in respect of tin, tin ore and tin mines (104).

Similarly, the Act provided that the Vice-Warden should thereafter exercise the stewards' common-law jurisdiction in the same way as they had hitherto *lawfully* exercised it, and this, too, was extended to other metals and metallic minerals as well as tin by the same words as were used to extend the equity jurisdiction (105). Nowhere in the Act was an attempt made to define the lawful extent of these existing jurisdictions, and the only two provisions which had any bearing on the matter were a procedural one requiring challenges to the Vice-Warden's jurisdiction to be made by the defendant taking the point within a limited time before the Vice-Warden himself (106), and a more general provision empowering the Court of King's Bench to transfer cases pending in the Vice-Warden's court to itself by issuing a writ of *certiorari*, which could be done whenever 'an impartial or sufficient trial' could not be had in Cornwall (107).

The Act did not attempt to solve the jurisdictional problem; it merely provided machinery by which the judges could be asked to solve it. But what criteria were they to apply? Those of the charters of 1201 and 1305 read with the Stannaries Act passed in 1641? Or were the words of the new Act which extended the Vice-Warden's jurisdiction to copper and other metals to be read back as applying also to his jurisdiction in respect of tin, as Parliament apparently assumed they did? If so, the new Act widened the existing jurisdiction considerably by merely confirming it. Throughout the nineteenth century the Vice-Wardens' and the superior courts at Westminster assumed that this latter, more liberal, solution was the correct one without expressly so deciding. It is worth noting, however, that one consequence of the Vice-Warden's equity jurisdiction being tacitly accepted as well founded legally was that the legality of mine creditors' suits was never challenged after 1836. The two questions were, of course, quite separate, and it is a wry comment on the clarity of contemporary legal thinking that it was assumed without question that both the major and the minor objections to the Vice-Warden's original jurisdiction made by the plaintiff in *Hall* v *Vivian* (108) were removed by the Act of 1836, whereas in fact it did not deal expressly with either of them.

After passing the Act of 1836 enthusiasm in Cornwall and among London investors for the reform or codification of stannary laws and institutions disappeared for over thirty years. This may have been because within a few years of his appointment in 1834 the new Vice-Warden, John Lucius Dampier, had clarified and expounded many of the unsettled questions of stannary law in judgments which were fully reasoned (unlike the decisions of his predecessors) and fully reported in the county newspaper, the *Royal Cornwall Gazette*. Much of the difficulty in ascertaining the content of stannary law previously lay not so much in the inaccessibility of the records of the courts, which had been open to public inspection since 1752 (109), but in deducing principles of law from the cryptic and unarticulated judgments given by Dampier's predecessors. The old stannary law was not unascertainable; it was merely not readily available in a concise and explicit form. Dampier and the *Royal Cornwall Gazette* remedied this, and although important and difficult points of law remained to be settled right up to the end of the nineteenth century, the bulk of stannary law soon became readily ascertainable by anyone who was interested and not only by the attorneys who practised before the Vice-Warden.

Dampier was born in 1792, the second son of Sir Henry Dampier, a judge of the King's Bench. After being educated at Eton and King's College, Cambridge, from which he graduated in 1816, he was called to the bar as a member of Lincoln's Inn in 1819 and soon established a reputation as a competent Chancery barrister. He was compelled to give up this practice two years after his appointment as Vice-Warden in Cornwall because the Stannaries Court Act, 1836, prohibited him from continuing, but in the following year he secured the recordership of Portsmouth, an office he held for two years. In 1850 he was appointed Vice-Warden of the Devon stannaries on the death of the previous incumbent, Thomas Commins, and held the Vice-Wardenships of both Cornwall and Devon until his own death in May 1853.

Dampier had a clear and orderly mind, as his judgments show. He was nevertheless impeded by a narrowness and illiberality of outlook, probably as a result of his Chancery background, and his decisions often reveal a coldness towards ordinary human feelings and aspirations. His great contributions to stannary law were establishing the legal character of tin bounds and the appropriate remedies for their protection; in developing the law relating to cost book companies and the rights and obligations of their members; and in enlarging the consequential proceedings after decree in mine creditors' suits so as to turn them into an effective winding up process. The basis for all this work had of course been laid by Dampier's predecessors, and he introduced few new principles;

but at least the law was more certain and more effectively administered at the end of his period of office than it had ever been before. Dampier was ably assisted by his Registrar, William Michell, a barrister who specialised in conveyancing work and a native of Truro, where he had been born in 1805. Michell was appointed Registrar of the Vice-Warden's court early in 1837, and he served continuously and conscientiously in that office under Dampier and his successor until his death in March 1869. As the winding up of mining companies became more complex, with the development of the proceedings after decree in mine creditors' suits and with the enactment in 1848 of general winding-up legislation affecting all companies, Michell's devotion to detailed work became invaluable, and the high public regard enjoyed by the Vice-Warden's court in the halcyon thirty years up to 1870 owed much to his labours.

On Dampier's death in 1853 Edward Smirke was appointed Vice-Warden of Cornwall and Devon by letters patent under the Great Seal of England dated 2 July 1853. This was the first occasion on which a Vice-Warden had been appointed in this way—under a provision in the Stannary Courts Act, 1836 (110), instead of by a warrant signed by the Lord Warden. Smirke also had the distinction of being the first Vice-Warden to be appointed to hold office during good behaviour, like the judges of the superior courts at Westminster. All his predecessors, including Dampier, had been appointed during the pleasure of the Lord Warden, though a Lord Warden had in fact exercised his right of summary dismissal of a Vice-Warden only once since Sir Joseph Tredenham was removed for political reasons in 1688. This one occasion was when the Marquis of Hertford removed John Thomas in 1817 for his refusal to support Sir Richard Vyvyan as a candidate for Parliament.

Edward Smirke was born in 1795, and after graduating at St John's College, Cambridge, in 1816, he was called to the bar as a member of the Middle Temple in 1824. At first he seemed destined for a career at the common-law bar in London, but during the 1840s he appeared in a number of mining cases originating from Cornwall, in particular in *Rogers* v *Brenton* in 1847, where he boldly contended before the Court of Queen's Bench that the tin bounding custom originated as part of the common law of the kingdom of Cornwall before its conquest by the Saxons, and as such tin bounding had become part of the common law of England (111). Smirke never appeared before Vice-Warden Dampier but his connections with Cornwall were close, and in December 1844 he was appointed Solicitor-General to the Duke of Cornwall, and in June 1852 Attorney-General of the Duchy. He therefore came to the office of Vice-Warden in 1853 with a long and extensive experience of stannary law, and this, allied with his great abilities and his enquiring and exact mind, made him undoubtedly the greatest of the Vice-Wardens.

As Vice-Warden, Smirke was little concerned with the law governing tin bounds, which was now obsolescent. His great contributions to stannary law were completing the exposition and systemisation of the law relating to cost book companies which Dampier had begun, and integrating the law governing such companies with the new voluminous legislation governing limited companies that Parliament enacted from 1856 onwards. Throughout Smirke's tenure of office, cost book companies out-numbered limited companies formed to exploit mines in the stannaries under the Joint Stock Companies Act, 1856, and the Companies Act, 1862, though these affected cost book companies to some extent, particularly in connection with winding-up proceedings. Smirke's clarity of vision in delimiting the areas of operation of stannary law and the companies legislation, and in resolving conflicts between them, was remarkable. He was as sure of himself when dealing with a complicated merger, sub-division or liquidation of a cost book company, or with an involved dealing in the shares of such a company, as he was when applying the Companies Act or the rules of equity to corresponding transactions affecting a limited company. Smirke's legal ability was accompanied by a lucidity of expression that enables the reader of the reports of his decisions to understand the rules of law involved immediately and completely, and to see them in perspective in their setting among related rules. The best examples of this lucidity are to be found in his exposition of the theory underlying the mine creditor's suit in his judgment in *Harvey* v *Read* (112), and in his explanation of the cost book principle for the benefit of the Court of Appeal in Chancery in *Re Wheal Emily Mining* Co (113).

Smirke also had a beneficial influence on legislation affecting the stannaries during his Vice-Wardenship. In February 1854 he addressed a lengthy memorandum to the Duchy Council on jurisdictional and procedural reforms which he considered necessary for the Vice-Warden's court (114). It seems that Smirke prepared this memorandum on his own initiative, but he was undoubtedly prompted to do so by a debate in the House of Commons a few weeks previously on the motion of Robert Collier, a barrister and acknowledged authority on mining law, for leave to bring in a bill to extend the jurisdiction of the Vice-Warden of Cornwall to Devon, to require cost book companies to be registered at the Vice-Warden's court, and to enable cost book companies to issue shares imposing only limited liability on their holders (115). Collier did not introduce a bill to achieve these objects, but left the field entirely to Smirke, who drafted a bill to realise his more limited proposals. The bill was introduced in the House of Lords on 30 March 1855, and, after an unopposed passage through that House and the House of Commons, it received the royal assent on 28 June 1855.

The main object of this legislation, the Stannaries Court Amendment Act, 1855, was to modernise the procedure of the Vice-Warden's Court in the same way as the recently enacted Chancery Amendment Act, 1852, and the Common Law Procedure Acts, 1852 and 1854, had done for the Court of Chancery and the superior common-law courts. In particular the procedure in mining creditors' suits and in pursers' suits was made more effective (116), but as in 1836 there was nowhere in the Act an express Parliamentary affirmation that such suits could be brought at all under the Vice-Warden's equity jurisdiction, although such an affirmation was obviously implicit in the Act's detailed treatment of the procedure for bringing them. Besides procedural provisions the Act contained two important provisions concerning the Vice-Warden's jurisdiction. The first gave him the same jurisdiction over mixed mines, containing both metalliferous and non-metallic minerals, as he already had over purely metalliferous mines (117). The other provision extended his jurisdiction to Devon, and united the two counties of Cornwall and Devon in respect of the constitution and procedure of the Vice-Warden's court, but not in respect of the substantive law of mining, which continued to be different in certain minor respects between the two counties (118).

The same person had been Vice-Warden in Cornwall and Devon since Dampier was appointed Vice-Warden of Devon in 1850, but the Stannaries Courts Act, 1836, did not apply to Devon, and so before 1855 Dampier and Smirke had presided over an unreformed court in Devon, to which the modernised practice and procedure of the court at Truro did not apply, and which did not have the common-law jurisdiction of the steward's court, which had been transferred to the Vice-Warden in Cornwall by the 1836 Act. The 1855 Act brought Devon into line with Cornwall in these respects, and also imposed the same levy of ¼d on each £1 realised on the sale of ores (other than tin) by Devon mines as the Cornish mines already contributed toward the cost of the Vice-Warden's court (119).

The Stannaries Court Amendment Act, 1855, was a sound, well drafted piece of legislation, and this was undoubtedly due to the fact that Parliament gave Smirke a free hand in a field where he was an expert. The same was equally true of the procedural rules he drafted under the rule-making power given to him by the Act (120), and the introduction to those rules, also written by Smirke, contained the clearest account which had yet been published of the scope of the Vice-Warden's jurisdiction (121).

Smirke's other involvement in legislation was an undoubted

success, again because he was given a free hand in drafting the enactment. Towards the end of 1868 a group of shareholders in Cornish mining companies headed by Thomas Bolitho, the tin smelter, and John St Aubyn, a member of Parliament and an extensive landowner, began to press for the reform of the law governing cost book companies to bring it more into line with the new legislation governing incorporated companies. A public meeting of mining investors was held at the Royal Hotel, Truro on 18 December 1868, and a committee was formed to draft a bill which the members of Parliament for Cornwall would introduce in the House of Commons (122). St Aubyn moved the House for leave to bring in the bill on 26 February 1869 and was supported by the Government. The Duchy Council referred the bill to Smirke for his opinion, and in March he expressed serious criticisms of it (123), which were unfortunately disregarded by its sponsors, much to the detriment of the subsequent law governing cost book companies. A little earlier, however, Smirke had drafted eighteen supplemental clauses dealing with the procedure of the Vice-Warden's court, and when the revised version of the bill was published before its second reading in the Commons on 12 March 1869, these clauses were added to it with the assent of the drafting committee.

The part of the bill which related to cost book companies will be discussed below in connection with the law governing such companies, and we will confine ourselves here to Smirke's own additions to the bill. He drafted them in the light of fifteen years' experience as Vice-Warden, and they reflect the very small changes he found to be required in the reforming legislation he had himself drafted in 1855 at the beginning of his period of office. The most important of his clauses empowered the registrar of the Vice-Warden's court to act as official liquidator in the winding up of a mining company if no one else was appointed by the Vice-Warden (124), and defined the circumstances in which a transfer of shares in a cost book company should be considered as fraudulent and void because of the transferor's intention to evade paying his share of the mining costs (125). The bill had an unopposed passage through the House of Commons and the House of Lords, where it was sponsored by Lord Portman, the Lord Warden of the Stannaries, and it became law as the Stannaries Act, 1869, on 24 June.

Smirke retired on 29 September 1870 at the age of 75 and was immediately granted a knighthood in recognition of his services to the stannaries. His successor, Herbert William Fisher, was appointed by letters patent under the Great Seal on 1 October 1870 to hold office during good behaviour, as Smirke had done. Fisher was an entirely different kind of man from Smirke. He was born in 1826, the son of the vicar of a country parish in Wiltshire, and was called to the bar as a member of the Inner Temple in 1855. Kind, liberal-minded and reserved, he was overshadowed as Vice-Warden by his registrar, Frederick Marshall, a 50 year old Truro solicitor whom Smirke had appointed in 1869. Marshall resided at Truro, and attended to the bulk of the routine work of the Vice-Warden's court, in particular the administrative work of winding up mining companies, which was now its principal occupation. He was efficient, an expert in mining law and had a very good memory for detail, but, unlike his predecessor William Michell, he was aggressive and tenacious, and it was an exhibition of this feature of his character that was a contributory cause of the closing of the Vice-Warden's court in 1896. Fisher attended at Truro only four times a year to sit as Vice-Warden; his sittings never exceeded fourteen days, and toward the end of his period of office fell as low as seven (126).

Undoubtedly Fisher was a competent lawyer, as the reports of his judgments show, and the liberality of his outlook led him to interpret stannary custom more favourably toward working miners than Dampier and Smirke had done, particularly in respect of the ownership of accident club funds paid for out of their wages. But the business of the court declined rapidly after Fisher's appointment in consequence of the growing practice of bringing suits concerning mines before the superior courts in London, in total disregard of the exclusivity of the Vice-Warden's jurisdiction under the Charters of 1305. In 1870 only nineteen new equity suits were brought in the Vice-Warden's court as compared with 125 in 1867, the most active year of Smirke's tenure; by 1881 this number had fallen to two new suits, and in the last ten years of the existence of the Vice-Warden's court, from 1887 to 1896, only fourteen new equity suits were entered (127). The winding-up jurisdiction of the court was more active during Fisher's earlier years, 132 winding-up petitions being filed between 1869 and 1879, but this number fell to forty in the next decade (128); winding-up proceedings were always lengthy and complicated, however, so that although only one new petition was presented after 1890, the court still had some winding-up work on hand when it was abolished at the end of 1896 (129).

The common-law side of the Vice-Warden's jurisdiction was obsolescent while Fisher held office, the decline having begun after the setting up of a county court for Cornwall in 1846. In 1870 six new actions were brought, and in 1880 two were begun; between 1890 and the closing of the court in 1896 there were forty-six new actions together with nineteen summary applications by miners for orders for the payment of their wages (130). It was obvious from these figures that the Vice-Warden's court would soon be extinct, whether Parliament intervened or not. In fact the Government did intervene, but for purely financial reasons.

The Vice-Warden's court met its expenses partly out of an annual payment from Duchy revenues, partly from the levy of ¼d in the £1 on metallic ores (other than tin) and partly by the fees it charged in connection with actions, equity suits and winding-up proceedings brought before it. The levy on ores yielded less than £700 a year after the sharp decline in Cornish copper mining in the 1880s (131), and the court fees, which were still below those charged in county courts (except in winding-up proceedings), dwindled from £130 a year in 1881 to less than £70 in 1890. The result of this was that in 1890 the expenses of the Vice-Warden's court exceeded its receipts by over £900, and the Treasury began to press the Lord Warden, the Earl of Ducie, and the Vice-Warden to make economies. Fisher wrote to Maurice Holzman, the secretary to the Duchy Council, on 12 January 1891 (132):

> The Treasury arrive at the conclusion that without some radical alterations, nothing short of speedy insolvency awaits the Stannaries Court, and no doubt this is true in the sense that it would be unable much longer to defray the salaries [of the Vice-Warden and the Registrar] at their present rate. But the Treasury go further, and appear to me to intimate pretty clearly that in their opinoin there is no sufficient reason for the continued existence of the Court upon any terms. . . . I should prefer not to say at the moment that I agree in the conclusion that the Court should be abolished, because it is possible, perhaps not probable, that persons interested in mining in Cornwall may, notwithstanding the little use which they have made of the Court lately, wish to be heard on the subject, and I should not in that case like it to be said that I have already recommended its abolition.

This diffident, impartial and seemingly rational attitude was unlikely to get a sympathetic response from the Gladstonian candle-snuffers and pinch-penny economisers at the Treasury. How differently would Smirke have fought for the survival of his court!

The following months were spent in negotiations between the Duchy Council and the Treasury for the reduction of the expenses of the Vice-Warden's court so as to prevent the Treasury having to bear any excess of expenditure over receipts out of the Consolidated Fund. Salaries were the obvious first choice for economies. The Vice-Warden's salary was fixed at £1,500 a year and the Registrar's salary at £500 a year by the Stannaries Courts Act, 1836, but on Smirke's initiative the Registrar's salary had in 1865 been supplemented by £300 a year (payable out of the fees received by the court in connection with winding-up proceedings under the Companies Act, 1862). Fisher was willing to take a substantial salary cut, and thought that Marshall, the Registrar, should do so too, but Marshall refused to suffer any reduction in his basic or supplemental salary despite the smallness of the volume of business he currently handled. He argued that much of the winding-up work he did was not as Registrar but as official liquidator of the companies wound up by the Vice-Warden's court, and for this work he received no additional remuneration at all. This was no real argument against a reduction, but when Marshall adopted this attitude of blank refusal Fisher declined to press him. Holzman wrote to the Lord Warden, the Earl of Ducie, on 26 October 1891 (132):

> . . . Mr. Fisher appears to have been shaken in his original resolution by the statement of the Registrar that in the event of the order [giving him £300 additional remuneration] being modified by your Lordship on the Vice-Warden's application to that effect, he would bring an action in the courts of law for the purpose of obtaining payment of the full amount of his salary, and the Vice-Warden may unconsciously be influenced by the effect which a public discussion of the matter would in all probability have on his own position. I have little doubt that if the Lord Chancellor became aware of all the circumstances connected with the actual state of business in the Stannaries Court, he would bring in a bill to abolish the court altogether, and in that case the Vice-Warden with one other officer might possibly, though not probably, be considered not to be entitled to compensation, whilst the Registrar and the other officers would have an undeniable claim to pensions.

The imputation that Fisher was motivated by concern for his future income was unfair; he had throughout shown a willingness to co-operate in making economies and to do so at expense to himself. What is amazing about Holzman's letter is that the Lord Chancellor, the vigorous and incisive Lord Halsbury, knew nothing of what was happening, and the future of the administration of mining law in Cornwall and Devon was being determined with the sole object of saving the Treasury expense.

In January 1892 Sir Robert Welby wrote officially on behalf of the Treasury requesting the Lord Warden and the Vice-Warden to consider what steps were needed to abolish the Vice-Warden's court (131). Three successive drafts of bills were then prepared by Treasury counsel in May 1892 and February and April 1893. All provided for the abolition of the Vice-Warden's court, but the first bill proposed the transfer of his jurisdiction to the Cornwall county court, whereas the second and third would have transferred it to such county court or courts as the Lord Chancellor should direct. The third draft was introduced into the House of Lords as a Government bill on 2 March 1895 (133), and proceeded as far as the committee stage, when it was abandoned. It was introduced in the Lords again in the following session on 10 April 1896 (134), and after an unopposed passage through the Lords and the Commons it became law on 14 August 1896 as the Stannaries Court (Abolition) Act, 1896. The Act took effect on 1 January 1897; on that day the Vice-Warden's court ceased to exist and its jurisdiction and all pending cases before it were transferred to the Cornwall county court, the recipient court nominated by the Lord Chancellor (135). It is perhaps fitting that the last action entered in the records of the Vice-Warden's court should have been brought on 7 November 1896 by Henry Roper, a solicitor of Helston, to recover £46 18s for fees payable by John Tremayne of Constantine, who was apparently a horse dealer as well as a tinner.

References to this chapter are on pages 197–203.

Chapter 2
Tin Bounding

EVERY SOCIETY AT SOME TIME PASSES THROUGH a period of economic development in which its natural resources, particularly its mineral deposits, are thrown open to exploitation by anyone who will do the necessary work to win and market them. This period always occurs when the society's population is small in relation to its territory, and in consequence not all its land is privately owned. The acquisition of the ownership of land or of some permanent and exclusive right to possession of land in such conditions, therefore, goes hand in hand with, and is the legal consequence of, the exploitation of the natural resources associated with the land. Mining, however, is different because it does not demand the exclusive use of large tracts of land surface, and because it is rarely possible in a technically unadvanced age to determine the exact limits of the land which must be worked to exhaust a mineral deposit. The law therefore inclines to give the speculative miner something less than ownership or the exclusive right to occupy the land. Instead he is given a right to take all the minerals found in a large and often ill-defined area, and ownership of the mineral is vested in him only when he breaks it from the parent lode.

The period in which distinctive mining rights originate comes to an end upon the extension of ownership to almost the whole of the surface. The law then inevitably tends to treat the owner of the surface as presumptive owner of the subjacent minerals as well, and the commonest form of acquisition of mining rights then becomes the grant of leases or licences by the surface owner as a matter of contract. In only a few countries like Germany, Austria, Spain and the former Spanish territories in South America did the concept survive of a distinctive kind of miner's right created independently of the agreement of the surface owner. Britain accepted the presumption of the surface owner's title to minerals early on as part of its medieval land law, and from the twelfth century onwards mines were worked principally under Crown or feudal grants and from the sixteenth century onwards under leases and licences granted by private landowners. Nevertheless in isolated parts of the country the older concept of independent miner's rights survived. In Cornwall and Devon this took the form of tin bounds and tin bounders' rights. Bounding was never extended to copper mining, partly because it did not begin seriously in Cornwall until the eighteenth century, by which time property rights had become too entrenched to admit of free mining; and partly because copper mining was deep mining, and bounding was originally and primarily a device for facilitating opencast mining or streaming.

The origin of free mining is probably to be found in north-western Europe during the centuries which followed the collapse of the Western Roman Empire. This was the period of small isolated agricultural communities, which banded together for self-defence, often putting themselves under the protection of local military potentates whose successors became the feudal baronage. The population was sparse, and although communities carried on intensive farming locally, there were wide bands of almost uninhabited country separating them. The ownership of these bands of country or marches was therefore of no practical significance at the time, and it was generally accepted that they were ownerless and could be used by any person for any purpose which did not prejudice the adjacent village communities or interfere with the satisfaction of their communal needs. This was just the setting for the establishment of free mining.

Unfortunately no documentary evidence survives to prove that free mining originated in this way, though deduction from the known social conditions of the time and the subsequent form of mining law during the medieval period shows that no other conclusion is possible. This was particularly so in respect of south-west England during the period from the fifth to the ninth centuries. The population at the time of the Domesday survey in the late eleventh century was less than 2.5 persons per sq mile in the districts which later became the stannaries of Penwith and Kerrier and of Foweymore, about 3 persons per sq mile on Dartmoor, and 4 persons per sq mile in what later became the stannaries of Tywarnhaile and Blackmore (1). In none of the tin-mining districts was there a village with more than forty inhabitants, and the moorland wastes were almost uninhabited (1). In earlier times the population must have been much smaller.

By deduction from the surviving records of contemporary law in Celtic and Germanic countries we can draw a picture of mining law in pre-Norman Devon and Cornwall with a fair probability of accuracy. Mining was an occupation open to any person who wished to undertake it; mines could be opened in ownerless land without any preliminary authorisation, but in land which had been appropriated by individuals, only with their consent; the miner could take the whole produce of the mine without delivering even a fraction to the king or his immediate overlord; and, finally, the miner's rights in respect of a mine he had opened or worked did not include ownership of the land, but were nevertheless recognised by law. The transition to medieval mining law required a number of adjustments to be made to this simple design, principally in respect of the render of toll tin to the owner of the land that was mined and the payment of coinage duty to the Crown.

THE CREATION OF TIN BOUNDS

The tinner's Charters of 1201 and 1305 gave no clear indication of the kinds of land which could be subjected to tin bounds. The Charter of 1201, which extended to both Cornwall and Devon, gave the tinners liberty 'to mine for tin and dig turves for smelting tin everywhere in the moors and fiefs of bishops, abbots and counts as they have been accustomed to do' (2), and the two identical Charters of 1305 for each county authorised the tinners 'to mine for tin and dig turves for smelting tin everywhere in our lands, moors and wastes and in those of all other persons whatsoever in the said county . . . as has formerly been done' (3). In each Charter the king had previously referred to the stannaries as being his demesne, and it may have been this which later led the Star Chamber, and several authors, including Pearce, to assume that the whole of the stannaries were in fact in the king's possession in 1201 and 1305, so that the Charters should be read as grants by the king of new rights of mining. In fact the charters merely confirmed the existing customary law of bounding, as the final words in the quotations given above clearly indicate, and, far from granting new rights or defining existing ones, they left the scope of the right of bounding unsettled.

Pearce, writing in 1725, thought that before the Charters of 1305 the tinners of Cornwall were entitled to mine 'in wastrel grounds and in the Prince's [ie the king's, later the Duke of Cornwall's] several lands only . . . excepting only sanctuary ground, churches, mills, houses and gardens' (4). This would mean that bounding never extended to land which was acquired by an individual before mining or prospecting began, except in the seventeen manors belonging to the Duchy of Cornwall, which were open to bounding subject to the exception in favour of houses, etc. Pearce's account substantially accords with a seventeenth-century manuscript now at the British Museum, which asserted that the pre-1305 customary law entitled the Cornish tinners to mine in wastrel and in the Prince's several land, but not under houses or highways (5). The Report of the Royal Commissioners appointed in 1525 to enquire into the stannary laws of convocation legislation for Cornwall expressed the position after 1305 in much the same terms (6), and it was obviously accepted that the Charter of 1305 had effected no changes. The most recent Convocation enactment in 1752 (7) provided that:

> . . . by the common usage and custom of the stannaries, any tinner may bound with tin bounds any wastrel lands within the County of Cornwall that are unbounded or void of lawful bounds; and also any several and inclosed lands that have been anciently bounded and assured for wastrel by payment of the toll tin before that the hedges were made upon the same; and also may cut bounds in the Prince's several and inclosed ancient assessionable Duchy manors according to the ancient custom and usage within the said several Duchy manors. . . .

Notwithstanding the general terms in which the right of tinners to bound inclosed land in the Duchy manors was expressed, it was subject to exceptions by custom. For example, in 1537 and 1538 a jury of the stannary of Foweymore presented that no one might mine in the king's inclosed land in the Duchy manor of Stoke Climesland without the king's licence (8). On the other hand a jury of the stannary of Penwith and Kerrier in 1636 presented that if inclosed arable or meadow land belonging to the king or a subject was worked for tin and toll tin was once accepted by the person entitled to it, the land should be treated as wastrel, and could be bounded or rebounded at any time thereafter (9). Churches and churchyards were always immune from mining operations (10), and houses were protected even though the land on which they stood had been bounded before they were built (11), but mining beneath highways was not prohibited (12) provided the surface was not damaged or endangered (13). In 1529 a jury of the stannary of Penwith and Kerrier presented that it was possible to bound land for underground lode mining even though the surface had already been bounded for a streamwork and *vice versa* (14). But it was not possible to bound lands which were subject to existing bounds so as to acquire a right to work them on paying toll tin to the original bounder (15), nor was it possible to bound such lands in reversion, that is, to acquire the right to work for tin in the future on the lapsing, forfeiture or surrender of the existing bounds (16). If existing bounds were not being worked or if they were not renewed annually, however, a stranger could rebound the land in question and the new bounds pitched by him replaced the original ones.

The categories of land which might be bounded in Devon were always wider than in Cornwall. In 1510 the Convocation of Devon declared that it was 'lawful for every man to dig tin in every place within the county of Devonshire where tin is found' (17). In 1574 the Devon Convocation accepted a limitation on the tinners' privileges by forbidding tinners to mine in future in or under meadows, orchards, gardens, mansions and houses and their respective outbuildings and curtilages, or in or under manured arable land or any other land while under corn or grain or within two years after the most recent crop was reaped, and it was also forbidden for tinners to cut down more than twenty timber trees in any wood or coppice (18). These acts could, of course, be performed if the landowner permitted, but if they were done without his consent, the offenders could be fined and were also liable to pay the owner treble damages (18). If permission was given, the landowner and his tenants (if any) were entitled to receive one-tenth of the profit made from working and selling the tin ore produced (19).

The result of the legislation of 1574 was to make the categories of land which could be freely bounded in Devon only a little wider than those in Cornwall. Apart from waste and moorland and land in the king's demesne, the only important land which could be freely bounded in Devon (but not in Cornwall) was rough pasture land, and after the decision of the Queen's Bench in 1847 in the case of *Rogers* v *Brenton*, which was concerned with tin bounds in Cornwall, it became very doubtful whether tin bounds in privately owned land in Devon were valid at all unless the land was wastrel when it was first bounded (20). By the time of this decision, however, most tin bounds in Devon were already extinct, since mining had ceased.

The procedure for bounding land in Cornwall and Devon was simple and was known technically as pitching a pair of bounds. Thomas Beare, writing in the second half of the sixteenth century, described it as follows (21):

> The manner of bounding is most commonly to make four corner bounds, two at the head of the work and two more at the tail, in cutting up three turfs in every corner, and so consequently their side bounds and head bounds with three turfs on every place, one directly against the other. . . .

Beare was writing of bounding streamworks, and 'the head of the work' was the higher part of the alluvial bed towards which the work progressed. The lower end of the bounds would have water brought to it through a channel called a tye or leat, so that the ore could be washed and the waste matter or tailings washed away downhill. Pryce, writing two centuries after Beare, was more succinct (22):

> They [tin bounds] are limited by holes cut in the turf, and the soil turned back upon the turf which is cut, in form of a molehill, and directly facing another of the like kind; these are called the corners of the bounds, containing sometimes an acre, sometimes more and often less. By drawing straight lines from the corners the extent of these bounds is determined.

In practice the corners of bounds were marked with stones, and not turves, in order to preserve permanent evidence of the limits of the bounds. The Convocation of Cornwall recognised either form of marking as sufficient, and required six stones or turves to be placed at each corner (23).

In the sixteenth or early seventeenth centuries a slight complication was introduced in the form of side bounds, a confusing term which could mean one of the sides of a pair of bounds other than the head or tail bounds or, alternatively, one of the additional sides which could be added to the original pair of bounds. The shape of the early bounds was a quadrilateral, which was not necessarily a rectangle. On moorland this shape was easy to mark out because there were no impediments, but when bounds were pitched near enclosed land it was often impossible to have a quadrilateral which took in all the tin-bearing alluvium yet did not cross the boundaries of the enclosed land. To overcome this difficulty triangular side bounds were extended from two of the corners of the original bounds, and the shape of the original and side bounds together would then be pentagonal, or if side bounds were extended from more than one of the original sides, hexagonal, heptagonal or octagonal. If owners of two adjacent pairs of bounds both wished to extend side bounds into the land lying between them, the owner to whose original bounds the additional land was nearest had the better claim (23). The validity of side bounds was recognised by the Convocation of Cornwall in 1687 (24).

In the early law of Cornwall and Devon a miner who intended to pitch bounds did not need to obtain the consent of the owner of the land in question, or even to notify him in advance. Devon law never required the owner of the freehold to be notified, but in 1532 and again in 1574 Convocation legislation made it necessary for a miner who bounded land which had previously been bounded but was no longer being worked (called 'alay') to notify the owner that he had rebounded them, and a formal procedure in the steward's court was provided to determine whether the rebounding was valid or not (25). This led to difficulties when the owner of the bounds was unknown or could not be found, and so in 1600 Convocation dispensed with notice of the rebounding in such situations (26).

By contrast with Devon law, the enactments of the Convocation of Cornwall did not require notice of an intention to rebound unworked bounds to be given to the owner of them, but in 1686 Convocation did require a bounder to notify the freeholder or his agent in writing within one year after any bounds were pitched, whether new or rebounded, so that the freeholder might claim his toll tin, and if the notice was not given the bounds became void as from the end of the year (27). This, of course, gave the freeholder no chance to prevent his land being bounded, though he was always at liberty to bound them himself and so forestall anyone else. The Convocation of 1752 extended the protection of the freeholder in this respect by requiring an intending bounder to give three months' written notice of his intention to the freeholder or his agent, and if the freeholder bounded his own land within the three months, and made a declaration on oath before the steward of the stannary before anyone else applied to the steward's court to proclaim bounds over his land, the freeholder's bounds were valid and the others' were made void (28). This curiously worded provision was never construed by the Vice-Warden or by any other court, but it seems to have given a freeholder who had received notice of an intention to bound the right to bound himself within the three months and to validate his own bounds by a sworn declaration without the need for the proclamations necessary in any other case; and it would also seem to have given such a freeholder priority for his own bounds over any two or more other persons who served separate notices of their respective intentions to bound his land, provided he bounded himself within three months after the last of such notices was served and made his sworn declaration before the steward received an application to proclaim bounds already pitched by any of the persons who had served notices. It was quite clear, however, that if a stranger did not serve a notice of an intention to bound three months or more before doing so, any bounds he pitched were void (28), and they were not validated by being proclaimed (29).

A freeholder could, of course, waive the three months' notice required by the Act of 1752 and the bounds were then pitched by the stranger with his consent (30). If he took no action to resist the pitching of bounds after the three months had expired, he was likewise considered to have consented to it, with the odd result that if the bounder enjoyed an asserted right against adjacent property—for example, a right to the continued flow of water from that land—he did so on behalf of the freeholder, who would after twenty years acquire the right permanently as an easement by prescription (31). Conversely, the fact that the bounder worked with the freeholder's implied consent made it possible for an adjacent owner to prescribe for any rights over the freeholder's land consequent on the bounder's acts or omissions—for example, prescription for the right to a continued flow of water if the bounder had allowed water to run from his bounds over the adjacent owner's land (32).

In 1752 the Cornwall Convocation also enacted legislation empowering any person to give notice of his intention to work bounds left unworked for twelve months to the owner of the bounds, and after going through certain formalities, to work for tin within the bounds as though the bound owner had granted a lease or sett to him (33). Such action by the stranger did not amount to a rebounding and the former bounds were not destroyed. Consequently, the stranger did not have to give notice of his intention to the freeholder, and the latter had no opportunity to bound the land himself and so forestall the reworking of the bounds.

THE REGISTRATION AND PROCLAMATION OF BOUNDS

Thomas Beare, writing in the second half of the sixteenth century, considered that the registration of tin bounds in the steward's court of the stannary where they lay was required by custom before it was prescribed by legislation (34). He did not say whether failure to register bounds in the court books, or failure by the steward to proclaim the registered bounds by oral announcement at the three following sittings of the court, invalidated the bounds. In fact no entries of bounds or proclamations appear in the court rolls of the stewards' courts of Devon or Cornwall before the first legislation was enacted requiring registration, and it is improbable that before that time anything further was required to perfect a bounder's title to bounds than pitching them in the manner already described.

The earliest legislation on the recording of bounds is found in the Act of a Devon Convocation passed in 1494 (35), the fifth article of which provided:

> . . . every tinner that hereafter shall pitch any tinwork, that at the next law court [ie sitting of the steward's court] after such pitch made the same pitcher shall enter the whole bounds of the same tinwork in the said court and the name thereof and as well to put in the names of all those that such pitcher hath named owners in the same work . . . and whosoever pitch contrary to this that then his pitch be void.

In 1496 Prince Arthur's Council enacted a similar ordinance for Cornwall (36):

> If any tinner shall hereafter pitch any tinwork he shall at the next law court enter the whole bounds of the same tinwork and the name of the tinwork with the names of his fellows . . . and the steward or his clerk shall take for every such entering but a penny for every name.

The Cornwall ordinance was revoked by the Charter of Pardon of 1508, but bounders continued to act as though it was still in force, and it was re-enacted by the Cornwall Convocation of 1588 in respect of the rebounding of old unworked tinworks, with the addition that the new bounder's entry had to show the date of rebounding and the old and new names of the work (37). The Act of 1588 significantly added that failure to comply with it made the new pitch void.

Meanwhile the Devon legislation had become more detailed and exacting. The Devon Convocation Act of 1532, relating nominally only to rebounding tinworks that were 'alay' or unworked, required the rebounder, after warning the owner of the existing bounds of the date on which he pitched new bounds, to 'cause the steward of the [stannary court] or his deputy for the time being to enter into his book, that shall remain in the court at all times of record, the name of the pitch, that is (to wit) his own name and all his fellows' names, named to be pitchers of the said tinwork, the tinwork's name, the owner or owner's names that were so warned, and the day and place where he gave such warning' (38). The steward was then to 'make the proclamation of the said pitch and warning of the said old owner or owners [of the bounds] in the same court [ie at the same sitting] and in the other stannary courts next following [ie the other three steward's courts of Devon] . . . when the steward or his deputy shall think most people to be present'.

If these formalities were not properly gone through the rebounding was 'to be void and of none effect' (38). Within three months after the last proclamation the existing bound owner could require the rebounder to attend at the tinwork so that the owner could prove that he was still in occupation of the tinwork, which would invalidate the newly pitched bounds (38). If he did not do this, his bounds lapsed, and the rebounder acquired a valid title to the new bounds he had pitched. If the bound owner proved his occupation, but the rebounder refused to accept his proof (because, for example, he considered that sufficient work was not currently being done to prevent the work from being alay), the bound owner had to enter a written summary of the proof he tendered at the next sitting of the steward's court, and the court then issued a writ of *scire facias* requiring the rebounder to appear and formally contest the proof (39). If he did not appear, or if the bound owner's occupation was verified by the oaths of four or five tinners and the rebounder could not prove that the work was alay or had not been renewed properly each year, the court confirmed the existing bound owner's title (39), but if the rebounder sustained the burden of proof imposed on him, the newly pitched bounds were formally confirmed. If the bound owner was unable to serve notice on the rebounder requiring him to hear the owner's proof at the tinwork because the rebounder was unknown or was out of Devon, the bound owner had to enter notice at the steward's court and at the other three stannary courts of a day within three months from the proclamation of the rebounder's new pitch when the owner would prove his occupation of the tinwork on its site, and that date had to be proclaimed in all four stannary courts (40). If the rebounder appeared at the tinwork on that day, the same procedure was gone through as if he had been individually notified, but if he did not appear his rebounding was invalidated (41). If under any of these detailed provisions the rebounder did not establish a valid title to new bounds, the existing bound owner was required to have an entry made in the court records against the original entry of the rebounder's new pitch, that the existing bound owner had proved the continued existence of his bounds (41), but failure to do this did not affect the validity of his bounds.

The Devon Convocation of 1574 simplified the procedure for recording the rebounding of tinworks by dispensing with proof of the existing bound owner's occupation at the tinworks themselves. Instead the existing bound owner was required to tender proof on oath of his occupation and of the successive annual renewals of his bounds at one of the four sittings of the steward's court following the sitting at which the rebounder's new pitch was proclaimed (42). If the existing bound owner failed to tender such proof, or if the steward rejected his proof, the rebounder's title was validated (42). The Convocation of 1600 obviously thought the burden of proving the continued existence of old bounds was unfair to the existing bound owner, especially since in the initial stages of the procedure under the Acts of 1532 and 1574 all the rebounder had to prove was that he had pitched new bounds—ie, had set up turves or corner stones. To counterbalance the burden and to protect old bounds as property rights, the legislation of 1600 gave an existing bound owner who proved his occupation and the successive annual renewals of his bounds the right to sue the rebounder for substantial damages for trespass (43). Technically the rebounder committed a trespass by setting up his corner stones if the old bounds still existed at the time, but the damages recoverable for this at common law were nominal. Under the new legislation, however, he could additionally be sued for damages for impeaching the existing bound owner's title and for the costs and expenses to which the owner had been put in defending it.

The Devon Convocation Act of 1600 also improved the position of a rebounder who did not know who was the owner of bounds which were alay. He was absolved from giving the existing owner any preliminary warning of having rebounded them before entering the rebounding in the steward's court, and on the expiration of one year after the last proclamation of his new pitch in the four stannary courts he became absolutely entitled to his new bounds, unless the existing bound owner entered a claim to the continued existence of his bounds in court meanwhile (44). It is not clear from the wording of the enacting part of this provision whether it applied only in favour of a rebounder who really did not know the identity of the old owner of the bounds (the kind of rebounder mentioned in the recital to the provision as its intended beneficiary), or whether all rebounders could avail themselves of the new provision instead of going through the more complex procedure laid down by the Act of 1574. It is possible to argue that a rebounder who knew the identity of the existing bound owner but did not give him the warning of the intended rebounding would have been guilty of fraud, and the validity of his new bounds would therefore have been impeachable by the old owner after the year had expired. On the other hand, an existing owner who did not act within the year must surely have acquiesced in the loss of his title, since he would have to renew it at least once within that time to keep it alive.

Also it may have been a subsidiary purpose of the legislation of 1600 to give the rebounder a title good against the whole world after the expiration of the year, although this idea is rather weakened by the presence of another provision in the legislation (45) which unequivocally achieved this only after the rebounder had been in occupation of his new bounds for two years. It could well be argued that the expiration of one year from the proclamation of the new bounds without the intervention of the existing bound owner gave the rebounder only a qualified title, which became absolute after a further year's occupation. Unfortunately no records of litigation in the Devon stannary courts survive to show which was the correct interpretation. It is clear, however, that the procedure of the Act of 1600 could be used when the land in question had never previously been bounded, and the bounder who remained in occupation for one or two years thereby obtained the same protection for his title as a rebounder would have done.

Although the Cornwall legislation on the registration of bounds followed the form of the early Devon legislation, in the seventeenth century it departed from that model radically, being designed to protect bounders' rights more extensively by making it difficult for anyone to attack them successfully. This reflects the growing interest in bounds of the landed gentry, from whose ranks the members of Convocation came. They did not work bounds themselves, but by granting leases or setts of bounds they owned to working miners they acquired a share of the produce, called farm tin, and so had every reason to protect their interests as property rights.

The ordinance of 1496 and the Cornwall Convocation Act of 1588 merely required bounds to be entered in the records of the sitting of the next steward's court after they were pitched, and it was not provided that failure to register made the bounds void until the Act of 1588. Nevertheless, Vice-Warden Beare held, either on appeal or at a joint sitting with the steward of Blackmore, c 1540, that it was necessary for bounds to be proclaimed orally in three successive courts following their entry in the court records, and that if either the entry or the proclamations were omitted, the bounds became void (46). According to the report, Beare also issued an injunction against the former owners of the bounds in dispute, which were currently unworked, and thereby directed the bailiff to put the new bounder, who had entered his rebounding and had it proclaimed, into possession of the tinwork. Such an injunction or warrant to deliver possession of bounds must have been the precursor of the writ of possession that became standard in the seventeenth century. It is interesting to note from this case, however, that the original purpose of the warrant was to remove the former bound owners in favour of the rebounder. In later practice the writ of possession was issued even though the land had never previously been bounded, and in such circumstances, which were by then the commonest, the issue of the writ was merely a formality. In the sixteenth century its precursor, the bailiff's warrant, probably was not.

The Cornwall Convocation of 1624 re-enacted the requirement that rebounders should enter the fact of their having pitched new bounds at the next sitting of the steward's court, though it curiously referred to the bounder as then making 'his proclamation' (47). The Act of 1636 covered both bounding and rebounding and imposed the same requirements in both cases, directing that the bounder's entry must show the date of the pitch, his name and the names of his fellow owners, the old and new names of the bounds and their locality (48). Both the 1624 and 1636 Acts made bounds void if any of these formalities were not complied with. These bare enactments obviously did not set out the current practice completely. This was more explicitly enunciated in the presentment of a grand jury of the stannary of Penwith and Kerrier on 23 May 1636 in which the tinners declared their customs as follows: a bounder must have his bounds proclaimed at three successive sittings of the steward's court; if bounds were entered and proclaimed in their new name but not in their old, the old owner might sue to recover his old bounds within a year and a day and could also sue for the value of the tin worked meanwhile; and on a rebounding the old owner could enter a plaint of trespass against a new bounder at the next sitting of the steward's court after the last proclamation of the new bounds, and thereupon the court had to restore him to possession of his old bounds until the question of their validity and that of the new bounds was tried (49).

The Convocation Act of 1686 was far more explicit than the earlier legislation. It provided (50):

> . . . that whosoever shall pitch any bounds shall enter his proclamations of the same in the stannary court where the ground lieth at the first court that shall be held after the pitch; in which proclamation he shall put down the day of the pitch, the names of his fellow owners and the party that cut them, and the true bounds and limits of the corners thereof, otherwise the said pitch to be void: and that also when any pitch of new bounds shall be entered in the stannary court, the same shall be openly proclaimed at the court and two courts following before writs of posses-

> sion shall be granted, and shall be ingrossed and posted up in some open place in the court during the continuance of such three courts before a writ of possession. And if any person shall in any of the three courts make claim or title against the said new pitch, either by reason of old bounds or several [ie privately owned] land, he shall forthwith enter his action of trespass against the person that cut the said bounds and the person to whose use the bounds were cut, and the person so cutting shall likewise give notice to the lord or lords of the fee of the lands on which such bounds are cut . . . within one year after such pitch and shall prove such notice given before the steward of the stannary in which the bounds are. . . .

TOLL TIN

Toll tin was the render or counterpart due to the freeholder when his land was mined for tin by a bounder or his lessee. It resembled a rent reserved by lease of land in that it was payable whether or not the land was worked profitably, but it was not a contractual render like rent, and so in strict law the freeholder could not sue the bound owner for breach of contract if it were not delivered. Nevertheless in equity the Vice-Warden's court allowed the freeholder to sue for damages (ie the value of his share of the tin broken) just as though he had granted a lease or sett to the bounder (51), and if the tin had been sold he was also allowed to sue for his share of the proceeds (52) or for an account of the proceeds so that payment of his share might be directed (53). Tolls were recoverable at common law by an action of debt or *indebtitatus assumpsit*, which pre-supposed the existence of a debt, and so direct actions for the freeholder's share of the proceeds of sale of tin could have been brought in the stewards' courts. Nevertheless suits for an account of the proceeds were quite properly brought in the Vice-Warden's court despite the availability of legal remedies because account was a distinctive equitable remedy. No doubt the Vice-Wardens before the reforms of 1836 would have justified their entertainment of suits in respect of toll tin on the ground that they had a general equitable jurisdiction over all matters concerning bounds. This idea was exploded in 1842 (54), but by then the Vice-Warden had acquired the stewards' common-law jurisdiction, and so the question whether claims for toll tin should be brought by action and not by a petition in equity affected only matters of procedure. In 1852 Vice-Warden Dampier decided that either method could be employed (52).

If two or more persons owned the same bounds in shares, they were jointly and severally liable for toll tin, which meant that the freeholder could sue all or any one or more of them at his choice for the whole amount of the toll tin due (55). He could also sue any adventurer in a partnership or company which worked the mine under a sett from the bounders (55). He could not sue the purser of the mine if the bounders worked it themselves as adventurers, however (56), and since the freeholder's claim was a purely personal one and he did not become a part owner of the tin ore broken, he had no claim against anyone who subsequently received or dealt with the ore, such as the smelter who converted it into white tin (57). In practice freeholders took toll tin in the form of a share of the proceeds of sale of the tin ore, but, if they wished, they could insist on receiving a share of the black tin as soon as it was washed, and they would then arrange for the sale of their share themselves (58). This right to take a share of the black tin had another important practical consequence: since toll tin became due as soon as the black tin was washed, the freeholder could thereafter seize or distrain the tin or any other chattels of the bounder or his lessee at the mine, and could retain them until the toll was rendered. In this respect the freeholder was better placed than the grantor of a mining sett who had no right by law to distrain for farm tin (59).

In Devon the freeholder of privately owned land and his tenants were entitled to receive one-tenth of the profit of tinworks on their land as compensation for damage done to the surface (60). Unlike toll tin, which was a share in the produce or gross proceeds of the mine, this entitlement was to a share of the net proceeds, so that if the cost of working the mine exceeded the proceeds of sale of the tin ore broken, the freeholder and his tenants received nothing. Their position closely resembled that of adventurers in a mining partnership with the bounders, but they were not in fact partners, and so were not personally liable to mining creditors for debts incurred by the bounders or the miners to whom they granted a sett in carrying on the mine.

In some parts of Cornwall it seems that the freeholder could commute his rights into an entitlement similar to that of his counterpart in Devon, by taking a 'land dole' or fractional share of the net profits of the mine on permanently renouncing his right to toll tin. The Convocation Act of 1686 provided that if a freeholder 'where land dole is customary do take and receive his toll tin before he enter his land dole' he was barred of his land dole, that is, he could not subsequently opt to take a land dole in exchange for toll tin; 'but if he enter into his land dole before he takes his toll tin, then he shall have, possess and enjoy both land dole and toll tin, else he shall have the toll tin only' (61). What this seemingly unjust provision seems to mean is that the freeholder who took toll tin could not subsequently convert it into a land dole, but if he claimed a land dole before receiving toll tin, he could still claim toll tin on converting his land dole into a share in the adventure operating the mine, so becoming an ordinary adventurer liable to pay his share of costs. The land dole in this case was usually called a pleasure dole, and it seems that a freeholder who took it could later convert his retained right to toll tin into a further land dole carrying no liability to pay a share of costs (62). The size of land doles and pleasure doles depended on custom, which might vary from locality to locality, though Carew, writing in 1602, said that pleasure doles were usually one-fifteenth shares (63). The tinners of Foweymore in 1613 presented their custom to be that land dole should be the reciprocal of the number of the adventurers' shares plus one (64), so that if the adventure was divided into six shares, the land dole would be one-seventh, and if the adventure consisted of twenty shares, the land dole would be one part in twenty-one.

Under such a custom it would seem to pay the adventurers to divide their undertaking into as many shares as possible, for even in the early seventeenth century there was no limit on the number of shares that might be created.

THE RENEWAL OF BOUNDS

The early customary law of both Cornwall and Devon required bounds to be renewed on the anniversary of the day following that on which they were pitched, and on every subsequent anniversary of the first renewal. If bounds were first pitched on 1 August 1500, therefore, they had to be renewed on 2 August 1501, 2 August 1502 and so on. Thomas Beare, writing in 1586, stated that by custom tinners 'must diligently observe and keep yearly from time to time bound to bounds, and most chiefly their corner bounds every year upon their very day of bounding' (65), but he then went on to cite a decision given by himself as steward of Blackmore in the very year he wrote, by which he ruled that the renewal should take place on the day after the anniversary of the first pitching. The renewal in that case had been effected on the anniversary of the pitching, and as the bounds would not have been void at the end of that day for want of renewal, the renewal was invalid, and Beare held, therefore, that another person who pitched new bounds on the same tinwork a few days later had a good title and could register and proclaim his bounds (66).

Beare's ruling is supported from a number of other sources for Cornwall. The proper interval between pitching and first renewal was given as a year and a day in a presentment of the customs of Penwith and Kerrier by a jury of tinners of the stannary in 1518 (67), by a similar jury for Foweymore in 1613 (68) and in the Act of the Cornwall Convocation of 1686 (69). The Act of 1686 contemplated that the first renewal was effective itself for a year and a day, as were also the second and subsequent renewals, so that according to the Act the second and subsequent renewals themselves had to take place on the anniversary of the day following the preceding renewal. This may seem a small point, but it could be of practical significance, as the Blackmore case of 1586 showed. Furthermore, the extension of the year and a day period to all renewals in the seventeenth century produced the idea that the bounder's interest itself lasted for a year and a day only, but was renewable for successive like periods at his option. The original conception was that bounds were perpetual but defeasible, that is, that they could be destroyed on the initiative of the landowner or a new bounder if they were not renewed. This concept was adopted by the Devon Convocation in the sixteenth century and remained the law in Devon throughout. The Devon Convocation Acts of 1532 and 1574 required bound owners to 'keep their tinworks . . . yearly between the feast of St Peter Advincula [1 August] and the feast of St Michael the Archangel [29 September]' (70), so that the first as well as subsequent renewals took place on the anniversary of the first pitching. The same enactments also referred to the bounder's interest being a fee simple, that is a perpetual interest, and stated that the bounder and his heirs were entitled to the bounds for ever. This clearly contemplated that in Devon, unlike Cornwall, bounds conferred not a yearly interest that was indefinitely renewable, but a perpetual interest subject to termination if it were not renewed annually.

The difference between bounders' interests in Cornwall and Devon is clearly shown by a comparison of the consequences of a failure to renew. Thomas Beare stated the original customary law of Cornwall to be that 'if a tinner do not renew his bounds within a year and a day, if he afterwards, finding his fault, doth renew his old bounds before any other, this saveth his work' (71). In other words, non-renewal merely exposed the bounder to the risk that the landowner or a new bounder might take over his tinwork, thereby destroying his interest, but if no one intervened he might save his interest, which still continued, by renewing late. Already the germ of the altered Cornish law had gained a place, however, for in 1518 the tinners of Penwith and Kerrier had declared their custom to be that 'bounds shall keep a tinwork for twelve month and one day and no more' (72), though in 1613 the tinners of Foweymore declared their custom to be what Beare had stated (73). The Foweymore presentment contained the clearest exposition of the original law. It stated:

> . . . that the said corners must be renewed after twelve months and one day, otherwise they are void if they are thereafter occupied by new bounders. But if after such a default the said tinwork is not pitched anew, the old owners of the same tinwork may renew after the year and the day and that shall suffice to continue the tinwork [ie interest in the tinwork] of the old owners.

In 1624 Convocation tried its hand at spelling out the consequences of failure to renew. It provided equivocally that if a bounder who had not renewed '. . . shall afterwards come again and renew the old corners before any new tinner shall put a new pitch upon them, that such renewing shall be taken as a good renewing against any other pitch' (74). The final words of this enactment opened up the possibility of treating the old owner of bounds as having a right of late renewal only against any bounder who entered after the proper renewal date had passed, but as no longer having any interest in the land as against the freeholder or any other person. This was assumed to be the meaning of Convocation by the Vice-Warden's court throughout the seventeenth and eighteenth centuries (75). The only exceptions were that bounders were permitted to sue lessees to whom they had granted leases or setts for farm tin due thereunder (76) and also to sue agents who had collected such farm tin for them (77), without in either case proving that they had duly renewed the bounds up to date. The exceptions were more apparent than real, however, for they rested on the general rule of law that a lessee may not dispute the title of the lessor from whom he has accepted his lease, nor an agent the title of his principal. In 1838 the Court of Exchequer confirmed the accepted opinion as to the effect of non-renewal of bounds, and held that if a bounder failed to renew on the proper date his interest in the land expired, and he could not revive it as against the freeholder by purporting to renew at a later date (78). The bounder could, of course, rebound the same tinwork by a new pitch if it had not been bounded meanwhile by the freeholder or anyone else, but since Convocation in 1752 had required three months' notice of intended bounding or rebounding to be given to the freeholder (79), so that he might prevent it by bounding himself, this alternative course had no practical value.

The Devon Convocation enactments by contrast constantly protected the bounder against loss of his bounds. The Convocation Acts of 1510 and 1533 enabled bounders who were in possession of their tinworks at Michaelmas of those respective years to register the fact in the records of the steward's court, and unless an adverse claim by any other person had previously been made to the court, on registration the bounders became entitled absolutely to their bounds (80), so that the fact that they had not previously renewed could not subsequently be raised against them by anyone. In 1600 Convocation extended this provision to any bounder who had received farm tin in respect of a tinwork or had actually worked it continuously for a period of two years, with the same consequence that any failure on his part to renew his bounds annually before registration could not be used by anyone subsequently to impeach his title (81). These preclusive provisions were, of course, as effective against the freeholder of the land as against anyone who attempted to rebound it. The effect of the Act of 1600 was to make biennial registration by a bounder an alternative to the annual renewal of bounds. Unfortunately no records have survived to show how much use was made of this alternative facility.

Even apart from these enactments Devon law treated a bounder as having a permanent interest in the land in question until his title was successfully impeached in court proceedings by someone who wished to rebound the land or by the freeholder. The procedure by which a new bounder could have the steward's court set aside the old bounds for non-renewal or failure to work them has already been described in connection with the registration in court of the new bounder's claim. It is significant to note that the enactments governing this procedure did not make unrenewed bounds immediately void, but only alay, that is to say available for rebounding by others. The old bounds remained valid until the court ruled otherwise (82), and in the meantime the old bound owner could continue working the tin ore for his own benefit.

The procedure for renewing bounds was quite simple. The bounder or his agent placed six turves or stones at the corners of the bounds in the same way as when they were first pitched. In fact the purpose of renewal was simply to ensure that the corners of the bounds were always marked with distinctive and visible evidence of the bounder's continued occupation. Thomas Beare considered that it was unnecessary to renew side bounds (83), but the Cornwall Convocation Act of 1686 declared that if they were not renewed at the same time as the principal bounds they became void, though this did not affect the validity of the principal bounds if they were properly renewed (84). Presumably the procedure for renewing bounds in Devon was the same. In neither county was it necessary to register or proclaim renewals of bounds in the way required when they were originally pitched.

THE WORKING OF BOUNDS

In the early law of the stannaries it was necessary for a bound owner to work his bounds continuously as well as to renew them annually. The whole purpose of recognising the bound owner as having a legal interest in the land subject to bounds was to ensure that the tin ore lying in it was worked for the benefit of the market, for the benefit of the landowner in the form of the toll tin rendered, and for the benefit of the king or the Duke of Cornwall in the form of the coinage duty paid. These benefits did not accrue if the bound owner merely renewed his bounds annually without working for tin ore. The requirement of annual renewal served the quite different purpose of publicising the bounds. The obligations to work and to renew were therefore independent and cumulative.

If either obligation was not satisfied, the bound owner's interest could be terminated.

There was never any precise criteria as to the amount of work required to keep bounds on foot. In 1518 the tinners of Penwith and Kerrier presented their custom to be that the bound owner must renew his bounds annually and

> . . . must do reasonable cost, and because that the reasonable cost was doubtful the said twelve tinners swore . . . and did find and present that the reasonable cost shall be three months cost of one man his working or one month cost of three men or else the same work [bounds] to be void at the fourth year if continually were not continued (85).

In 1586 Thomas Beare expressed the custom of Blackmore to be less strict:

> . . . that the first year [after pitching bounds the bounder] may keep [his] work by bounds, in the second year it behoveth [him] to bestow some charge, and in the third year [he] must deliver toll tin within their said bounds, and so maintain forth the bounds by renewing (86),

and this was enacted in substance as the rule by Convocation in 1752 (87). Here again working and renewing bounds in the second and subsequent years were expressed to be cumulative duties. A little earlier in his book Beare gave an alternative to the obligation to renew bounds, namely fetching 'water from the leat [the nearest natural or artificial watercourse] of another man's work . . . [and paying] a farm [rent] to the work whence you take your water for the use of your work' (88). It can readily be seen that this would provide some evidence of the continued existence and also, possibly, the continued working of the tinwork so served, but it is difficult to understand how taking water for washing ore from an adjoining streamwork could be any substitute for renewing corner turves or stones so as to indicate clearly the limits of the bounds. However, this is the first instance we encounter of a different act being substituted for one of the bound owner's two obligations to work and to renew, and it marks a stage in the development toward treating the performance of one of the obligations as a substitute for performing the other.

The change to treating either renewal or working as sufficient to keep bounds on foot was brought about by the increasing acquisition of bounds during the sixteenth century by landed gentry who did not work the bounds themselves but let them to working tinners under leases or setts. Under such arrangements it was impossible for the bounders to ensure continuous working, but they could and did ensure that the corner stones or turves of the bounds were renewed annually. Gradually the law came to accept that what they could ensure should be the full extent of their obligation, and, conversely, that the working tinners, who had no power to renew bounds unless they were expressly authorised by the bounders, should not be prejudiced by the bounders' failure to renew, provided the tinners worked for tin ore continuously.

The acquisition of tin bounds by non-working proprietors began early in the sixteenth century, but there may have been some isolated instances in the previous century. One of the earliest recorded tin bounds entered on the steward's court roll for Foweymore in 1506 appears to be made for a non-working proprietor. The bounds were stated to have been cut jointly by Richard Code, esquire, and Edward Trewynnek, but it is unlikely that Code, who was a member of a family of landowners at St Austell and Morval, actually took part in pitching them. It is more likely that Trewynnek did so as his agent, and the registration of the bounds was made in their joint names because the device of the pitcher bounding to the use or on behalf of the intended proprietor had not yet been adopted. In 1539 a plea in an action of trespass brought by a landowner against a bounder in the steward's court of Penwith and Kerrier, which expressly set out the bounding custom as entitling a bounder to pitch bounds either himself or by his men, was upheld by the Vice-Warden, Sir William Godolphin (89), thus clearly recognising the legality of vicarious pitching.

Convocation enactments were slow to recognise the changed conditions under which bounds were owned by non-working proprietors. The Devon legislation of 1510 and 1533, which validated the titles of bounders who held bounds at Michaelmas in those years despite defects in their titles that had arisen beforehand, applied only to persons who were then 'peaceably seised of and in any tinwork' (90), an expression which could have excluded bounders who had granted leases or setts, but which may not have been intended to do so. This equivocal wording contrasts with the more precise language of the corresponding Devon legislation of 1600, which gave the same protection to persons who were 'peaceably seised in fee of any tinwork . . . either by working or taking the profits thereof or by renewing or keeping it to his or their uses, and so [continued] seised by the space of two years' (91). By 1600 bounds in Devon could obviously be kept by working *or* by renewing. The Cornwall Convocation Act of 1636 produced much the same result by providing (92):

> That an owner working his tinwork by himself, his wages man or farmer [lessee] paying toll once a year and a day, or otherwise continuing his working without fraud in driving an adit into or sinking a shaft upon the said work, and withal preserving the four corner bounds . . . if they or any of them shall be newly or casually or maliciously defaced, so long the said owner shall not lose his bounds for want of renewing.

It could be argued that this enactment only made working a substitute for renewing and not *vice versa*, but any doubt on this score was removed by another provision of the same enactment, which enabled any person who wished to work bounds that 'hath lain . . . unwrought for the space of seven years' to notify the owners of the bounds and to enter his claim on the steward's court records, whereupon, if the bound owners failed to grant a sett to him within a year, he could work the bounds as though a sett had been granted to him, reserving one-seventh or one-ninth of the ore broken as farm tin, depending on whether water had to be pumped out of the work (93). This enactment was reaffirmed in 1752, with the modification that the bounds need be unwrought for only twelve months, and the claimant could enter if the bound owners failed to grant him a sett within two months of notification and recording of his claim; the farm tin he had to render to the bound owners was to be 'the usual and accustomed farm', which varied from one locality to another (94). Both the earlier and the later enactments obviously considered that the unworked bounds were still valid by reason of annual renewals, for if non-working alone caused the bounds to lapse, the claimant would not need to demand a sett under which he would render both toll tin to the freeholder and farm tin to the bound owner, but would simply rebound the land and render toll tin alone.

Until the middle of the nineteenth century, writers (95), the stannary courts (96) and the royal courts at Westminster (97) assumed that bounds could be kept alive either by continuous working or by renewal. The disputes occasioning litigation always concerned bounds that had been renewed, but not worked for periods often exceeding thirty years. The bound owner or his lessee had usually abandoned mining because the bounds were thought to contain insufficient tin ore to cover costs, but the bounds were renewed in the hope that adjacent workings would eventually reveal a payable lode. The freeholder or his lessee, often in ignorance of the continued existence of the bounds, then worked the ground again at a much later date, and often after incurring considerable expense discovered a lode, whereupon the bound owner or his successors would assert a prior claim to the mine, or at least to the payment of farm tin. The position was clearly unsatisfactory, for there was no means by which the bounder's rights could be extinguished, or even discovered, apart from searching for recently turned corner turves or stones. John Basset proposed than an Act of Parliament should be passed extinguishing bounders' rights which were merely kept alive by renewal unless they were registered in the Vice-Warden's court by a certain date, and that in any case it should be possible for the freeholder or his lessee to buy out such rights for compensation to be fixed by a jury of that court (98). This was a sensible compromise, but nothing came of it.

In 1847, however, the court of Queen's Bench struck a death blow at bounds which had been preserved by renewals without working (99). Rejecting Edward Smirke's contention that the law governing bounds was part of the Celtic law of Cornwall before it was annexed to England by the Saxons, and that the Celtic law should therefore be applied by English courts in the same way as the existing law of a conquered colony in force at the date of annexation, the court ruled that bounding could only be justified as customary law observed since the beginning of legal memory in 1189, and to be accepted as part of the law of England it must therefore be shown to be reasonable. The court held that the bounding custom was reasonable insofar as it permitted bounds to continue as long as the minerals under the land were being worked, for the freeholder whose property was occupied by the bounder or his lessee was at least compensated by the receipt of toll tin during that time. But this was not so when the custom went further and allowed unworked bounds, yielding no marketable tin for the benefit of the public nor toll tin for the benefit of the freeholder, to be kept in being by formal annual renewal. If this were permitted, the uncompensated freeholder would be unable to work the minerals himself or build on or develop his land.

The argument that a bounder should not be required to work continuously, because in times when ore prices were low it might not be profitable for him to continue incurring operating costs, was rejected for the counter-argument that the bounds might have been pitched at such a time and the freeholder then have been constrained to enclose the land for agriculture simply because there were no prospects of profit from using it for mining. The court asked rhetorically: 'Why then is he [the freeholder] to lose his earlier and better right for ever and under the same circumstances the bounder to preserve his?' The court did not attempt to define what amounted to continuous working, and in the case before it it was unnecessary to do so because the defendant staked his whole defence on the validity of the bounds by renewal. In a slightly earlier case, however, a jury had held that three months' work after a period of thirty-four years of idleness, did not amount to continuous working (97), and, since the defendants in the present case had only worked for a few weeks before the action was brought after eighteen years without working, there was no hope of satisfying the court that working had been continuous.

No one could doubt that the Queen's Bench's judgment was just, and it is significant that only one more case concerning tin bounds came before the Vice-Warden's court after it had been decided. Subsequently the royal courts dealt with two cases in which bounds were incidentally involved, but it was not disputed in either of them that the bounds had been continuously worked (100). In a case in the Queen's Bench court in 1858 concerning the validity of the mining customs of the Forest of Dean, the court treated its own pronouncement in 1847 about the validity of bounds in Cornwall while continuously worked as being extra-judicial because not necessary for the decision of the case before it, and the court refused to uphold similar customary claims for the Forest of Dean (101). It is true that the 1847 pronouncement was itself extra-judicial, but the question whether bounds could exist in law at all was by now merely theoretical, for all the mining in Cornwall and Devon in the second half of the nineteenth century was deep mining under setts granted by the freeholders of the land worked.

Nevertheless claims to bounds could be made again even today as a matter of law, though this would be a practical proposal only for streamworks near stream and river beds which still bear mine waste washed away from the deep mines years ago. It would certainly be a bold man who would nowadays seek to establish rights to prospect and sink shafts on land that had been urban or agricultural for generations, on the strength of nothing more than setting up corner stones and entering his bounds and having them proclaimed in the Cornwall county court as the successor to the Vice-Warden's court. The capital costs of prospecting and shaft sinking are too great to hazard work on the strength of so flimsy a title, and in any case deep mines work for other metals as well as tin, and those ores would belong to the freeholder if the mine were worked under bounds. Nevertheless, the threat to pitch bounds may one day be used by a mining company against a landowner who holds out for too high a price for the grant of a mining lease, and so litigation about the right to bound may yet come before the courts again.

References to this chapter are on pages 203–6.

Chapter 3
Mining Setts and Leases

THE GRANT OF MINING LEASES WAS UNCOMMON in Cornwall and Devon until the sixteenth century. Before then tin mining was carried on almost wholly under the bounding system, which did not entail the execution of private documents to regulate the relationship between landowner and miner. Nevertheless it is probable that in those early days, when landowners mined their own land, they took the precaution of bounding it first so as to prevent anyone else from doing so, and when they employed miners to work their bounds they entered into tribute contracts resembling mining leases for the division of the ore broken. It may well be also that when bounds were pitched by persons other than the landowner, special bargains were struck between landowner and miner as to the fraction of the ore broken that should constitute the landowner's toll tin. This may account for the variation in the fraction in the same localities over periods of time, and the striking of bargains over this matter would certainly involve a contract resembling a rudimentary lease (1).

By the sixteenth century two factors were combining to bring about an increase in the number of mining leases granted. First, more waste land was being enclosed for farming or as the demesne lands of manor houses than in earlier times, and this meant that, unless the enclosed land had previously been bounded, it could only be mined 'according to covenant and agreement between the lord of the freehold and the tinner made' (2). Secondly, the ownership of bounds was increasingly passing to landed proprietors who did not work for minerals themselves or employ miners to do so, but granted subsidiary mining rights to mine operators who agreed to deliver a fraction of the ore broken to the bounders as farm tin in addition to the toll tin rendered to the freeholder. The contract between the bounder and the mine operator would inevitably be, or resemble, a lease.

FORM OF SETTS

The form of mining setts or leases in the sixteenth and seventeenth centuries was derived from the grants of mining rights made by the kings of England from the thirteenth century onwards. At first most of these royal grants had been made gratuitously to members of the royal family or to court favourites, but occasionally they were also made as commercial transactions in return for a fraction of the ore broken or, less frequently, a money payment. The earliest example was a grant of Henry III to Adam de Greynvill and John Silvester in 1263 by which the king granted (*concessimus*) the royal mines of gold, silver, copper, lead and all other metals in Devon to hold during the king's pleasure, but the grantees had to answer at the royal exchequer for the produce thereof (*ita quod de exitibus inde provenientibus nobis respondeant ad scaccarium nostrum*); the grantees were also given full disciplinary and civil jurisdiction over the workmen in the mines to the exclusion of other jurisdictions, such as the stannary courts (3). The grantees' share of the metal produced was not specified, but clearly they were intended to receive more than a fee or wage. Nearly 100 years later, in 1358, Edward III granted and leased (*concessit et dimisit*) to John Balancer and Walter Goldbeter the royal mines of gold, silver and copper in Devon with liberty to dig in all places they thought fit but not in gardens or under houses; the grant was made for two years at a rent of 20 marks for the first year and the render of one-fifth of the metal coming from the mines during the second year (presumably in the form of ore) (4). The render of the rent and share of ore to the king was secured simply by the promise of the grantees, and no condition for forfeiture was added if the render was not made.

After a further century the royal grant had developed into the more sophisticated form that private grantors imitated in the sixteenth century. In 1452 Henry VI granted to John Botright, the governor of the king's mines of gold and silver in Devon and Cornwall, all mines of copper, tin and lead in those counties from which gold might be extracted to have and hold to his own use so long as he was of good behaviour in his office of governor and rendered to the king and his heirs one-tenth of the refined gold, silver, copper, tin and lead after deducting the expenses of smelting (5). In this grant the duration of the grant and the quantum of the render were more formally expressed and were made conditions for the continuance of the grant, and in the last part of the grant something akin to what later became the grantor's covenant, that the grantee should quietly enjoy the exploitation of the minerals without interruption, was included in place of the command addressed by the king to his subjects not to interfere with the grantee commonly found in earlier grants.

The earliest surviving mining lease or sett granted by private persons in Cornwall or Devon was of tin bounds in Polgooth (St Austell) and is dated 29 September 1666. The operative words of the grant were that the grantors 'have granted sett and to farm let' the tinworks and bounds in question. The word 'sett' is one peculiar to mining grants, but had no particular technical meaning; its earliest appearance was in the fourteenth century, when it was used in the sense of setting or fixing conditions for the grant or sale of a thing. The use of the expression 'to farm let' means that bound owners joined in the grant. A bound owner originally exploited his interest by him or his workmen working for tin, and when he delegated the working to another in return for a share of ore or a fixed money payment, he received an agreed fixed return or *firma* instead; when anglicised this word became the noun and verb 'farm'. From it comes the term 'farm tin', which was the fraction of the ore received by the bound owner. Often in early private mining leases the grantor let the minerals to farm, as well as granted and sett them, even though he was the freeholder and not a bound owner. This was to ensure that whatever kind of interest the grantor had was validly granted to the grantee, but in law there was no rule requiring particular formal words to be used, and a sett by a bound owner which simply 'granted' mining rights was fully effective. Because of this the operative words 'to farm let' were dropped in the early eighteenth century, and the expression thereafter used was that the grantor 'hath granted and sett, sett and confirmed, and in and by these presents doth grant and sett, sett and confirm unto' the grantee, etc (6), which was later simplified into 'doth give and grant unto' the grantee.

It was never the practice in Cornish mining setts for the grantor to demise the land in question to the grantee, and so give him a term of years or leasehold estate in the land. Strictly speaking, therefore, a mining grant should not be called a lease, and the commonly used word 'sett', although it has no technical meaning, is a useful substitute if strict accuracy is insisted on. The legal nature of the grantee's interest in the land will be considered below, but it is appropriate here to emphasise that it was not the absence of the word 'demise' from the grant which prevented the grantee acquiring a leasehold estate, but, as the court at Westminster held in 1819 (7), the fact that in the developed form of lease or sett what was granted to the grantee was not the land, but 'full power, liberty, licence and authority to dig, work, mine and search for' metallic ores. The use of the term 'demise' was avoided in the developed form of mining lease because the grantor was granting a new and limited right to mine his land, so that the word 'grant' was the appropriate operative word. The word 'demise' is appropriate only when an existing estate in land is being granted for a term of years, so that during that time the grantee will have almost the same full powers of exploitation as the grantor had previously.

The duration of the mining lease of 1666 mentioned above was set out in the *habendum* clause which followed the description of the property over which mining rights were granted. The lease was granted for twenty-one years, the normal period employed from the sixteenth century onwards. Leases for the working of tin were at first often not granted for any fixed period because of the special rule entitling the grantee to hold his lease so long as he actually worked for tin (8). However, after the middle of the eighteenth century it became rare for leases to be granted for working tin alone, and leases for fixed terms of all metallic minerals (other than gold and silver) then became almost universal. A render of one-tenth of the ore broken was reserved to the grantors in the lease of 1666, and this was provided for by the *reddendum* clause which followed the *habendum*. The grantor's share of ore was delivered by the grantee in the form of black tin, or, in the case of leases for mining other metals, in the form of crushed ore ready for smelting. The cost of smelting this share was borne by the grantor, not the grantee, but in practice the grantor would either sell his share to a smelter or deliver it to him for smelting on commission and take a tin bill from him as security. It was an obvious convenience for the grantee to arrange for the sale or smelting of the grantor's share of ore while making the arrangements for his own share, and the practice grew up in the eighteenth century of the grantee accounting to the grantor for the sale price or market value of the grantor's ore in cash instead of delivering ore in *specie*. This was particularly sensible with copper ore, which was always sold to the smelters after copper ticketings or auctions of copper ore were introduced in 1725. When smelters ceased to smelt tin on commission in the 1830s, legal draftsmanship at last caught up with this century-old practice, and grantees henceforth obliged themselves to pay the grantor's render in cash.

THE GRANTEE'S INTEREST UNDER A SETT

At common law an oral or written permission given by a landowner to another person to search for and work minerals under his land created a mere licence and not an interest in the land itself. That is to say, the licensee acted lawfully in exploiting the minerals and committed no trespass against the landowner until he notified the licensee that he revoked the licence (9), but the licence conferred no legal rights on the licensee against third persons, so that if they interfered with his working or abstracted the minerals themselves, he had no remedy against them (10). If the landowner granted the licence for valuable consideration and revoked it prematurely, the licensee could of course sue him for breach of contract, but the licensee could not contend that the licence still existed, and, if he continued to work minerals in pretended exercise of the licence, he was liable in damages to the landowner for trespass to his land and conversion of the ore broken (11). However, if the licence incorporated a promise by the landowner to grant the right to work minerals by a deed, the Court of Chancery would compel him to do so, and in the meantime would restrain him from revoking the licence (12). Later cases, not connected with mining, have extended the availability of an injunction to situations where there was no promise by the landowner to execute a deed of grant, and the licensee's only interest was a contractual right to timber or any other thing in or on the land which the landowner had agreed to sell him (13).

If the right to search and work for minerals was granted by deed, it gave the grantee a legal interest in the land which could not be revoked by the landowner, and which was also effective against third persons. Consequently, if either the landowner or anyone else disturbed the grantee's exploitation of the minerals, he could sue them for damages for trespass or nuisance (14), and in equity he could obtain an injunction as an auxiliary remedy to prevent interference with his rights in the future. The grant by deed might create either of two quite different legal interests, which may easily be confused, because the remedies for protecting them were the same. If the grant were a perpetual one made to the grantee and his heirs, or if it were made for a fixed number of years, as Cornish mining setts always were after the middle of the eighteenth century, the grantee acquired an incorporeal legal interest in the land called a *profit à prendre*, which was a servitude or incumbrance on the land (15). If on the other hand the grant was made to the grantee personally, or if the duration of the grant was not specified and the extent of the rights of the grantee and his successors was fixed by reference to the tonnage of mineral they might take away, the grant created a licence and not a profit, which could exist only if granted for the duration of one of the estates in land known to the law. The licence in this case was irrevocable, however, because it was coupled with a grant of the ownership of the minerals (16), and the fact that the extent and value of the minerals could not be ascertained until broken from the strata in which they lay did not seem to affect the validity of the grant. The consequence of the grant vesting the ownership of the unbroken minerals in the grantee, either immediately as a vested interest, or contingently on the ascertainment of the extent of the minerals, was that the licence to search and get the minerals was annexed to a proprietary interest as the means of realising it, and it could therefore no more be revoked by the grantor than the proprietary interest itself. For the same reason the annexed licence was effective against third persons, and the grantee could sue them for damages if they interfered with him or took the minerals granted to him (17).

The customary law of Cornwall in respect of tin mining setts departed from the common law rules in two respects. In the first place a valid sett could be granted by writing signed but not sealed by the grantor (18), or even by word of mouth, despite the statutory requirement that the grant of interests of uncertain duration in land should be made in writing signed by the grantor in order to be valid (19). The grantee of such a sett acquired the same legal interest in the land as he would have done by a grant made by deed at common law. Consequently, if a landowner first granted a sett for tin to one man, and subsequently granted a sett by deed in respect of tin or all minerals to another, the first oral sett had priority over the second for tin mining, and the second grantee could not take tin from the land comprised in the first sett until it expired. Secondly, a grant of a sett for mining tin in Cornwall which did not specify the duration of the grant was construed as a grant to the grantee for as long as he personally worked the minerals, or if the grant was made to him, his executors, administrators and assigns, it was construed as continuing in perpetuity so long as he and his successors worked the minerals (18). An oral or written grant of the right to mine for tin in Cornwall was, however, effective as a legal grant only in respect of that metal. If it included the right to mine for other minerals as well, it was governed by the common-law rules as to form, and was therefore ineffective in creating a legal interest in the land in respect of them.

It was, of course, possible at common law to grant a true lease of land containing minerals, and as an incident of the lease to give the lessee power to extract the minerals and to make them his own property. The principal distinction between such a lease and a licence or sett in Cornish form was that the lessee had possession of the land and the minerals while unbroken, and so could recover possession from the lessor or any other person who evicted him by bringing an action of ejectment at common law, whereas a grantee of a sett was at most only in occupation of the head gear, shafts, levels and engine houses and other buildings of the mine without being in possession of the surface of the land or the subjacent minerals (20), and so could sue for damages for interference with his rights but could not recover the mine by an action of ejectment if he was evicted (21). However, the rights of the grantee of a sett were also protected by the Court of Chancery, which could issue an injunction to restrain the grantor and third persons interfering with them (22), and the practical result of obtaining an injunction was the same as obtaining judgment for possession in an action for ejectment.

The differences between leases of mines and mining setts or licences went farther than the different remedies available at common law to the evicted lessee or grantee. A lease not only gave the lessee possession of the land, which a licence or sett did not; it also created a tenurial relationship between him and the landowner, which did not exist when the landowner merely granted a licence to work minerals. Consequently, a landowner who granted a lease could distrain on the lessee's goods on the land leased if he failed to pay the render reserved by the lease, whether in the form of a fixed money rent, a royalty on the value of the mineral worked, or a share of the ore broken. On the other hand, a grantor of a licence or sett could not distrain for farm tin or for a money render, whether fixed or related to the quantity or value of ore broken (23). Nevertheless, the other incident of leases, that covenants by the lessor and lessee in the lease which related to the land demised and were not merely personal ran with the lease and the reversion so as to be enforceable by and against their respective successors in title, did apply also to licences and setts. It was therefore possible for the grantor of a sett to sue a person to whom the grantee assigned it for failure to erect and maintain a smelting house (24), although Vice-Warden Smirke, while holding that covenants could run with setts, declined to hold that a covenant by the grantee to install machinery was enforceable against an assignee (25). A covenant to work the mine continuously was enforceable against an assignee by an award of damages to the grantor for the loss he suffered as a result of breaches of the covenant, though not by an order requiring the assignee to perform the covenant specifically (25). Similarly, a covenant by the grantee to pay compensation for the surface area around the mine rendered unusable by the sinking of shafts or the deposit of mine refuse was enforceable by the grantor against an assignee of the sett (26), and by a purchaser of the land from the grantor against the grantee of the sett (27).

THE OBLIGATIONS OF THE PARTIES TO A SETT

In the developed form of sett used in Cornwall the grantee entered into numerous covenants with the grantor relating to the render of his share of ore or its value, the method of working the minerals and many other matters; and the grantor entered into certain limited covenants with the grantee. The sett was always granted to one or several grantees, but never to more than four, and they were all expressed to be jointly and individually liable in damages for the full loss suffered by the grantor as a result of breaches of the grantees' covenants, it being insufficient for a grantee to tender his proportionate share of the damages if the others did not pay theirs (26). With all but the smallest tinworks, the grantee or grantees of the sett would form a partnership or company, usually a cost book company, with several other persons, and by agreement the mining undertaking was divided into shares, which were used as the basis for calculating the shareholder's liability to contribute toward the costs of the mine and the amount he was entitled to receive out of its profits. But the grantees of the sett did not assign the sett they had taken to themselves and the other shareholders together in order that they might all have the same shares in the legal interest created by the sett as they had in the other assets of the mine. Instead the grantees declared themselves trustees of the sett for all the shareholders, including themselves, and the shareholders thereby acquired beneficial equitable interests in the sett. The grantor often anticipated the formation of a company by granting the sett to the named grantees and their executors, administrators, assigns and co-adventurers. It was held that this did not make the adventurers co-owners of the legal interest vested in the named grantees, but it was sufficient as a declaration of trust by the grantees to give all the adventurers equitable interests in the sett (28).

Because the shareholders or adventurers of a mining company

(other than the grantees of the sett) did not hold the legal interest created by the sett and did not enter into covenants with the grantor, they could not be sued by the grantor for farm tin or whatever render was reserved to him, nor for damages suffered by him as a result of breaches of the grantees' covenants (29). But the adventurers could be made indirectly liable to the grantor in equity for breach of certain covenants. For example, if the grantees became insolvent, the grantor could compel the adventurers to account to him for his share of the ore broken or its value (30), and if the adventurers worked the mine in breach of the covenants contained in the sett, the grantor could obtain an injunction to restrain them from continuing to do so (31). On the other hand Vice-Warden Smirke held that the grantor could not claim to be put in the place of the grantee so as to enforce the grantee's claim to be indemnified by the adventurers against his liability for dues or royalties payable out of the proceeds of sale of ore (32), although Vice-Warden Dampier once said *obiter* that he could do this (33). The grantor's strongest hold over the adventurers was the threat to exercise the power to forfeit the sett which its terms usually empowered him to do if the grantees broke any of their covenants. If the grantor exercised this power the adventurers' equitable interests would be completely destroyed.

Farm tin, renders and dues

Until the third decade of the nineteenth century the grantor of a sett was usually given the right to a physical share of the ore broken by the grantee as his return for the grant of the sett. By custom the ore had to be spalled or crushed and properly mixed so that its quality was uniform, and the grantor or his toller or agent had to be notified of the time when the division was to take place at the mine or the stamps where the ore was crushed for smelting so that he could sample the ore before his share was set aside for him (34). In practice all these matters were dealt with expressly in the sett. By the 1830s the grantor's rights had universally been changed to a share in the proceeds of sale of the ore.

The grantee's covenants were now usually (1) to spall, dress and render fit for sale all ore broken; (2) to sell the tin and copper ores by public sale in the usual manner as often as conveniently may be (ie at the ticketings), and to sell other ores by public sale or private contract; (3) to pay the grantor his share of the proceeds; and (4) not to mix the ores with those from any other mine or to sample or sell such mixed ores.

Later it became usual for the grantee to covenant to pay the grantor's share of the proceeds 'free from all charges', that is to say without any deduction for the cost of operating the mine or the sale of the ore, and to make the payment within two months of the sale. In the 1860s it became common for the sett to reserve a minimum or dead rent, so as to ensure a minimum income for the grantor; this was taken into account in calculating the dues payable to the grantor, so that if his fraction of the price realised by the ores came to more than the dead rent, he received his fraction without any supplement. Dead rents were rarely substantial, £10 or £20 *per annum* being the average. Finally, in the 1870s the practice was adopted of taking a covenant by the grantee to keep accounts of the minerals broken and removed from the mine, showing their quantity and weight, and to give seven days' notice to the grantor or his agent before removing ore from the mine for sale. It is curious that this covenant did not appear earlier, since proper accounting was obviously necessary if the grantor was to be sure of receiving his dues in full, and it was even more curious since it had been usual since the 1820s for setts to reserve the right to the grantor to inspect and copy all books and accounts voluntarily kept by the grantee concerning the mine.

Covenants in respect of mining operations

Cornish mining setts always contained a general covenant by the grantee to work the mines comprised in them continuously, and during the late eighteenth and the nineteenth centuries further covenants dealing with specific matters were added, most of them prohibitory. This is significant, for the landowner did not consider it his function to prescribe in detail what operations should be carried out. He was only concerned to see that he was paid as large an income as possible in the form of dues, that he was kept informed of developments in the underground workings, and that the surface of the land was as little damaged as possible.

The following are the grantee's covenants in respect of mining operations contained in a sett of 1804 (35):

> *And* [the grantee] shall and will at all times during the term hereby granted work and carry on the mine or adventure agreed to be undertaken and prosecuted within the limits of the sett hereby granted and the bottoms thereof regularly and in every respect according to the practice of good miners *And* shall and will bring into and drive through the said limits hereby described the deep level or adit from Cobbernoon Mine adjoining on the south (36) *And* also shall and will at all times during the said term firmly bind, secure and keep open with timbers and fixed stemples (37) and props or by other good and effectual and durable means all adits, shafts and other workings which shall be cleared or newly driven sunk or made within the limits of the sett hereby granted, and the same in good repair and firmly bound, secured and kept open as aforesaid and the said mine or adventure agreed to be so undertaken as aforesaid within the said limits so regularly worked according to the practice of good miners as aforesaid and in good order and condition for the future prosecution thereof, shall and will at the expiration or other determination of the said term quietly and peaceably leave yield and deliver up to the [grantor] his heirs or assigns together with all and every the engines, erections, buildings and all manner of machinery, and the materials thereunto belonging, he or they paying a reasonable price for such machinery or such parts thereof as he or they shall choose to take, such price (if necessary) and the time of payment thereof to be fixed by two indifferent [ie disinterested] persons one of whom shall be chosen by the [grantor] his heirs and assigns and the other by the [grantee] his executors, administrators or assigns, and in case of their disagreeing the same shall be ascertained and fixed by such third person as the said two persons shall choose *And* also shall and will once in every year at his and their own expense provide for the [grantor] his heirs or assigns and deliver to him or them or to his or their known agent a full and correct plan and section of the said mine or work and all lodes and veins discovered therein *And* also shall and will preserve and lay aside in heaps all the meal earth or soil [ie topsoil] which shall be

dug up in the prosecution of the said adventure and shall not within twelve months after lay any ores or rubbish thereon *And* shall and will make sufficient fences round every shaft and open part of any adits which shall be dug or sunk within the limits of this sett *And* further that it shall be lawful unto and for the [grantor] his heirs and assigns and his and their known agents and agent, either alone or with any other person or persons, when and as often as he or they shall think proper during the term hereby granted to go down examine, and measure all or any of the shafts, adits and other workings of the said mine so to be undertaken as aforesaid and for that purpose to use the tackle and other conveniences then and there being.

These covenants were standard for all setts, and in substance amounted to obligations accepted by the grantee to work the ground specified in the sett continuously and systematically and not to strip the mine of ore indiscriminately so as to impede future development; to keep the mine properly timbered and to give it up in proper condition on the termination of the sett; to leave fixtures and loose equipment at the mine at that time if the grantor wished to buy them, the price to be settled by arbitration if necessary; to provide the grantor annually with plans showing the development of the mine and to allow him to inspect the mine; to separate topsoil raised in shaft sinking so that it might be put to agricultural use; and to fence shafts to prevent persons and animals falling down them.

It is doubtful whether an obligation to work the ground for ore was implied on the part of the grantee of a sett for mining tin in the absence of an express covenant; it would seem that, if the grantee did not work effectually, the grantor's only remedy was to forfeit the sett, but not to sue the grantee for damages (38). If this is correct, there could have been no implied obligation on the grantee to yield up the mine in proper condition either, and so the court could not have enjoined him from mining in an inexpert manner, though it could have prohibited him from deliberately rifling or damaging the mine by stripping ore from it wastefully (39). If a grantee covenanted to make improvements to the mine—for example, by erecting engine houses, sinking shafts or driving adits or levels—it was implied that he also obliged himself to keep the improvements in repair and good condition and to deliver them up in good condition to the grantor at the termination of the sett (40). But the Vice-Warden's court would not compel the grantee to perform such covenants by ordering specific performance of them or issuing a mandatory injunction; the grantor's only remedy was to sue for damages (41). The same consideration applied to the grantee's covenant to work the ground comprised in the sett effectually; this covenant, too, would not be specifically enforced, because the court had no effective machinery for doing so (41). The fact that the grantor had an option to purchase fixtures and equipment brought on to the mine by the grantee did not induce the court to take a different view of specific enforcement of covenants to work the mine and to make improvements, particularly if the sett still had several years to run (41).

The customs and practices of miners had some influence on the judicial interpretation of setts, especially when they were in skeleton form and contained few or no express covenants. For example, if a sett for mining tin said nothing about the erection of buildings or the installation of equipment, the grantee was entitled to claim from the grantor the value of such items as he provided and left at the mine on the termination of the sett, but the grantor could avoid such a claim by showing that the sett was granted in return for a smaller fraction of the ore raised than was usual because it was understood that the grantee would carry out the improvements (42). But custom and usage could not be invoked to vary the clear meaning of a sett. Consequently, when a sett specified the standard of working to be kept up by the grantee, he was not allowed to escape liability for breach of covenant by showing that the usual standard of working in the locality was less exacting (43).

During the nineteenth century the grantee's covenants usually inserted in setts became more extensive and more refined. Soon after the beginning of the century grantors habitually took power to work the minerals specified in the sett if the grantee failed to fulfil his covenant to work them effectually, but the grantor usually had to give the grantee one or two months' notice of his intention to allow him a last opportunity to remedy his default. This was a far more effective inducement to the grantee to work properly than the threat of litigation. In the second decade of the century the provision became more precise, the grantor's power being made exercisable after he had given the grantee one month's notice of the existence of a vein or lode the grantee had not worked for six consecutive months. This ensured that the grantee worked every accessible lode continuously. As the nineteenth century progressed, covenants for effectual working were made more effective by requiring not less than a stated number of workmen to be continuously employed in the mine specified in the sett, and were reinforced by detailed covenants for improvements, such as the erection of steam engines and pumps and the sinking of shafts and driving of adits. Furthermore, negative covenants against harmful practices were employed to ensure that effectual working did not result in nuisance to the grantor and his tenants. It became common, for example, for the grantee to covenant not to carry on more than one mining adventure on the land specified in the sett, though such an obligation was implied in any case in a sett for tin mining (44). It also became common for the grantee to covenant not to erect more than one burning house or calciner, or not to erect a calciner at all without the grantor's consent.

In the 1820s grantees' covenants to make good damage done to the surface of the land and to fences, hedges and gates, or else to pay compensation to the grantor or his tenants, began to appear. In the 1840s this became more precise by the grantee covenanting to pay the grantor on the termination of the sett a certain number of years' annual or rental value of every acre of the surface taken for use by the mine and rendered unusable for any other purpose. In the 1860s compensation for rendering the surface unusable came to be fixed at a specified sum per acre, usually £80 for each acre of cultivated land and £40 for each acre of common or waste, but an allowance of one-eighth of an acre for every shaft sunk by the grantee was generally conceded. A provision for compensation in a sett only regulated the calculation of the damages which the grantor would otherwise have been able to recover from the grantee for trespass on the surface beyond the confines of the shafts, buildings and dressing floors of the mine. It did not affect the right of a tenant of the surface to sue for trespass or nuisance in respect of loss suffered as a result of the deposit of mine waste on his land (45). Nor did the provision, when read with the grantee's covenant to work the mine effectually, authorise the grantee to infringe the grantor's right to have the surface of the land supported, so that, if underground workings caused it to subside, the grantor could recover damages from the grantee in addition to compensation at the agreed rate for the deposit of waste on the surface (46). Still less did covenants to work effectually and to pay compensation permit the grantee to work the mine opencast, like a quarry, unless the sett clearly indicated that the land contained alluvial tin that the grantee was to work by streaming (47).

FORFEITURE OF SETTS

English common law did not imply a term in leases or setts enabling the grantor to forfeit or terminate them if the grantee failed to fulfil his obligations under them, or if he was in a position which made it certain that he would fail to fulfil his obligations at some future time. By custom, however, it was possible for the grantor of a Cornish sett of a tin mine or streamworks which had been granted orally or by a signed but unsealed instrument for an indefinite period, to forfeit the sett if the grantee failed to deliver the grantor's share of the ore broken (48) or, presumably, if he failed to pay the grantor's share of the price realised by the ore. The grantor could also forfeit the sett if the grantee in breach of his agreement failed to notify the grantor of the time when and the place where the ore would be washed, so that the grantor or his toller might attend to take his share (49). Perhaps more important than either of these cases, the grantor could forfeit the sett if the grantee failed to work the mine or streamworks effectually (50), and the grantor's power in this situation was expressly confirmed by the Cornwall Convocation Act of 1752, which made it exercisable if the grantee 'shall not work the [sett] effectually at all working times and seasons, or shall leave the said work unwrought at any time without reasonable cause' (51).

Although all the decisions of the Vice-Wardens assumed that failure to work effectually merely entitled the grantor to forfeit the sett if he wished, and this view was strengthened by the enactment of 1752, there was earlier authority that total cessation of working automatically terminated the sett without the grantor re-entering, and in view of the fact that the grantee's interest in the land had no fixed duration, it is probable that this was the correct view (52). In practice, however, this made little difference, for the Vice-Wardens of the eighteenth century considered that they had no discretion to withhold a decree of forfeiture if there had been a cessation of working, even though the grantee would thereby suffer hardship. The grantor's right of forfeiture could be exercised either by evicting the grantee from the land specified in the sett, by obtaining a decree of forfeiture in the Vice-Warden's court, or by the grantor making a new sett in favour of another person of the whole or part of the land and that other person entering under the sett granted to him (53).

If a sett was granted by deed, it could be forfeited only if it expressly so provided, and the causes of forfeiture specified in it were construed strictly against the grantor. Consequently, when the sett permitted forfeiture if the grantee and his co-adventurers ceased to work effectually, it was held that the grantor could not forfeit when a cessation had not occurred but was likely because the adventurers had exhausted their capital and mine creditors were threatening proceedings against the mine's assets (54). In early setts it was common to provide that the sett should be void if the grantee failed to work it, or if he broke any of his other obligations; and at first the proviso was construed literally, so that the sett terminated immediately the breach of obligation occurred. The result was that the grantee could terminate his sett prematurely against the wishes of the grantor by deliberately failing to fulfil his obligations, and so in later cases the proviso was read as if it gave the grantor alone an option to terminate by re-entering on the sett, the grantee having no choice in the matter (55). Because of this construction it became standard form for the proviso simply to confer a right of re-entry on the grantor in the following words:

> *Provided always* nevertheless and these presents are upon this express condition that if the [grantee] his executors, administrators or assigns shall at any time hereafter during the term hereby granted refuse, neglect or fail to observe, fulfil and keep all or any of the exceptions, reservations, payments, covenants, provisoes and agreements hereinbefore contained on the part of the grantee to be observed, fulfilled and kept, then and thenceforth for all or any of the causes aforesaid and as often as it shall so happen it shall be lawful for the [grantor] his heirs and assigns immediately thereupon, or at any time thereafter, into the ground hereinbefore described and hereby set to re-enter and the same to have again, repossess and enjoy as in his or their former estate, anything hereinbefore contained to the contrary notwithstanding.

This proviso was in exactly the same form as those contained in leases, and came into effect after the ground for forfeiture had arisen, either by the grantor giving the grantee formal notice requiring him to yield up the mine and bringing a common-law action for trespass if he did not do so, or by the grantor suing in the Vice-Warden's court for a decree that the sett was forfeit and an order for its delivery up to the grantor for cancellation (56).

In the seventeenth and eighteenth centuries the Court of Chancery gave liberal relief to lessees and other grantees of limited interests in land against the forfeiture of their interests under contractual stipulations for forfeiture. At the beginning of the nineteenth century this liberality contracted considerably. The rule came to be that relief could only be given if the reason for forfeiture was the lessee's failure to pay rent or to make a render which could be valued in money terms, and any relief given was conditional upon the requisite money payment being made in full (57). In the case of setts this meant that relief would be given if the grantee had defaulted in paying dues to the grantor or in delivering to him his share of the ore broken, but not if he had failed to perform or observe any of his other obligations in the sett (58).

The statutory protection of lessees against forfeiture of their leases for failure to pay rent or for breaches of certain other covenants, which Parliament enacted in the middle of the nineteenth century (59), did not apply to mining setts, because they were not leases within the meaning of the statutes, and so the grantee's only protection continued to be the limited intervention of the Court of Chancery under its rules of equity. By the Conveyancing Act, 1881, however, lessors were required to give their lessees written notice of breaches of their covenants and also a reasonable opportunity to remedy the breaches before taking proceedings for forfeiture, and the court could in its discretion give relief against forfeiture if the lessee applied to it before the lessor obtained judgment against him or before he actually re-entered (60). This provision did apply to mining leases, which were defined as including 'a grant or licence for mining purposes' (61), and so for the first time grantees of setts were given full protection against arbitrary forfeiture. However, the new enactment did not apply to forfeiture for non-payment of rent (62), which was defined as including 'toll, duty, royalty or other reservation by the acre, the ton or otherwise' (63), nor did it apply to forfeiture for assigning setts without the grantor's consent (if the sett required this), nor for breach of the grantee's covenant to allow the grantor to inspect the mine or its records, nor because of the grantee's bankruptcy or the seizure of the sett by way of execution of a judgment against the grantee if the sett made these events causes for forfeiture (64). The grantee therefore had to rely on the equity rules for protection against forfeiture for non-payment of dues, but had no protection whatsoever against the other excepted causes for forfeiture.

THE MINING LEASES BILL

Until the second half of the nineteenth century grantees of mining setts encountered little difficulty in negotiating the terms on which setts should be granted or renewed by landowners, who as a class were quite happy to accept dues of between one-seventh and one-eighteenth of the proceeds of tin, or between one-tenth and one-thirtieth of the proceeds of copper and other metals (with or without tin). The dues for a particular mine became established by experience of its ore content and the difficulty of working it, and grantees assumed, usually with justification, that when they asked for a renewal of their sett it would be granted on the same terms as the current sett or on more favourable terms if the mine was becoming deeper or was approaching exhaustion. In the 1860s, however, some landowners began demanding substantial capital down payments or premiums as well as the usual dues for the renewal of setts of prosperous mines. They were no doubt encouraged to do this by the example of mine company promoters, who often took setts in return for dues only and sold them for substantial, and usually inflated, prices to the companies they formed. Landowners saw no reason why they too should not cash in on the capital gains which could be made. In 1858 the Duke of Bedford had extracted £20,000 in this way from the Devon Great Consolidated Mining Co, then at the peak of its career as a copper mine. But in most cases promoters' profits were totally unjustified by the value of the setts they assigned, and when landowners sought to exact comparable premiums from established companies, capitulation to their demands would often have made the companies insolvent or at least stripped them of all working capital (65).

Such a case occurred in 1883 when Gustavus Lambert Basset of Tehidy, the heir of the Basset estates, demanded a premium of £40,000 for the renewal of Dolcoath Mining Co's setts, and at the same time proposed to raise the dues from one-twentieth to one-fifteenth. The company had some bargaining strength, however, for its current sett did not expire until 1887, and it made it clear to Basset that unless his demands were moderated it would strip ore from the mine during the four remaining years without regard to future working, and would close down the mine and discharge its workers at the end of that time. At this point Thomas Bolitho, the smelter, intervened as a self-appointed arbiter, and the matter was settled after three months haggling by Dolcoath conceding dues of one-fifteenth and Basset reducing the premium to £25,000.

The Dolcoath affair did not end with this compromise. The mine workers and adventurers in mining companies were now alive to the risk to their livelihoods if landowners remained free to impose arbitrary demands when setts came up for renewal. As was usual in Cornwall whenever a crisis loomed, meetings of adventurers were held to devise protective measures, and consideration was soon given to drafting legislation which would be introduced in the House of Commons by the county's members. A Mines Leases Committee was set up, consisting of the county members led by Sir John St Aubyn and the leading shareholders of the big mines, and after holding fourteen meetings the committee produced a Mining Leases Bill and a second bill dealing with mining operations generally, which were discussed at a public meeting at Tabb's Hotel, Redruth, on 27 April 1886 and unanimously approved (66). At an earlier public meeting on 2 March 1886 a rival Mining Leases Bill, which Charles Conybeare, county member for the Mining Division of Cornwall, had introduced in the Commons and then withdrawn, had been discussed along with the first drafts of the Mines Leases Committee's bills, but Conybeare's proposals were rejected by the meeting in favour of the other bills, and, though Conybeare for a time persisted in his intention of reintroducing his bill in the Commons, it was in fact not revived. The Conybeare bill was the more radical of the two proposals in that it provided that landowners would always have to renew a sett if the grantee wished, unless the grantee had been guilty of serious breaches of covenant; it also provided that dues should henceforth be payable only out of the net proceeds of ore sales, that is out of the profits of the mine after deducting operating expenses from gross receipts. Under all existing setts dues were payable out of the gross proceeds of ore sales, and, although some landowners accepted a lower rate of dues when the proceeds were less than operating costs or when ore was selling below a certain figure, it was not uncommon for mining companies to be paying heavy dues even though they were operating at a loss.

The Mining Leases (Cornwall and Devon) Bill was introduced in the House of Commons on 5 May 1886 by Sir John St Aubyn, but in the debate on the second reading Conybeare opposed it as too accommodating to the rich landowners and successfully moved its adjournment. The Bill was reintroduced by St Aubyn in the following session on 1 February 1887, and after an unopposed second reading on 9 March it was referred to a select committee consisting of St Aubyn and the other county members for Cornwall and Devon, three of whom had backed the bill, together with Conybeare. The select committee held twenty-one sittings between 30 March and 29 July 1887, but all of these were taken up with hearing evidence upon and discussing the general bill, and when the committee reported to the Commons on 29 July it stated that it had not had time to consider or take evidence on the Mining Leases Bill.

The St Aubyn bill proposed a variety of improvements to the existing law. If the freehold of land was held by co-owners and those holding two-thirds or more of the beneficial interest had granted a sett, the grantee could apply to the Vice-Warden to license him to work the minerals in respect of the interests of the remaining co-owners on the terms and conditions of the sett, and the Vice-Warden could make such order as he thought fit for that purpose if satisfied that the remaining co-owners were either under a disability, or had 'refused or neglected after reasonable notice to grant their share in such minerals' (67). Grantees of setts were given the right to remove all buildings they had erected on the land specified in the sett notwithstanding any contrary stipulation therein (68), but the grantor was given the right to purchase the buildings at their value to a new grantee within six months after the termination of the sett (69), and, if he did not exercise this right of pre-emption, the grantee had to remove the buildings within eighteen months after the sett terminated (70). Stipulations in setts for the compensation of the grantor for damage done to the surface of land were subjected to an overriding rule that he should not be able to recover from the grantee more than the fair value of the land, or, in the case of land still usable for certain purposes, more than the loss actually suffered (71). The most important provision of the bill, however, was that which gave the grantee an absolute right to renewal of his sett, or to compensation in lieu of renewal. It provided that (72):

> The lessees under any existing or future lease shall be entitled to a renewal of such lease from time to time for a similar period as the existing lease, or during a term customary in the district, as the lessees require . . . upon equitable and fair terms, or to compensation on the non-renewal thereof, provided that within the last two years and not less than eighteen months before the expiration of such lease they give the lessors notice in writing that they claim such renewal, and if within six months of the delivery of such notice the lessors and lessees have not agreed upon the terms of such renewal, such terms shall be settled by reference [to arbitration], and under the same reference the amount to be paid by the lessors to the lessees by way of compensation, if any, in the event of the lessors refusing to renew on the terms fixed by the award shall be determined: Provided that no premium or fine or other payment of a like nature he awarded to the owner for such renewal, unless by mutual agreement between the parties, in which case the amount shall be settled by reference [to arbitration].

If this provision had been enacted, it would have been an improvement on the existing law, but it would nevertheless have left grantees in a weak and uncertain position. Grantors were not obliged to renew setts without qualification; they could avoid doing so by choosing to pay compensation instead after the terms of the new sett had been determined by arbitration. There was no formula for calculating the compensation to be paid by a grantor who refused to renew, so that a grantee who was offered what he considered inadequate compensation had to go through the farce of arbitration as to the terms of a renewal he would not get in order to exact a fairer amount of compensation. The amount of compensation was apparently left to the discretion of the arbitrator, who might limit it to the immediate loss suffered by the grantee having to vacate the mine (that is, the cost of stripping and bringing up pitwork and pumps and moving equipment and ores), or at the other extreme, might award the grantee the capitalised value of the profits anticipated from working the known reserves of ore in the mine. The final proviso, directing arbitrators not to award premiums on renewals, was well intentioned, but unlike Conybeare's bill, did not outlaw premiums altogether. It would still have been possible when grants were made in the future for the grantor to exact the consent of the grantee to a renewal premium as a term of the original sett, and the proviso would then leave the arbitrator powerless to reduce or cancel the agreed renewal premium, though presumably he would have been able to take it into account when fixing the amount of dues payable by the grantee under the new sett, and make them correspondingly smaller.

A new Mining Leases Bill in the same terms as the St Aubyn bill was introduced in the Commons on 13 February 1888 by Charles Acland, one of the backers of the St Aubyn bill, and on 7 March it had an unopposed second reading. Owing to pressure on Parliamentary time it was never considered in committee, and on 4 July 1888 it was withdrawn. With its withdrawal passed the last opportunity for reform of the unsatisfactory legal substratum on which Cornish mining setts were based. The fact that the grantee's position under the unregulated common law and customary rules was tolerable was because the behaviour of the owners of mineral-bearing land was generally fair and sensible. If they had all adopted the attitude of Gustavus Lambert Basset towards Dolcoath Mining Co's application for the renewal of its sett in 1883, the Cornish mining industry would have declined much earlier than it did.

References to this chapter are on pages 206–9.

Chapter 4
The Refining and Coinage of Tin

CONTRACTS FOR STAMPING AND SMELTING

IN EARLY TIMES TIN STREAMERS CARRIED OUT the dressing and smelting of tin ore themselves near their works. Stream tin required little dressing, since the alluvial deposits were usually in fine grains or particles which could be smelted immediately. Smelting was carried out in the small granite-built and thatched blowing houses which dotted the countryside where streamworks were found, and the smelted tin was cast immediately into blocks, which were coined at the nearest stannary town and then sold. The mine operators, therefore, marketed their own tin, and there were no intermediate transactions with other parties before the white or refined tin reached the merchants, mostly London and foreign pewterers, or, if the royal right of pre-emption was currently being exercised, the king or his lessees of the pre-emption.

In the sixteenth century the advent of deep mining made the dressing of ore a more complicated proceeding. The ore was broken from the rock in lumps of varying dimensions which were reduced by bucking and spalling but remained too large for smelting. The spalled ore therefore had to be crushed to powder by a crazing mill or, later, by stamping, and not all mines possessed their own mills or stamps, even as late as the eighteenth century. So numerous mining adventurers had to have their ore stamped by another mine's stamps or by independent stamping mills at so many pence per cwt of black tin. If the charge was not paid, the owner of the stamping mill could sue the adventurers, in the eighteenth century by a creditor's suit (1), and, if the stamping had been commissioned by the purser, the adventurers were personally responsible for the charge made (2). Few suits for stamping charges were brought in the stannary courts, no doubt because the owner of the stamping mill had the far more effective common-law remedy of retaining possession of the stamped tin until he was paid in exercise of his lien for the value of his work. This lien attached to each parcel of tin only for the charge of stamping that parcel; the owner of the stamps had no general lien at common law over all black tin belonging to the adventurers in his possession for their general indebtedness to him. But if he brought a creditor's suit against them for the total amount of their debt, he could obtain an injunction preventing them from removing any of their black tin from the stamps pending the trial, and this in effect gave him a general equitable lien for all unpaid stamping charges (1). If tin ore sent for stamping was left in the hands of the owner of the stamps for twelve months without being claimed, it became his property by the custom of the Stannary of Foweymore (3) and possibly in the other stannaries as well.

It seems likely that, when adventurers first sent their black tin to be smelted by the owners of blowing houses, they agreed to pay a fixed sum for each cwt smelted and themselves received back the white tin produced from the black. There is no direct evidence to support this, but three of the early rules of stannary law clearly presupposed that the smelter did not purchase the black tin outright; these rules were the requirement that the owner's distinguishing mark should be put on the blocks of white tin as well as the blower's mark (4), that owners of blowing houses were forbidden to smelt their own tin (5), and that there was no lien to owners of blowing houses for unpaid smelting charges (6). The first requirement would be purposeless unless the adventurers or the persons delivering the black tin for smelting retained the ownership of it, and the third rule, which took away the smelter's common law lien so as to ensure that white tin was coined as soon as possible after smelting, would have had no meaning at all if the adventurers did not employ the owners of blowing houses to smelt their tin for them at an agreed charge.

From early in the sixteenth century, however, it seems that owners of blowing houses undertook smelting work on the far more practical basis of agreeing to deliver to the adventurers in time for the next coinage so many hundredweights of white tin for each thousandweight of black tin sent for smelting; the actual number was determined by the smelter's assay of the metal content of the black tin, and usually ranged between 8 and 13 cwt for every ton of black tin. This meant that the smelter's remuneration was now variable, its amount depending on the quantity of white tin he could in fact extract from the black tin and on the ruling price for tin on the delivery date. It also meant that the white tin to be delivered to the adventurers need not be refined from the black tin sent by them, and that, although the adventurers might remain the legal owners of the black tin or co-owners with other adventurers if it was mixed with theirs, the owner of the blowing house was merely under a contractual obligation to have ready for the adventurers at the next coinage an agreed quantity of white tin acquired from any source. This obligation was evidenced by a short document given by the owner of the blowing house to the person who delivered the black tin for smelting. It was originally called a precept, and had to be produced at the next coinage in order to obtain delivery of the white tin from the blowing house owner. Later on it developed into the tin bill, which by custom was treated as embodying the title to the tin it represented so that the holder of the bill was considered as being the owner of the tin (7). The sixteenth- and seventeenth-century convocation enactments recognised this changed way of dealing between adventurers and blowing-house owners by continuing to require the blowing-house owner's mark to be impressed on blocks of white tin, but dropping the rule that the mark of the owner of the black tin should be shown as well (8).

So long as black tin was smelted nominally, at least, on behalf of the adventurers to whom the smelter had issued a tin bill, there was no need or reason for implying an undertaking by the adventurers that the black tin delivered to the smelter was of any particular standard or would yield a particular amount of smelted tin, or that any sample assayed by the smelter was representative of the quality of the whole. But when smelters began to purchase crushed tin ore outright in the 1830s, the question unavoidably arose whether such undertaking should be implied in contracts for the sale of black tin in the same way as they were currently being implied by the common law courts in other contracts of sale. Vice-Warden Smirke held in the only case on this question to come before the stannary courts (9) that no promises could be implied on the part of the adventurers as to the quality of the ore sold or as to its conformity to sample, and the adventurers could only be sued for breach of contract if they or the officers of the mine (the purser, mine captain or bottom captains) had 'prilled' the sample tendered, that is had put better quality black tin broken from another mine or another part of the same mine in the sample, or had mixed inferior ore from elsewhere with the ore delivered, or if the adventurers knew or were grossly negligent in not discovering that other persons, such as tributers or tutworkers, had done any of these things. In other words, the adventurers were liable to a smelter only if they were guilty of fraud or of conduct closely approaching fraud.

CONVOCATION ENACTMENTS IN RESPECT OF SMELTING TIN

Convocation enactments regulated the smelting and transportation of tin closely for three purposes: (1) to prevent the evasion of the coinage of tin and the payment of the coinage duties, (2) to ensure that the weight and quality of tin was satisfactory and (3) to prevent the theft and misappropriation of tin.

The Devon Convocation early on prohibited the movement of black tin from a tinwork unless notice of the intention to move it had first been given to the owners of the tinwork (who would usually be the bounders) (10). If any black tin was taken without the consent of the owners or occupiers (ie lessees or tributers) of the tinwork, they could apply to the steward of the stannary court to have it seized by his bailiff until the question of title could be tried; if the takers were found to have no title, a penalty of £40 could be recovered by the owners or occupiers of the tinwork (of which one-half went to the Duchy), and, if the taking was forcible, the takers could also be fined and imprisoned (11). By Cornish custom it was unlawful to buy black tin otherwise than at the wash (ie at the time of the division between the adventurers) or to buy the leavings of a blowing-house or white tin from anyone other than an adventurer, the owner of a blowing-house or a worker in white tin (12). In 1636 this custom was reinforced by a rule requiring purchases of black and white tin to be made before at least two sufficient witnesses, and, if this rule or the customary one as to clandestine purchases was broken, the seller and buyer were liable to a penalty of twice the value of the black or white tin sold (12). In 1686 purchases of black tin from the owners of the land or bounds where it had been broken were permitted if the purchase took place at the wash, but on the other hand all sales of black and white tin at night were prohibited (13). By the middle of the eighteenth century these restrictions on sales of tinstuff had become impossible to enforce, since most sales of black tin were by sample and took place at the smelting house, and so in 1752 the rule was altered to prohibit purchases of black tin or leavings of a blowing-house or smelting-house 'otherwise than openly . . . of persons of honest repute who are known to be adventurers in mines, or owners of blowing-houses or smelting-houses, or owners of lands or bounds, or known proprietors of tinstuff or black tin' (14). The category of permitted sellers had now been widened sufficiently to include all habitual dealers in tinstuff, and no restrictions were placed on the time and place of sales.

The earliest legislation on smelting required owners of tin and blowing-house owners to register their respective marks in Devon at the steward's court of their stannary, or in Cornwall at the Duchy Exchequer at Lostwithiel, and to put these marks on every block of tin smelted by or for them (15). The purpose of marking tin was to enable it to be traced back to its first owner and smelter after it had been marketed, so that any unpaid coinage duty could be collected, and also, more importantly at first, so that deceived purchasers might recover damages if the tin was of poor quality and the smelter might be punished in that case. The legislation directed that if a merchant should buy (16)

> . . . any false [ie poor quality] tin and . . . be deceived, that if he bring to the court the mark of the blowing-house and of the owner in [the metal], let him come thither with sufficient evidence and prove that the tin whereupon the said mark was set was false and untruly meddled [smelted], that they the Prince's officers shall make search . . . who be the owners of those marks and give notice of their names to the Warden or his deputy . . . in open court, and he forthwith shall commit them to ward [prison] that owneth the marks and the blowers, and to compel them to satisfy the merchant of all such hurt and damage as he hath taken by such false tin and then the blower to remain in ward and make such fine as shall be thought reasonable. . . .

The provisions for the protection of merchants were elaborated in later legislation. In 1510 the Devon Convocation directed that in proceedings in respect of false tin the owner's mark and the blowing-house mark must still be visible when the defective tin was produced in court and the block must not have been melted since it was coined (17). The tin was to be tried by smelting in open court, and if it was not merchantable the owner whose mark appeared on it and the blower who smelted it were to 'recompense the merchant for his costs and charges' and the tin was forfeited to the Duchy; but if the tin was found to be merchantable the merchant who complained was liable to a penalty of £5, half of which was paid to the owner or blower who had been impugned (17).

The earliest legislation of Devon and Cornwall had already prohibited the smelting of sinder tin (whether alloyed with better quality tin or not) 'or any other manner of hard tin unless the blocks were marked with the letter H' (18), and this was repeated in the Devon legislation of 1510 (19). All the existing enactments for Devon were repealed in 1552 and were replaced by more precisely drawn provisions for the protection of purchasers. The new enactment began by providing that all tin blown in the customary fashion and not mixed with hard tin should be taken 'to all intendments for good and pure tin' (20), and so a purchaser could not complain about its quality. Tin blown with a *pyte* or short float (21), whether alloyed with good tin or not, was to be deemed to be sinder tin, and was to be marked with an H (20), as, presumably, by implication was real sinder tin. If tin should have been marked with an H and was not so marked when coined or sold, or if unmarked good tin contained hard tin hidden inside it, or if hard tin marked with an H contained worse metal hidden within, any buyer of the tin could bring it before the steward's court with the first owner's and the blowing-house marks intact and have it tried by re-smelting (20). If the defect complained of was thereby proved, the first owner of the tin forfeited its value to the Duchy and was liable to a penalty of £10, half of which was recoverable by the buyer, but if the tin was found to be good the buyer paid the same penalty to the Duchy, half of which went to the impugned first owner or blower (20). Furthermore, buyers of tin were encouraged to have hard or falsified tin condemned by the steward's court instead of reselling it by another provision of the 1552 enactment, which imposed a penalty of £10 on any buyer who by 'privy contracts, payments or otherwise' conspired with the first owner of hard or falsified tin to conceal its true character (22).

Convocation legislation for Cornwall similarly protected

buyers by enabling them to have blocks on which the first owner's and the blowing-house marks were still intact tried by re-smelting in the steward's court by two blowers, one assigned by the buyer and the other by the first owner (23). Instead of entitling the buyer to recover the penalty of £5 per block of unmerchantable tin as the Devon enactment of 1552 had done, however, the Cornish legislation followed the early Devon enactments and simply gave the buyer the right to sue for damages (23). The Cornish legislation also required tin other than good soft tin to be marked with an appropriate letter indicating its quality: H for hard tin, P for pillian tin, S for sinder tin and R for relistian tin (24). With the exception of hard tin, these categories seem to have been based upon the method of smelting employed rather than the assayed quality of the tin. All the enumerated kinds of tin were obtained otherwise than directly from the first smelting, and in Devon were known simply as hard or sinder tin, which were interchangeable terms. In Cornwall, sinder tin must have been obtained from a second or third smelting of the slag or 'cinders' left from the first smelting. Pryce defined pillian as 'the tin which remains in the scoria or slags after it is first smelted'; he explained that it consisted of the globules of melted tin disseminated through the slag, and that they were separated from the latter by spalling but not by stamping (25). In the Convocation legislation requiring poorer grade tin to be marked, the categories appeared in the descending order pillian, sinder and relistian, and from the derivation of the words it would appear that sinder tin was obtained from slag which had to be stamped before being re-smelted, unlike pillian, and that relistian was obtained from the slag of a second, third or fourth smelting.

The later Cornish legislation dropped the treble classification of re-smelted tin, and by the eighteenth century it was all called pillian. The Convocation Act of 1624 provided that the owner of a block of tin might appeal to the steward's court against the taring of the block, that is marking it as defective, by the Duchy assayer at the coinage (26). It also provided that 'casing' tin, that is hiding poorer quality metal inside the block, should be punished by a penalty of £5 imposed upon the owner of the block whose mark appeared on it at the time of coinage, or, if the casing was done without the owner's privity or consent, by the imposition of a like penalty upon the blower who smelted the block, half the penalty in either case being payable to any buyer of the tin (27). The Act of 1636 dealt with the falsification of tin, that is casing blocks or alloying tin with poor quality tin or any other metal. If the block of tin complained of was sent to the steward's court with the owner's and the blowing-house marks intact and was found to be defective, the owner was liable to a penalty of £3 and the blower to one of £5, and any buyer of the tin could recover double damages from the owner who coined the tin (28). Because some difficulty arose under these enactments in determining the responsibility of the owner of a blowing-house and the blowers employed by him, the Act of 1686 provided that they should be liable only for their respective faults (29). The blowing-house owner was consequently exonerated from liability for his employees' errors, though he could, of course, still be liable to the penalties and liability in damages imposed by the enactment as owner of the defective tin. Finally the Convocation Act of 1752 amplified the provision in the Act of 1624 for appeals to the steward's court against the taring of tin by the Duchy assayer. The assayer had henceforth to bear the costs of the appeal only if he marked the value of the block of tin down by more than 150 per cent of the amount it should have been marked down, but on the other hand he was made liable in damages to any buyer of coined tin which he should have tared but did not (30). The Act of 1752 also repeated the enactment of 1636 on the falsification of tin, raising the penalty recoverable from the blower or smelter to £40 for each offence, but exonerated the first owner of the tin from any penalty or liability to pay damages (31).

Although the Convocation enactments of the sixteenth and seventeenth centuries imposed penalties and liabilities in damages on the first owner of bad tin which bore his mark, no legislation after the earliest required owners' marks to be registered along with blowers' marks. This may have been because the owners of blowing- and smelting-houses were themselves the first owners of most newly smelted tin, and the impressing of the blowing-house mark on a block of tin was therefore sufficient to establish its origin. Nevertheless it seems more likely that the increased importance attached to the blowing- or smelting-house mark was due to the wish of the Duchy officials to prevent any tin escaping the coinage, for if an uncoined block of tin bore such a mark, it would be a simple matter to find out from whom the coinage duty and penalties should be exacted. With this object the Devon legislation required both blowing-house owners and blowers, whether employed in blowing-houses or blowing their own tin, to register their respective marks in the steward's court (32). The Cornish legislation went further. By the Convocation Act of 1624 blowing-house owners were required to register the names of the blowers they employed in the stewards' courts half-yearly (33), and the blowers were sworn not to falsify tin and 'to deal justly with every man', and, most important, to certify to the steward's court half-yearly the number of blocks of tin they smelted and the names of the owners of the blocks (34). These rules were substantially re-enacted in 1636, with the addition that the blowers' half-yearly certificates were also to be signed by the owner of the blowing-house or his agent (35).

In 1752 Convocation extended the registration rules to smelting-houses, as there had been some doubt whether the earlier enactments applied to smelting tin by reverberatory furnaces; it also required principal blowers and smelters to be registered and sworn before they began work, but dispensed with the registration of other blowers and smelters; and it remoulded the blowers' oath so that principal blowers and smelters now had to swear to the blocks of tin they smelted and the names of the persons to whom they were delivered within six weeks after the end of each coinage, and to make only merchantable and unfalsified tin (36). Furthermore the Act of 1752 required every blowing- and smelting-house to keep a record of all purchases of black tin (37); ostensibly this was to enable stolen tinstuff to be traced, but in fact it was another check on the evasion of coinage duty, for the record book was principally resorted to by the supervisors of blowing- and smelting-houses, who were Duchy officers. The record book could also be inspected by 'any person at all seasonable hours, paying sixpence for each time' (37), which appears to have made it a public record. Vice-Warden Wallis held that the record book was not a public document, however, and that a private person could only obtain an order for it to be produced if he showed that he had a special interest in inspecting it and made out a *prima facie* case of fraud on the part of the persons responsible for keeping it (38). Blowing- and smelting-house owners or their agents were additionally required to keep tin scale books, in which were recorded the numbers, weights and dates of casting of all the blocks of tin they produced, and this book was open to inspection by all holders of tin bills issued by the blowing- or smelting-house (39). Such holders could select the blocks of tin they wished to take in satisfaction of their tin bills, provided the numbers of the blocks they chose were consecutive, and they could demand delivery on giving six days' notice (39).

THE TIN COINAGE

The earliest detailed account of the coinage or taxation of newly smelted tin is in William de Wrotham's letter of 1198 to Hubert Walter, Richard I's justiciar. In it he related how he and the sheriffs of Devon and Cornwall and certain other commissioners took evidence from named 'wise and discreet' tinners at Exeter and Launceston as to the weights customarily used for the weighing of tin and the rate of duty paid to the king. The Devon tinners deposed that 'it has anciently, now and always been obligatory to weigh tin on its first smelting by the weight of the City of Exeter for the second smelting, allowing a ninth weight for every eight, and this is because out of every thousandweight calculated by this greater weight there are given to our lord the king by ancient custom (*de antiqua consuetudine*) 30 pence for the farm of the stannaries in Devon and for the customary duty of waggons [or for entry?] in the market towns (*pro custo vecturae ad villas marcandas*), and because an amount of tin is lost on the second smelting'. The tinners of Cornwall for their part deposed 'that the true and ancient weight for the first smelting has allowed and ought to allow an eighth weight for every seven of the weights of the second smelting, and that the true and ancient weight for the first smelting of tin in Cornwall has formerly, now and always been accustomed to be, and ought to be, greater by 30 pennyworth of tin than the weight for the first smelting in Devon, and this is because out of every thousandweight calculated by this greater weight there are given to our lord the king by ancient custom five shillings for the farm of the stannaries in Cornwall and for the customary duty of waggons [or for entry?] in the market towns, and because an amount of tin is lost on the second smelting'.

These complex passages require elucidation. Before the additional duty of 1 mark per thousandweight was imposed by de Wrotham and the other commissioners in 1198, coinage duty was paid on the first smelting of tin, but no coinage stamp was impressed on the tin, for it still had to be smelted a second time to make it merchantable. Obviously on the second smelting the tin would be reduced in volume by the removal of impurities and the loss of some tin in the furnace, and allowance was made for this in calculating the coinage duty by assessing it on eight-ninths of the weight of the tin after the first smelting in Devon, and on seven-eighths of that weight in Cornwall. But the allowance of one-eighth or one-ninth covered the cost of the coinage duty as well; this rested on the plain man's logic that if a fraction of the tin or its value belonged to the king, the tinner should not pay duty on that fraction as well as the residue he kept. The statement that payment of the coinage duty satisfied not only 'the farm of the stannaries' but also the 'customary duty' for bringing the tin into the coinage towns is explained by the fact that the king was exempt from tolls payable in markets or for bringing goods along ancient highways, and, because the tinners were specially protected by the king, he extended his personal exemption to them, but only for a price. It may be assumed that the price paid by the tinners for exemption from toll was the same in both counties, and so the difference between the allowances made to the tinners on the first smelting in the two counties, namely the difference between one-ninth and one-eighth of the gross weight, was attributable to the 30 pence extra coinage duty which the Cornish tinners paid. This means that one seventy-second of a thousandweight of tin was considered to be worth 30 pence, and this put a value on refined tin of £9 per thousandweight which was three times the current market value. In other words the allowance made to the Cornish tinners for the duty they bore was inadequate in comparison with that made to the tinners of Devon, and the Cornish tinners paid duty at a higher rate, a situation which continued as long as the coinage lasted.

The Charters of 1305 contained only a few provisions in respect of the tin coinages. They directed that all tin should be coined in the presence of the Lord Warden by Michaelmas (29 September) each year, and that coinages should be held at Lostwithiel, Bodmin, Liskeard, Truro and Helston for Cornwall, and Tavistock, Ashburton and Chagford for Devon (40). In 1328 Plympton was added as a coinage town for Devon on the petition of the Devon tinners, who complained that it was burdensome for them to have to carry their tin as far as Tavistock from their tinworks on Dartmoor (41). The patent appointed Plympton to supersede Tavistock as a coinage town, but coinages continued to be held at Tavistock, and in the eighteenth and nineteenth centuries it became a busy centre for the coinage and sale of tin mined in east Cornwall. As a result of the westward movement of tin mining in Cornwall from the fifteenth century onwards, the coinages held at Truro and Helston became inadequate, particularly in view of the great volume of tin mined in the Land's End district, and so in 1663 Penzance was appointed by royal warrant to be an additional coinage town for Cornwall on the tinners undertaking to meet the cost of building a coinage hall there (42).

The Charters of 1305 contemplated the holding of only one coinage annually at each of the coinage towns, but during the first half of the fourteenth century two coinages were held each year, at Easter and Michaelmas, and in 1357 the Black Prince directed four coinages to be held in Cornwall (43), though it seems that practice soon reverted to the original two. By the sixteenth century regular coinages were held twice-yearly at Midsummer and Michaelmas in Cornwall (44), but only one regular coinage was held in Devon, at Michaelmas (45). From the beginning of the century, however, occasional coinages had been held at other times of the year, at least in Cornwall, and the tinners had the right to have such coinages if they were prevented from presenting their tin at the regular coinages by flooding or a lack of water to wash their black tin (46). By the end of the century these occasional coinages had become regular events and were held at Christmas and Lady Day (25 March) (47), so that in fact there were now four quarterly coinages. But the Cornish tinners only claimed a right to the Midsummer and Michaelmas coinages and to occasional or post coinages in case of necessity (48), and they accepted that the holding of post coinages at other times was at the discretion of the king or the Duchy. Tin coined at a post coinage bore the additional duty of 4d per cwt, and these duties were known as post groats. It was, of course, of vital importance to the tinners and smelters to have their tin coined promptly, so that it might be sold, and in 1686 the Cornwall Convocation emphasised this by laying down the duration of the coinages at each coinage town (49) and imposing penalties on the officers of the coinage if they did not hold them at the proper times (50).

The proceedings at a coinage have been well described by Lewis in the following passage (51):

> As the day [for the beginning of the coinage] drew near the controller [of the coinage] and the receiver journeyed from town to town carrying

in a sealed bag the stamping hammer and the weights. At the towns they were met by other functionaries, the weigher and the assay master, together with the requisite number of local porters. Thither also came the tinners, despatching their metal in advance by packhorses or carts, while from London and the southern ports came the would-be purchasers, including country chapmen, London dealers, pewterers' factors and a sprinkling of Italian or Flemish traders (52). At noon on the first day of the coinage, all assembled by the coinage hall, a warehouse-like structure near the market place, in which tin had previously been stored in anticipation of the official inspection and public sale. An open space was roped off in front, the King's beam was brought out and rectified by the controller and weigher, the weights were solemnly unsealed and handed to the weigher, the assay master made ready his hammer and chisels and the steward, controller and receiver took their seats facing the beam. When all was in readiness, the porters brought out the blocks one at a time and placed them upon the scales. Each had been stamped with the private mark of the owner, and as the steward carried with him a register of these marks no difficulty occurred in identification. The weight of each [block] was shouted out by the weigher and taken down by the three officials. The blocks, on leaving the scales, were taken in hand by the assay master who chiselled a small piece from the corner of each and rapidly assayed it to make sure that the metal was of the proper quality. If so the controller with a blow from the hammer struck upon the block the Duchy arms; but should it be below standard it was 'tared' by the assay master, that is to say, a relative figure was placed by him upon each block at which it might be sold below the price for tin of standard quality. If hopelessly corrupt it was set aside for re-melting.

A few details need to be added to this account to complete the picture. When a tinner or smelter delivered his blocks of tin to the coinage hall shortly before the coinage began, the receiver of the coinage gave him a receipt for them, which was known in the seventeenth century as a ticket or coinage bill, the latter name being generally used in the eighteenth and nineteenth centuries. Unfortunately none of these coinage bills have survived, but probably they were nothing more than lists of the blocks deposited by the tinner or smelter and were prepared by him in duplicate, one copy being left with the receiver of the coinage, and the other receipted by him so that the tinner or smelter might prove his right to receive back his blocks after they had been coined. The stamped blocks of tin were, of course, retained by the receiver until the coinage duty had been paid. At first purchasers of tin were given until All Saints' Day (1 November) to pay the duty on tin coined at Michalemas (53) and tinners and smelters availed themselves of this concession too, and customarily delayed payment for another four weeks until 28 November. The concession was withdrawn in Cornwall in 1636 and the duty was made payable ten days after the tin was coined (54). If the duty was unpaid for a year and a day after the tin was coined, the Duchy claimed the right to sell the tin and satisfy the duty out of the proceeds of sale (55).

On payment of the coinage duty the receiver of the coinage was safe in returning the stamped tin to the person who had deposited it at the coinage hall if the latter produced the coinage bill or accounted satisfactorily for its loss, because the receiver was merely a bailee or depositary of the blocks and so was not guilty of the wrong of conversion, even if the person producing the bill had no title to the tin. In fact stannary law went farther than this, for the person who presented the coinage bill could demand the return of the blocks duly stamped, and could sue the controller and the receiver for damages if delivery was refused (56). If the person who deposited the tin for coining had agreed to sell it to another, the purchaser, or his sub-purchaser if he had resold, would take the coinage bill and use it to recover the stamped blocks from the receiver. Here again the receiver was safe in re-delivering to the person who produced the coinage bill duly endorsed with memoranda of the sale or sales, but this time because of the special quality of the bill by stannary law. If tin had been stolen or misappropriated, therefore, the owner was at considerable risk that it might be coined and delivered to the thief or anyone who had bought it from him. To prevent this happening the owner could serve a *caveat* or warning on the controller of the coinage setting out his claim to the blocks in question, and the receiver would then retain them until the owner's claim had been tried by the stewards' court in an action brought by him, or by the Vice-Warden on an application to remove the *caveat* made by the person who held the coinage bill (57).

From the sixteenth century onwards Convocation legislated to prevent offences against the coinage system. The Devon Convocation of 1510 enacted that if tin was not presented for coining within the period allowed by law, or if anyone presented tin at the coinage in his own name on behalf of another whose name was not disclosed, the tin should be forfeited and the person presenting it fined (58). In 1552 the Devon Convocation prohibited the sale of uncoined tin, ordering that such tin should be forfeited and the seller and buyer fined (59). The Cornwall Convocation created an elaborate network of offences as sanctions against the evasion or attempted evasion of coinage duty. The Convocation of 1588 began by outlawing the movement of uncoined tin, even within the stannaries, unless it was for the purpose of coining it (60), and this legislation was repeated in 1624 with a proviso that if tin had not been coined at the coinage following its smelting, it might be retained by the owner until the next coinage without committing the offence of unlawful carrying (61). In 1636 a more positive enactment required tin to be carried directly from the blowing-house to the nearest coinage town under penalty of forfeiture, but an owner might retain uncoined tin until the next coinage but one after its smelting provided he notified the controller of the coinage of the quantity and whereabouts of the uncoined tin by the end of the next coinage (62). This was re-enacted in 1686 with an addition of prohibition on the movement of tin by night, the time when most smuggling took place; the penalty for contravention was increased to a fine equal to the value of the uncoined tin as well as its forfeiture, and the accused could also be imprisoned for up to six months (63). The legislation of 1752 repeated the provision of the 1686 Act with the omission of the proviso permitting owners to retain uncoined tin temporarily, and it directed that prosecutions for the movement of uncoined tin should be brought in the steward's court, and that if the accused was convicted, the tin should be forfeited, or if the tin had been taken outside the stannaries, the accused should be ordered to pay its value to the Duchy (64).

The problem of the sale of uncoined tin was dealt with in detail by the Cornwall Convocation of 1624. If the seller and buyer were apprehended while negotiating the sale, they were fined the value of the tin sold and the tin was forfeited, but if the sale could only be proved by inference from the buyer being in possession of the tin, the fine was reduced to £3 (65). A buyer of uncoined tin could not be sued by the seller for the unpaid price because the contract of sale was illegal, nor for the same reason could the unpaid seller recover the tin, but the tin was not the buyer's undisputed property because the Duchy could forfeit it for non-payment of the coinage duty. If the tin had been transported outside Cornwall, however, the Duchy's right of forfeiture could not be enforced, and in that case the 1624 legislation permitted the Duchy to recover the unpaid purchase price from the buyer, and he could not plead the illegality of his purchase as a defence (65). The enactment of 1624 remained in force until the coinage was abolished, and was altered only in two respects by the legislation of 1752, which made sales of uncoined tin punishable by a fine equal to the value of the tin in all cases, whether the parties were caught in *flagrante delicto* or not, but the legislation also put the burden on the Duchy of proving that the accused seller or buyer intended to defraud the Duchy of the coinage duty if a conviction was to be obtained (64).

During the second half of the eighteenth century the smelters and adventurers repeatedly requested the king and the Duchy officials to abolish or reduce the coinage duty, on the ground that it put an undue burden on the tin trade, but their requests were unavailing. In the 1820s, however, the abolition movement became more determined, and the tin interest began to take action itself. Apart from the burden of the duty, the smelters and adventurers complained of the loss they experienced by the unavoidable delay between the smelting and coining of tin: the tin could not be sold to merchants until it had been coined, and the fact that large quantities came on to the market at the same time, when the quarterly coinages were held, tended to depress its price. The smelters attempted to gain concessions by filling the narrow streets of the coinage towns with their blocks of tin when the coinage halls had been filled to capacity, which caused the greatest inconvenience to everyone; the risk of theft to the smelters was not great, for each block of tin weighed 3 cwt or more. In March 1833 the Whig Government met the tin interest's grievance about the delays imposed on sales by adding Calstock, St Austell and Hayle to the coinage towns, and coinages were directed to be held at each of the eight coinage towns every six weeks (66). This meant that coinages were held on over 160 days each year, and the longest delay between one coinage and the next in the area bounded by Truro, Helston, Penzance and Hayle was less than two weeks.

But this administrative rearrangement did not lighten the financial burden of the coinage. On the death of William IV the lords, adventurers and merchants interested in the Cornish tin industry therefore petitioned the House of Commons to abolish the coinage duty altogether when enacting the new Queen's civil list (67). On 2 and 3 August 1838 the House debated the proposal after the Queen had signified her consent to it, and on 4 August the Chancellor of the Exchequer, Spring-Rice, was directed to bring in a Coinage Abolition Bill. The bill encountered no opposition in the Commons, but in the House of Lords it was opposed by the arch-Tory the Duke of Wellington and the arch-Whig Lord Brougham, who together with the future Lord Chancellor, Lyndhurst, objected that a confidence trick was being practised on the young and inexperienced Queen (68). Nevertheless the bill became law on 16 August 1838 (69). It provided that as from the following 10 October it should 'not be necessary to coin any tin dug, raised or taken . . . and that the duties which would but for this Act be payable on the coinage of tin after that time shall cease and determine' (70). The Queen was compensated by a perpetual annuity equal to the average net annual yield of the coinage over the last ten years; this was charged on the Consolidated Fund and attached to the Duchy of Cornwall (71). To help make good the loss of revenue, a customs duty was imposed on imported refined tin at the rate of 15s per cwt, and on imported tin ore at the rate of 10s per cwt (72).

References to this chapter are on pages 209–12.

Chapter 5
Mining Companies

ORIGINS OF THE COST BOOK COMPANY

ALTHOUGH NO RECORDS SURVIVE OF PARTnerships between tin miners earlier than the seventeenth century, it is certain that partnerships or joint adventures, to give them a neutral name, existed since tin mining was first undertaken. The nature and extent of the work involved in operating tin streamworks demanded the labour of more than one man, and except in the minority of cases where the undertaker was rich enough to employ mineworkers at wages, the labour must have been provided by those who shared the black tin produced. The method of sharing was undoubtedly one share for each participant (1), so the adventure was simple in structure, there was no need for drawing up a formal agreement between the adventurers, and the adventurers and the courts rarely had to characterise the legal nature of the adventure. It was not until the sixteenth century that writers began to speak of the adventure as being a partnership, and they were induced to do this not by the commercial character of the adventure but because they envisaged the adventurers as part-owners of the produce and the assets of the stream-work they operated.

Indeed, when the law had to classify an adventure between tinners, it looked almost exclusively at the feature of co-ownership necessarily present. Before the adventurers began work, one or more of them had to acquire a proprietary interest in the land in the form either of tin bounds or of a sett granted by the freeholder or bound owner. This interest was vested in the adventurers as co-owners because it was their intention that the produce of their working should be shared between them, and their shares or doles were taken to extend to the *corpus* as well as the produce (2). This was so even if the bounds were pitched or the sett granted in the name of one of the adventurers only; in that case he held the bounds or sett in trust for himself and his co-adventurers for their respective shares. Most of the legal problems which arose between labouring co-adventurers could be solved by reference to the law of property governing their shares. If one of the adventurers incurred or satisfied an obligation for the purpose of carrying on the mine, he could obtain a contribution from the others in proportion to their shares; if he incurred expense voluntarily, for example by providing or repairing necessary equipment, he could recover a contribution from the others in the same proportion even though they had not assented to the expenditure. The Devon Convocation provided that if one adventurer incurred expense in defending the adventurers' title to their tinwork, he could recover a rateable proportion of his costs from his co-adventurers (3). Fiduciary duties between co-owners, and even between true partners, were not worked out by the courts until the nineteenth century, but their beginnings are found as early as the sixteenth century as regards co-adventurers, again based on the proprietary interests of the parties. Thus, if one co-owner of bounds procured the freeholder's bailiff or bounds keeper to renew them for the benefit of himself and persons other than his co-adventurers, the inclusion of himself 'let in' his co-adventurers, and the renewal was taken to be for his and their benefit alone, the strangers being excluded (4). By Convocation enactment this was extended to cases where the collusive renewal was wholly for the benefit of strangers, and here too the original adventurers alone benefited (5).

The solution of questions arising between co-adventurers by reference to property law alone ceased to be satisfactory when in the fourteenth or fifteenth centuries owners of capital began to put funds at the disposal of labouring tinners in return for a share in the produce of the mine. This involved making a contract which not only specified the share in the adventure which the investor should take but also laid down to what extent he was to be responsible for the future cost of operating the mine and to what extent the labouring tinners should satisfy their obligations to contribute by providing labour and by putting up money. At first no doubt labouring tinners resorted to these cost-sharing contracts only when a sudden expense beyond their means had to be met, such as replacing equipment or constructing a leat or conduit over a long distance, but by the sixteenth century it was common for such contracts to be entered into as soon as work began in a mine.

As the seventeenth century progressed, adventures in which working miners participated became rarer, though they did not become extinct until the eighteenth century in respect of deep mines, and they continued into the nineteenth century in respect of streamworks. By the end of the seventeenth century adventurers were almost all investors, largely from the merchant class. The principal disputes between adventurers were now as to their respective rights to supply the mine with equipment and materials from their privately owned businesses, of course at a profit and often in excess of the mine's real requirements. This question was sometimes settled by the agreement entered into by the adventurers when work on the mine was begun, some of the adventurers being designated 'in-adventurers', who could satisfy their obligation to contribute toward the costs by supplying materials, and the remainder being 'out-adventurers', who had to contribute in money. When no agreement was reached over this matter, Convocation enactment gave each of the adventurers the right to provide his share of the materials required (6), a most impractical rule, which gave rise to more disputes than it avoided. By the last quarter of the eighteenth century most mines had come under the unified management of a mine captain or purser, who placed orders for equipment and materials as he thought fit, though often no doubt with an eye to his own profit or to currying favour with influential adventurers.. Nevertheless the adventurers' right to participate equally in supplying materials to the mine was still recognised by the Vice-Wardens, and occasionally suits for enforcing it were brought (7).

What was the legal character of the association between investing adventurers of the seventeenth-century type? In Convocation enactments and elsewhere the adventurers were frequently referred to as partners, but it is clear that they did not regard their adventures as trading partnerships, for this would have exposed them all to unlimited liability for debts incurred by any of their number in managing the mine. In fact in 1686 the Cornwall Convocation expressly enacted that creditors of the mine should sue only the adventurer or adventurers 'who bought or contracted for the . . . goods [supplied] or hired or contracted with the labourers to work in the [mine], and not any other adventurers'; but if this resulted in the adventurer who was sued paying more than his share of costs, he was entitled to recover contributions from his fellow adventurers (8). If the enactment had been given full effect, adventurers who took no part in managing the mine would have enjoyed a form of limited liability denied to true partners; this notion was voiced even as late as 1847, when the court of Common Bench at Westminster was prepared to limit an adventurer's liability to the amount of calls for costs properly made on him on the ground that if he took no part in the management of the mine he could not be exposed to the full liability of a partner to its creditors (9). Stannary law, however, equated the position of adventurers with that of trading partners as far as personal liability for obligations incurred in connection with the mine was concerned.

This was the result of a number of decisions by Vice-Warden Tredenham both before and after the legislation of 1686, and of two leading cases in the eighteenth century.

In 1683 Tredenham held without hesitation that adventurers were jointly and individually liable to mineworkers employed in their mine for payment of the wages contracted to be paid them by the adventurer who managed the mine (10), and he reaffirmed this in another case four years later (11). In 1687 he applied the same rule of personal liability of adventurers when the plaintiff mineworkers were engaged by the mine captains (12). In 1684 Tredenham also made it clear that it was no defence for an adventurer who was sued for a mining debt to show that the purser had been paid sufficient costs by the adventurers to meet the debt (13), though in such a case the adventurer who was compelled to pay was entitled to be indemnified by the purser (14). After Tredenham's enforced retirement, it seems that the Vice-Wardens were not so strict as he was in making adventurers personally liable for mining debts. The next case that followed Tredenham's lead was decided by Vice-Warden Borlase in 1759 (15), when he held adventurers personally liable to a supplier of materials to the mine on the order of the purser. The adventurers appealed to the Lord Warden, and argued in their petition of appeal that Borlase's judgment denied them the exemption from personal liability conferred by the Convocation enactment of 1686; but Borlase replied that the Convocation enactment of 1686 did not apply when the adventurers had appointed a purser, for he was the agent of each adventurer and so empowered to pledge the personal credit of all the adventurers. The Lord Warden accepted this advice and upheld Borlase's judgment. In 1789 Borlase's argument was taken a stage further in a case where creditors sought to recover from adventurers the price of goods supplied on the order of a purser whose authority to contract the adventurers had publicly repudiated by newspaper advertisement on discovering that he had fraudulently misrepresented the condition of the mine to induce them to take shares in it (16). The Lord Warden, on appeal from the Vice-Warden of Devon, held that notwithstanding the purser's fraud, the fact that the adventurers had supplied the purser with sufficient cash to meet the expenses of the mine and their repudiation of his authority to contract on their behalf, they were personally liable in their capacity as adventurers to creditors of the mine who were unaware of the fraud and the repudiation.

After this the floodgates were down, and it was held repeatedly that adventurers could be sued for mining debts incurred by the purser without proving the extent of the authority expressly conferred on him by the adventurers (17), and also that they were liable for debts properly incurred for running the mine even though no purser had been appointed (18). Moreover, it was held that a mine creditor could sue an adventurer even though he was unaware of his membership of the adventure at the time the debt was incurred (19). In 1829 and 1837 Vice-Wardens Wallis and Dampier respectively justified this apparent disregard of the Convocation enactment of 1686 conferring immunity on adventurers for mining debts not contracted by them individually by treating the immunity as confined to adventures in which all members exercised the right to supply their share of materials and labour (20). This smacks of justification *ex post facto*, and the fact that the immunity was conferred by the section of the 1686 enactment which followed one that gave adventurers the right to supply materials and labour afforded little real justification for reading the sections as complementary.

Although important rules of partnership law applied to adventurers or cost book companies, as they came to be called during the eighteenth century, they were not treated as partnerships by the law in all respects. In particular the feature of co-ownership of the bounds or sett the adventurers held continued to influence legal thinking about the quality of adventurer's shares. Because the share was originally nothing more than a share of ownership, and because the adventurer's interest in the sett or bounds was still the most important element among his rights, his share was freely transferable in law, unlike a share in a partnership, which was purely a personal association between the original partners. The fact that the adventurer's share comprised personal rights and obligations as well, such as his right to require the purser and his co-adventurers to account to him for his share of the produce of the mine and his obligation to contribute toward the costs of operating it, did not in any way diminish the transferability of the share. Such rights and obligations were regarded as incidental to the co-ownership of the mine's assets, and passed to a transferee of the adventurer's share along with that co-ownership (21). From an economic standpoint a share in a cost book company was now simply an investment, like a share in a company incorporated by royal charter or Act of Parliament. Even the sett held by trustees for the adventurers could no longer be regarded as a beneficial interest owned by the adventurers for its own sake, but instead was more properly looked on, even by the courts, as an asset held by the trustees for the purpose of producing dividends for the adventurers (22). This meant that the adventurers ceased to be beneficial owners of any of the assets vested in the company from time to time while it was working the mine. Their shares were now simply collections of disembodied rights and obligations, but paradoxically the free transferability of cost book shares resulted from the fact that originally adventurers' shareholdings involved the ownership of physical assets, and this was the one feature that distinguished them originally from partnerships.

The conversion of the seventeenth-century mining adventure into the eighteenth-century cost book company centred round the office and functions of the purser. The number of adventurers in the average mining company was now far larger than it had been, and the identity of the adventurers changed more often than it did formerly because of the increased turnover of shares. It was therefore impossible for rights and obligations of the company to be enforced by and against the numerous and fluctuating body of adventurers, yet the company could not sue and be sued in its own name, because it was unincorporated and was therefore not recognised in law as a juristic person. The difficulty of litigating could only be overcome if some permanent officer of the company could sue and be sued on its behalf. Common-law and equity would not permit actions and suits to be brought in this way, with a nominee or agent representing the real parties, but the eighteenth and nineteenth century Vice-Wardens adapted their equitable procedural rules to enable the purser of a cost book company to fill this role. Thus the purser could sue for debts payable to the adventurers (23), including those falling due before he was appointed (24), and conversely he could be sued for debts owed by the adventurers (25), whether he was himself an adventurer or not, and whether he had received sufficient money from the adventurers to pay the debts or not.

If a purser died or retired or was removed while litigation was pending, it did not terminate; the adventurers simply appointed a new purser, and the litigation continued with his name substituted for that of the original purser as plaintiff or defendant (25). Finally, if an adventurer wished to have an account of the company's assets and liabilities or receipts and expenditure so as to calculate the surplus or deficit attributable to his shares, he did not have to bring a suit for an account against all his fellow adventurers, but could bring such a suit against the purser alone as custodian of the company's records and money (26). By these devices the cost book company was made as manageable an instrument for acquiring rights and obligations as an incorporated company, and it was on the basis of this practical accommodation of stannary law to the needs of adventurers and their creditors that the substantial body of law governing cost book companies was developed during the nineteenth century.

THE FORMATION AND ORGANISATION OF COST BOOK COMPANIES

Formation of the company; the original adventurers

The early cost book companies were formed by the original adventurers executing a deed or signing an agreement setting out the terms on which they were associated, or more usually in the nineteenth century, by the original adventurers holding a meeting and adopting cost book regulations drafted beforehand and passing various consequential resolutions—for instance, for the appointment of a purser and trustees (if not named in the regulations) and for the appointment of the subordinate officers of the mine. Unless the company intended to issue a prospectus inviting the public to subscribe for its shares, the original adventurers usually agreed to divide all the shares between them, and they subscribed the cost book of the company at the meeting for this purpose.

If a cost book company issued a prospectus inviting the public to subscribe for shares in it, the first meeting of the original adventurers was held in the way described above in order to form the company, but only a few of its shares were allotted to the promoters or their nominees at that meeting. Alternatively, the promoters issued a prospectus inviting the public to apply for shares before the company was formed, and the meeting held to form the company and adopt its regulations was then attended by the members of the public who had applied for and been allotted shares. In that case the prospectus would outline the intended regulations of the company or would say simply that it was to be conducted on the cost book principle; if the regulations adopted at the first meeting were inconsistent with what was stated in the prospectus or conflicted with the cost book principle, any allottee of shares who did not vote in favour of the regulations adopted at the first meeting could rescind or cancel his allotment, and he was thereupon treated as never having been an adventurer (27).

An allottee of shares under any prospectus could rescind the allotment made to him if it contained any misrepresentation of a material fact, such as a statement that the promoters held a sett of the mine when they only had hopes of acquiring one (28). In order to rescind, the allottee had to show that he had been a victim of the misrepresentation, which was not the case if he knew of its falsity when he applied for shares, or if he relied on his own judgment or on independent advice in deciding to apply and not on the statement in the prospectus (29). Moreover, if the allottee was a professional dealer in mining shares, the court would not allow him to rescind unless he had not only been misled but had also taken the steps dictated by common prudence to verify unlikely statements in the prospectus and had reasonably concluded that they were true (30).

Another ground on which an allottee could rescind an allotment of shares was that less than all, or substantially all, the shares offered by the prospectus had been subscribed for (31). The reason for this rule was that the debts of a cost book company were the personal liability of the adventurers, and each allottee of shares was entitled to an assurance that the liability would be shared with other persons who were sufficiently numerous or substantial to diminish the risk he was taking. If a material fraction of the shares offered to the public were left unallotted, any allottee could rescind within a reasonable time after discovering that fact, even though he had meanwhile signed the cost book in respect of his shares (32), but he could not rescind after accepting his shares or acting as an adventurer with knowledge of the under-allotment (33), and until he did affirmatively cancel his shareholding the purser could treat him as an adventurer and sue him for calls (34). Moreover, it appears from two judgments of Vice-Warden Dampier that the allottee's right of rescission could not be used so as to deprive creditors of their right to hold the allottee personally liable for the company's debts incurred before the rescission took place (35). This qualification of the right to rescind was, of course, logical and necessary to protect creditors who might be unaware of the under-allotment or of the allottee's ignorance of it when his shares were allotted.

Registration and inspections

Originally cost book companies were not required to register or publish the fact of their formation or the contents of their regulations. In 1869, however, statute required all existing and future cost book companies to file a copy of their regulations with the Registrar of the Vice-Warden's court, and any member of the public could inspect the filed copy at the Registrar's office without payment of a fee (36). The only sanction against failure to file copy regulations was that any adventurer or creditor of the company could apply to the Vice-Warden for an order compelling it to do so (36); this was an inadequate incentive, and in fact copies of only thirty-four sets of regulations were ever filed. In 1887 cost book companies filing copies of their regulations or any returns required by law with the Registrar of the Vice-Warden's court were also required to send duplicate copies, and the Registrar was to transmit the duplicate to the Registrar of Joint Stock Companies in London so that it might be available for public inspection there (37).

The only other return required to be made to the Registrar of the Vice-Warden's court by a cost book company was a four-monthly statement showing the number of shares into which its undertaking was divided, the number of shares issued, the total amount of calls made, received and outstanding, and the total number of its shares which had been forfeited for non-payment of calls (38).

Wholly apart from statute, adventurers were entitled by cost book custom to inspect their company's cost book (39), accounts and papers (40), and to have them kept at the account house of the mine (41). Creditors of the company, however, had no right by cost book custom, at common law or in equity to inspect any of the company's records and papers (42). In 1855 statute enabled both adventurers and creditors of a cost book company to make a summary application to the Vice-Warden for an order compelling the purser to produce a list of the present adventurers showing the number of shares they held and the dates on which they became adventurers, or an order for the production of the cost book or other books and documents relating to the mine (43). Under the statutory provision for inspection of the company's records,

Vice-Wardens Smirke and Fisher held that production of a list of adventurers or the cost book would always be ordered at the suit of an adventurer, unless the purser proved that his motives were improper or that the application was vexatious (44), and the fact that the applicants' shareholding was small or that he was a dealer in mining shares was irrelevant (45). On the other hand, in a case where the applicant sought production of a list of adventurers, and such a list had been offered to him for inspection at the last two monthly meetings of adventurers, his application was held to be vexatious and was dismissed (46). One particularly useful purpose served by a summary application for inspection of the company's records was to enable an adventurer to decide whether to relinquish his shares or to petition for the company to be wound up (47).

THE WORKING OF COST BOOK COMPANIES

The controlling organs of the cost book company were (1) the general meeting of adventurers and (2) the purser. If the regulations of the company provided for the election of a committee of management by the adventurers, usually from among their number, the regulations always vested 'the direction of the affairs of mine or adventure' in the committee and it then took the place of the purser, who became a subordinate official like a secretary. But in that case it was common to provide that the committee should be 'subject to the directions and resolutions passed at meetings of the adventurers', and the committee was then obliged to conform to directions given by the general meeting, even in matters of day to day management. Even if there were no such provision in the regulations, the purser (if there were no committee) or the committee of management were considered in law to be the agents of the adventurers collectively, and so were bound to give effect to all directions addressed to them by general meetings of adventurers, whether of a broad nature or in respect of a single transaction, however trivial (48). Nevertheless, as far as an outsider was concerned, the purser or the committee were the representatives of the company with whom he might safely deal, and if they entered into a transaction on the company's behalf which was normally within the powers of a purser, and the outsider was unaware of any restriction placed on those powers by the company's regulations or by a resolution passed by a general meeting, the company was bound by the transaction (49). Furthermore, if the regulations did not specify the extent of the committee's or purser's powers, it or he had the normal authority of a purser, and so, in the absence of any resolution or direction by a general meeting diminishing that authority or requiring it to be exercised in a particular way, the committee members or the purser acted properly as officers of the company as long as they kept within that normal authority.

The authority of a purser or committee of management

In a number of cases judges expressed the view that the nature of cost book companies required them to be managed on a ready money basis, which meant that goods and services were to be paid for when received, and the adventurers only subsequently charged by the purser or committee of management with the cost (50). According to this view, therefore, no purser or committee of management had implied authority to buy anything on credit or to borrow money. Following the ready money theory, the Vice-Wardens repeatedly asserted that a general meeting of adventurers had no power implied by law to make calls on their number otherwise than for the purpose of defraying costs that had already been incurred, and that no call to meet prospective or future costs could be made unless the company's regulations expressly permitted it (51). If both these principles were good in law, the only way a purser or committee of management could have conducted their company's affairs would have been by advancing money out of their own pockets to meet the company's expenses and recouping themselves out of the proceeds of calls subsequently made on the adventurers. There was no doubt that if the purser or committee of management chose to make advances, they were entitled to be indemnified by the adventurers (52), though it was also once held that they could claim an indemnity only if they had no ready money in hand and no saleable ore to raise money at the time they incurred an expense (53). But there was never any obligation on the purser or committee to make advances, and so it was obvious that the ready money theory had to give way in part, if not entirely, if the courts were to make the operation of cost book companies practicable.

In determining the extent of the adventurer's personal liability for debts of his company, the first and simplest question to be asked was whether a purser or committee had implied authority to order goods or services on credit for carrying on the mine and so make each adventurer personally liable to the supplier for payment of the agreed price. After an initial refusal to imply such an authority in a case where the purser had given a bill of exchange to secure a loan made to enable him to buy goods (54), the courts at Westminster held consistently from 1840 onwards that where the claimant had at the instance of the purser sold goods on credit to the company or performed services for it, he could sue each adventurer for the price, provided the goods or services were of a kind required for carrying on a mine (55). In fact the courts were not breaking new ground in so deciding, for there were at least three earlier decisions to the same effect (56). Moreover, throughout the eighteenth and nineteenth centuries the Vice-Wardens held adventurers personally liable on contracts made by the purser for the purchase of mining materials, such as timber (57), chains and hauling tackle (58), coal and steel (59), and steam engines (60). Adventurers had also been held liable on contracts made by the purser for the performance of services for the company, such as draining the mine (61), repairing the engine house and other mine buildings (62), or repairing ore waggons (63). Adventurers were also liable for the payment of wages to mineworkers engaged by the purser (64), and for the payment of engine dues to the patentee of the engine used at the mine (65). But pursers and committees of management could only negotiate contracts needed for the day to day management of a mine; long term and major contracts required the approval of a meeting of adventurers, unless the company's regulations expressly empowered the purser or committee to enter into them. Consequently, although a purser could contract for the use of tin stamps to crush a particular parcel of ore, he could not bind the adventurers by taking a twenty-one year lease of stamps (66), nor, of course, could he bind them by taking a sett of another mine (67).

The second litigated question in respect of a purser's powers was whether he had authority to bind the adventurers by issuing, accepting or endorsing bills of exchange in the name and on behalf of the company. In two early cases in the Court of Common Pleas (68) and before Vice-Warden Vivian (69) it was held that adventurers could not be sued on bills accepted by the purser as security for a loan to the company unless they had assented to the acceptance of the bills. Since the payee of the bill in such a case could not have sued the adventurers for repayment of the loan contracted by the purser unless they had expressly consented to it, it is not surprising that the adventurers could not be sued on the bill either if they had not consented. Vivian's ruling was based on the view that the purser's power to issue or accept bills was dependent on the binding character of the underlying transaction, so that if he gave a bill for a debt recoverable from the adventurers, the holder of the bill could sue them on it. According to this view it was impossible to deal with the validity of a bill issued by a purser in the abstract. In two later cases Vice-Wardens Dampier and Smirke accepted this idea, and allowed the holder of a bill to sue the adventurers on it when it had been accepted by the purser in payment of the price of mining materials sold to the mine (70). But in four other cases the Common Bench (71), the Court of Exchequer (72) and Vice-Wardens Dampier and Smirke (73) affirmed the original ruling of the Common Bench, that the purser's inability to issue or accept bills was unqualified, so that if he issued a bill in payment for goods, the adventurers could not be sued on the bill, even though they could be sued under the contract of sale for the price of the goods. The consequence of a purser issuing or accepting a bill in the name of his company, therefore, was simply that he made himself liable for payment of its amount (71).

Attempts to establish an implied power for pursers to borrow gave rise to the greatest number of litigated cases among those concerned with the personal liability of adventurers. At first the Common Bench ruled that a purser had no power in any circumstances to borrow on the credit of the adventurers (68), but in 1832 Vice-Warden Wallis permitted a bank, which had advanced money on overdraft to a purser to finance current operations, to recover the amount advanced up to the date the mine closed plus interest from the adventurers (74), and in 1839 Vice-Warden Dampier similarly held adventurers liable to a lender who had advanced a lump sum to finance current work (75). This promising start was cut short in 1841, however, by a decision of the Court of Exchequer that adventurers were not liable to repay loans raised by a purser to meet the necessary and immediate expenses of the mine or to pay miners' wages (76). The decision of the Exchequer was affirmed by the same court in 1847 and 1851 in cases where the adventurers had deliberately abstained from approving the purser's accounts, so that he was forced to borrow in order to keep the mine going (77). In 1847 the Common Bench, too, ruled that in no circumstances whatsoever could a purser borrow without the express authorisation of the adventurers, and that their approval of his opening a bank account did not make them personally liable to the bank if he overdrew on it (78). The ready money principle reached its summit with this ruling, but the court's adherence to it caused great inconvenience to cost book companies, which now found it impossible to borrow on the strength of a contract signed by the purser alone. The application of the principle was also illogical, since the courts at Westminster had already conceded that the purser might buy goods and services on credit, and economically there was no difference between taking credit from the supplier and borrowing from a third person so as to pay the supplier immediately.

In the following years the courts at Westminster and the Vice-Wardens' set about modifying the stark prohibition on borrowing by pursers, so as to do justice between the parties and to bring the law into line with commercial reality. In 1858 the Court of Exchequer held that a lender could recover from the adventurers if the purser borrowed in order to pay an existing debt of the company (79). This meant that loans raised to finance the purchase of mining goods or payments for services to which the company was already contractually committed were recoverable if the company's commitment had not been discharged before the loan was raised. Consequently, loans raised to pay wages to mineworkers for work already completed or work currently being done were binding on the adventurers (80). In 1881 Vice-Warden Fisher carried this exception to the basic prohibition a step further by holding that a lender might recover if his loan was expended on working the mine, even though the company was under no contractual obligation to incur the expenditure at the time the loan was made (81). The original exception rested on the substitution of the lender for the creditor whose debt was paid off with the loan, an equitable process known as subrogation; the extension of the exception involved the equitable concept of tracing the lender's money into the assets acquired or benefited by its expenditure. Both were perfectly respectable equitable devices for doing justice in cases where the loan contract itself was not directly enforceable, and neither involved the complete abandonment of the rule adopted by the common-law courts that the purser did not act as an agent of the adventurers when he accepted a loan.

Another line of cases adopted a third equitable device, that of the indemnity, to modify the effects of the purser's lack of authority to borrow. In 1854 the Chancery Court had held that directors of a joint stock mining company, who, like pursers, had no implied borrowing powers, were entitled to be indemnified by their shareholders for the repayment by them personally of loans raised to meet expenditure required to preserve the mine or continue its working (82). The decision was justifiable, because the directors would have been entitled to an indemnity if they had incurred the expenditure out of their own pockets in the first place, and the decision was used by the Chancery Court two years later to justify awarding an indemnity to a purser who had incurred expenses in running the mine partly by advancing money himself and partly by borrowing from others (83). The interesting point about this latter decision is that the purser had not repaid the loans at the time he sought the indemnity, but the court held that since he was entitled to repay the loans at any time, he was also entitled to be indemnified in advance. Again, this equitable modification of the common-law position did not entail a reversal of the common-law rule. Like the subrogation and tracing exceptions, it only applied when the loan had been spent on improving the mine or carrying on mining operations; if the adventurers had benefited in neither of these ways, the purser could not recover an indemnity.

The decisions of the common-law courts denying pursers power to borrow did not amount to an absolute prohibition, but only to a refusal to imply an authority for them to make the adventurers personally liable to repay loans. If the regulations of the company permitted the purser or committee of management to borrow, all the adventurers would be taken to have authorised them to do so, and so would be personally liable for repayment. Furthermore, if the adventurers passed a resolution in general meeting authorising the purser to borrow, the adventurers who voted for the resolution were personally liable to repay loans contracted under it. It was also possible to make non-assenting adventurers personally liable for future loans to the company by altering the company's regulations so as to give the purser or committee power to borrow. This could be done either under the terms of a provision in the original regulations permitting them to be altered by resolution of the adventurers, or by resorting to the statutory power to alter the regulations by a resolution passed by a simple majority vote and confirmed at a meeting of adventurers held not less than fourteen days later by a three-quarters majority vote (84). A company formed before 24 June 1869 could not, however, exercise the statutory power of alteration to authorise its purser or committee to borrow (84).

The powers and proceedings of meetings of adventurers

Meetings of adventurers of cost book companies were always held at much more frequent intervals than the annual or semi-annual general meetings of joint stock companies. During the eighteenth century, when most of the adventurers resided in Cornwall or Devon within easy distance of the mine, it was customary to hold a meeting once a month, or at least once every two months. Meetings were held frequently because the company had no fixed capital with which to carry on its operations, and unless its current receipts exceeded its expenses and liabilities, it was necessary to make a call on the adventurers to provide the money required. Even if a company had made profitable sales of ore over an extended period, frequent meetings might still be necessary. Under cost book practice the whole of the profits of a company were immediately divided once its accounts were approved by the adventurers; no reserves were kept in hand to meet the outlay of the ensuing financial period, and so a call would be necessary at the end of it unless receipts meanwhile were adequate to cover the outlay on the mine. Since companies sometimes had to wait months before receiving payment for ore sold to the smelters, the occasions when receipts were sufficient to meet current expenses were fewer than they would have been if the smelters had paid cash on delivery, and the need for frequent meetings was so much the greater. During the nineteenth century three-monthly meetings of adventurers became the commonest arrangement to suit the convenience of adventurers who lived at some distance from the mine, but cost book regulations often prescribed other periods for meetings. By the Stannaries Act 1887 cost book companies were required to hold a meeting of adventurers at least once every sixteen weeks (85), though there was of course nothing in the Act to prevent them from being held more frequently.

The procedure for calling a meeting was always prescribed by the cost book regulations. The purser or committee of management were usually directed to call a meeting at specified intervals by sending postal notice of it and sometimes also of the business to be transacted at it to each adventurer at his address registered in the cost book at least seven days before the meeting was to be held, and the posting of the notice was usually deemed to be sufficient communication of it to the adventurer. A Cornwall Convocation Act required the purser to give the adventurers or their agents whose names had been notified in writing to the purser, at least seven days' notice of a meeting called to approve the purser's accounts (86), but otherwise there was no statutory minimum length of notice required for meetings until the Stannaries Act, 1869, required at least seven clear days' notice to be given of meetings called to pass certain important resolutions (87). Adventurers and members of the committee of management individually had no statutory or customary right to call meetings of adventurers, but it was common for a company's regulations to empower adventurers holding a certain number of shares or a certain fraction of all the issued shares to require the purser or committee to call a meeting for a specified purpose, and if the purser or committee failed to call the meeting, the requisitionists were usually empowered to call it themselves.

A quorum was rarely fixed by the company's regulations, and if no quorum was specified, a meeting could be held if it was attended by two or more adventurers or, if the regulations permitted the appointment of proxies or if the company was formed after 24 June 1869 (88), by two or more persons who were adventurers or their proxies (89). Before 1869, however, a meeting to approve accounts or to make calls could not be held unless a majority in number (90) or value (91) of the adventurers or their proxies attended it and voted in favour of approving the accounts or making the call. This requirement was derived from the customary rule that a majority of adventurers had to sign the accounts in the cost book before the purser could sue each adventurer for his appropriate share of costs—that is the excess of the company's expenses and liabilities over its receipts as shown by the accounts (92). The signature by the majority operated as a call without any formal resolution or notification to each adventurer, of the amount payable by him, and when in the nineteenth century cost book regulations formalised the business of meetings of adventurers by making the approval of accounts and the making of calls the subjects of separate resolutions, the same majority presence was required for both resolutions.

The same requirement did not apply to any other resolutions (93). Furthermore, in the case of companies formed after 24 June 1869, resolutions approving accounts and making calls could be validly passed by the simple majority vote of the adventurers or their proxies present at the meeting, without the need for a majority in number or value of all the adventurers to be present or represented (94).

Meetings of adventurers were governed in most respects by the same rules of law as meetings of shareholders of other kinds of companies. Unlike partnerships, in which each partner had one vote irrespective of the amount of capital he contributed, shares in cost book companies carried one vote each, unless the regulations provided otherwise. This was also the rule usually set out in the regulations, though often subject to the qualification that only shares on which all calls had been fully paid might be voted. The Stannaries Act, 1869, likewise attributed one vote to each share by implication from its provision that a resolution passed by a majority in *value* of the adventurers should be binding on all of them, unless the regulations of the company otherwise provided (95), as they might do by disqualifying adventurers in arrear with calls from voting. In respect of the two statutory resolutions for which a three-quarters' majority was required (96), however, it would appear that the regulations could not deprive any share of the single vote attached to it, unless the company was formed before 24 June 1869 (97), and upon such resolutions all adventurers were entitled to vote, whether in arrear with calls or not.

Resolutions were passed by a simple majority of the votes cast, the votes of absent and abstaining adventurers not being counted. But not every transaction could be effected by such a simple majority vote. Although it was once held by the Chancery Court that the regulations of a cost book company could be altered, or at least waived on a particular occasion, by a simple majority vote (98), the better opinion was that before 1869 the company's regulations could not be altered without the consent of every adventurer (99), unless the regulations themselves sanctioned their alteration, as they often did by an absolute or by a two-thirds or three-quarters majority vote. After 24 June 1869 any company, whether newly formed or existing, could alter its regulations by a resolution passed by a simple majority at a first general meeting of adventurers and confirmed by a three-quarters' majority vote of all the shares represented at a second general meeting held between fourteen days and one month after the first (100). Such a power of alteration could not be excluded by the company's regulations, but no alteration could be made if it was inconsistent with the Stannaries Act, 1869 (for example, by excluding the statutory power to forfeit shares or to sell the mine as a going concern); moreover, in the case of an existing company, no alteration could change 'any special rules or regulations existing [on 24 June 1869] for the management of [the] company or authorise the company to borrow' (101).

Even if a company's regulations contained a power for a majority of its adventurers to alter them against the wishes of the minority, the majority could not before 1869 empower the purser to borrow on the adventurer's credit (102), nor resolve to sell the mine and its equipment and materials as a whole (103), nor make calls to meet costs to be incurred in the future in running the mine (104), nor forfeit shares for non-payment of calls (105); and although after the Stannaries Act, 1869, came into force the regulations could be altered for the latter two purposes by following the procedure laid down therein (106), the former two objects could still not be achieved without the unanimous consent of the adventurers. On the other hand, any company could by a simple majority vote resolve to sell its assets piecemeal (107), or to compromise a dispute with another mine, for example, as to boundaries (108), and a company could also perform any recurrent administrative act by a simple majority vote, such as appointing or removing a purser (109). The Stannaries Act, 1869, removed some of the other limitations on the power of the majority of the adventurers, apart from giving a three-quarters' majority power to alter the regulations. No general power to borrow was conferred, but a general meeting, of which seven clear days' notice had been given to the adventurers, could by ordinary resolution make a call to meet the estimated expenses of the company during the following three months (110), and could forfeit shares for non-payment of calls (111). By a resolution passed in the same way as one altering the company's regulations a general meeting could also authorise the sale of 'the machinery and materials belonging to the company with or without the legal or equitable interest of the company in the leases or sett' of its mine, but the sale had to be by public auction after advertisement in a local newspaper and a mining journal in two successive weeks (112).

The most frequent and important item on the agenda was the approval of the purser's accounts. By custom the purser was required to keep accurate records of the company's receipts and payments and stocks of unsold ore, and the Stannaries Act, 1869, clarified and extended this duty by requiring him to enter in the company's cost book at least once every four months all receipts and payments up to the end of the last preceding month, and to show therein all credits (ie amounts receivable), debts and liabilities of the company at the end of that month and all calls paid and remaining unpaid, together with a list of the adventurers (113). In 1887 the accounting period was shortened to sixteen weeks, and the adventurers were empowered to give further directions to the purser as to the detail his accounts should contain (114). The cost book and the purser's accounts had by custom to be laid before the periodic meetings of adventurers for audit and approval, and in 1887 this duty was made statutory and was amplified by requiring the purser also to lay before each meeting a list of adventurers showing arrears of calls owed by them individually; each adventurer was given the right to inspect the documents so laid without any restriction imposed by the company's regulations or otherwise (115). Custom imposed no obligation on the purser to send copies of his accounts to the adventurers either before or after the meeting at which they were laid, but the regulations of several companies required this to be done after the accounts had been audited. In 1887 every purser was subjected to a statutory obligation to circulate printed copies of accounts laid by him before periodic meetings of adventurers, whether approved by the meeting or not, both to the adventurers and to the grantor of the company's sett (116).

SHARES IN COST BOOK COMPANIES

Rights of adventurers: dividends

The principal rights of an adventurer, apart from those specially conferred on him by the company's regulations, were to take part in meetings of the company, to dispose freely of his shares and to receive dividends. The first of these rights has already been dealt with and the second will be dealt with below in connection with the transfer of shares in cost book companies.

It was never judicially settled whether adventurers were automatically entitled to receive their proportionate share of the surplus of their company's receipts over its expenses and liabilities as shown by the periodical accounts approved by meetings of adventurers. As long as the tin ore broken by a company was divided *in specie* between the adventurers after it had been washed, as was the practice until near the end of the eighteenth century, an adventurer had an absolute right to his share of ore if he had paid his share of the costs shown in the accounts approved by the adventurers (117), or if he was willing to pay his share of costs when the accounts had been approved (118), or if he could show that he had paid his share of the costs properly debited and that the accounts submitted by the purser included extra costs which had not really been incurred (119). It is tempting to deduce from this automatic entitlement of each adventurer to his share of ore that when companies went over to paying cash dividends, each adventurer was similarly entitled to his share of surplus receipts shown by the approved accounts without a dividend first being declared by resolution of the adventurers. This deduction was implicitly rejected by a judgment of Vice-Warden Dampier in 1844, however. In the case in question (120) the plaintiff sought a declaration that he was entitled to a certain share in a tin streamworks, the profits of which share the defendant had received in cash for several years. Dampier dismissed the suit on the ground that the plaintiff's claim should have been made against the purser; the plaintiff had no proprietary right to the money paid to the defendant, and so could not trace it into his hands even in equity; all he had was a personal claim against the purser for a sum equal to the dividends the adventurers had resolved to pay and which the purser had wrongly paid to the defendant in respect of the plaintiff's shares. Although this case was not primarily concerned with the legal nature of an adventurer's claim to dividends, it did show that by 1844 his right was as much dependent on a resolution of the company that a dividend should be paid as was the corresponding right of a shareholder of a joint stock company.

Nineteenth-century cost book regulations were remarkably vague on the question of dividends. None of them expressly provided for the declaration of dividends by resolution of the adventurers or, alternatively, for the automatic distribution of surplus receipts among the adventurers after the company's accounts had been approved. The only provision found in most regulations was for the closing of the register of transfers of shares for up to seven days before the dates of meetings of adventurers in order that dividend warrants might be prepared. In practice resolutions declaring dividends, like resolutions making calls, were passed separately from resolutions approving accounts, if only for the purpose of quantifying the dividend payable on each share.

Liabilities of adventurers

The liabilities of adventurers of cost book companies were twofold: first, to pay their respective shares of costs to the purser after the cost book accounts had been audited and a call to meet the deficit of expenses over receipts had been made, and secondly to satisfy the lawful debts and obligations of the company incurred by the purser or the committee of management or with the consent of the adventurers. The procedure for making calls, etc, has already been dealt with, and it only remains to consider here the nature of adventurers' direct liability to creditors for their companies' debts and the ways in which that liability and their liability for calls could be enforced.

By the end of the eighteenth century it had been established by a line of decisions of the Vice-Warden's court dating back to Sir Joseph Tredenham's time that, despite the Cornwall Convocation legislation of 1686 to the contrary, adventurers were jointly liable to creditors without limit for the debts of their adventure incurred by the purser or by those of the adventurers who had been deputed to manage the mine. During the nineteenth century the Vice-Wardens and the courts at Westminster worked out the details of this liability. Vice-Warden Dampier laid down definitively in 1840 that mine creditors could sue any one or more of the adventurers in debt at common law without joining them all as defendants, and could enter judgment for the whole amount owing against the adventurers who were sued (121). The remedy of an adventurer who was compelled to pay more than his proper share of the company's debts was to sue the purser (122) or the other adventurers (123) for an account, but in such proceedings the plaintiff could not recover more than each fellow adventurer's share of the debts, and so if any of them were insolvent the loss fell on the plaintiff (124).

Unlike partners, adventurers of a cost book company were both jointly and individually liable for its debts, which meant that if a creditor sued one or more of them he could later sue the remainder in separate actions (125), and did not lose his remedy against the others as he did if he sued only one or some of the members of a partnership. Because adventurers' liability was individual as well as joint, it became a common practice for pursers and mine creditors to co-operate in collecting calls from dilatory adventurers by a creditor collusively suing individual adventurers for parts of his debt equal to the calls they owed. Thus if a creditor were owed £300 for timber, ropes and mining equipment supplied to the mine, he would sue adventurers in arrear with calls up to an aggregate of £300, the claim against each adventurer being limited to the calls due from him. This was a convenient way of proceeding, since both the calls and the debt were satisfied when the defendant adventurers paid the creditor, but despite this it was held by the Chancery Court in 1858 (126) and by the Court of Queen's Bench in 1878 (127) that such actions were inequitable and would be stayed unless the creditor joined all the adventurers as co-defendants. It is difficult to understand why the courts at Westminster were opposed to creditors limiting their claim against individual adventurers to the amount of calls due from them when there was nothing to prevent creditors from suing adventurers individually for the whole of their claims. However, one result of the decision of 1858 was to stimulate the draftsmen of the Stannaries Act, 1869, to include a provision by which the purser was empowered to sue adventurers for unpaid calls by an action of debt on the common-law side of the Vice-Warden's Court (128).

If the regulations of a cost book company purported to limit the liability of the adventurers for its debts by reference to a nominal value attributed to their shares or otherwise, the limitation was effective between the adventurers themselves, and so restricted the amount an adventurer who had paid the company's debts could recover as a contribution from his fellows (129). The limitation provision was ineffective against creditors of the company, however, because it was inconsistent with the character of a cost book company, and so creditors could sue adventurers individually for the whole amount of their claims, even though they were aware of the provision when they contracted with the company (129).

Customary creditors' suits in equity

In addition to the common-law action of debt that mine creditors could bring against adventurers, they could enforce their claims by proceedings in the Vice-Warden's court of an equitable nature known as creditor's suits or creditor's customary suits. Creditor's suits developed from the rudimentary equitable remedies given to mine creditors by Vice-Warden Tredenham towards the end of the seventeenth century. By the middle of the eighteenth century they took the form of petitions against the adventurers or the purser, or both together, for a decree ordering the payment of the petitioner's debt. If the decree was disobeyed, the Vice-Warden made an order for the attachment and imprisonment of the defendants (130) or an order for the sale of the ore and materials at the mine (131), but the decree could not be enforced by execution against the private property and assets of the individual defendants, as in a successful common law action for debt. Because the Vice-Warden ensured that his decree for payment was carried out by ordering the sale of the adventurers' ore and materials, it became usual to anticipate the order for sale as a mode of execution by the creditor asking for it in his petition, and furthermore substantiating his right to have the ores and materials at the mine sold by alleging in his petition that he supplied goods or services 'as well on the credit of the said [purser] as of the said mine and the adventurers therein' (132), or 'later, as well on the credit of the said mine as of the [purser and named adventurers] and the other adventurers thereof, whose names are unknown to your petitioner' (133).

The change of emphasis in respect of the principal beneficiary of the credit given by the petitioner is significant, because it shows that creditors were now looking for payment primarily to the mining assets of the company working the mine, and that Vice-Warden Borlase's factual observation in 1759 that creditors often did not know who were the adventurers in the mine and relied for payment on the dependability of the purser and the sufficiency of the mine's assets (134), had now ripened into the idea that a mine creditor had rights enforceable against the mine's assets to exact payment. By the early nineteenth century this right had been characterised as a lien or equitable charge on the company's ores and materials at the mine (135), on its ores and tinstuff at the stamps (136), on its blocks of tin at the smelting house (137) and also on its machinery and mining equipment at the mine (138). The lien arose in favour of each creditor as soon as his debt was incurred, and was protected when he presented his petition by the court immediately issuing an interim injunction against the purser and the adventurers and their agents and servants to prevent them removing or disposing of the company's mining assets, including, after 1869, the sett of its mine (139).

The later development of the creditor's suit changed it from one brought by an individual creditor to exact payment out of the company's mining assets into a form of winding-up proceedings in which all mine creditors of the company participated, and under which the proceeds of its mining assets were distributed rateably between them if there was a deficiency. The change was initiated in 1822 in the litigation before Vice-Warden Vivian which resulted in the action in the King's Bench brought by the defendant, Hall, against Vivian in which the legality of the Vice-Warden's equitable jurisdiction was challenged (140). Despite the verdict in favour of Hall in that action after Vivian's withdrawal of his defence, the creditor's suit was revived in 1831 in a case brought before Vice-Warden Wallis (141). Thereafter its legality was repeatedly asserted by Vice-Wardens Dampier and Smirke (142), and no serious attempt was made to establish the contrary. The procedure in the creditor's suit was elaborated in detail by decisions of the Vice-Wardens during the next thirty years, and, until the extension to cost book companies in 1849 of the winding-up procedure for joint stock companies enacted by the Joint Stock Companies Winding-Up Acts, the creditor's suit remained the standard procedure for administering cost book companies' assets for the benefit of their creditors. In fact it was not until the Companies Act, 1862, repealed the earlier winding-up legislation and replaced it by a more workable body of rules that statutory winding-up proceedings began to supersede the creditor's suit.

There were strict limitations on the kind of claims that could be enforced by creditors' suits, and which were therefore protected by the mine creditor's lien, and there were also limitations on the classes of person who could be sued by a creditor's suit. The adventurers of a cost book company could obviously be made defendants to such a suit, though in practice it was brought against the purser as representing the adventurers. But a company incorporated under the Joint Stock Companies Acts or under the Companies Act, 1862, could not be sued by a creditor's suit (143), unless the mine creditor believed that he was dealing with a cost book company at the time the contract was made, and the agent who negotiated the contract for the company did not tell him that it was incorporated (144).

The debt on which a creditor's suit was founded had to be a liquidated claim for a definite sum and not merely a claim for damages for breach of contract (145); it had also to be a mining debt and not merely a debt incurred by the company in connection with its mine. Mining debts included all those within the authority of any purser or committee of management to contract on behalf of their company by implication of law without regard to any more extensive powers conferred by its regulations. Mining debts therefore included a mine captain's wages and loans made to pay miners' wages (146), engine dues in respect of a patented steam engine the inventor had licensed the company to use (147) and charges for building an engine house (148) or for repairing waggons or machinery used at the mine (149). The following, however, were not mining debts, even though the adventurers might be personally liable to pay them if sued in an action of debt, and because they were not mining debts, they were not secured by the mining creditor's lien: the price of a mining undertaking sold as a going concern, even though particular sums were assigned by the sale agreement to machinery, buildings and equipment (150); freeholder's royalties or dues under a sett, though toll tin and dues owing to bounders under a sett were mining debts (151); loans made by a bank or any other person to the company for its general purposes (152); the amount payable to a former adventurer for shares he had relinquished (153); and the costs of an adventurer who successfully defended a purser's suit for calls alleged to be unpaid (154).

Pursers' suits for the payment of calls

Actions of debt and customary creditor's suits were the direct means of enforcing claims by outsiders against adventurers. Pursers' suits were proceedings to enforce the adventurers' obligation to contribute toward the costs and expenses of the company's undertaking and toward meeting such claims by outsiders. A purser's suit presupposed the making of a call on the adventurers to meet these expenses and claims, or alternatively a refusal by them to make a call to meet liabilities already incurred by the purser; his suit was simply an equitable form of proceeding to collect the call or the shares of costs, and it was adopted because of its speed and cheapness compared with the alternative remedy—the equitable suit for an account between the adventurers. It is most probable that the purser's suit, like so many other procedural expedients peculiar to the stannary courts, was invented by Vice-Warden Tredenham to fill the gap in the contemporary rules of common-law and equity. By Tredenham's time both the common-law courts and the Chancery Court permitted a partner to recover a proper contribution from his fellow partners towards the expenses of running the partnership business and paying its debts, but the only forms of proceeding available for this purpose were the common law and the equitable suit for an account, both of which entailed the detailed examination and audit of all the dealings of the firm unless the partners had already agreed or settled a statement of the accounts between them.

In Tredenham's day adventurers did not keep their books of account with the meticulous care of the eighteenth-century cost book companies, and so the equitable suit for an account would have been a cumbersome method of enforcing adventurers' obligations to contribute their rateable shares of current costs. Far more appropriate was the equitable suit for a contribution order the Chancery Court had already evolved, since one co-debtor who had paid the whole debt for which he and others were jointly liable could recover the proper shares the others should have borne. The transaction in such cases was usually a single one, and the only apportionment the court had to make was of one sum of money, so that the taking of accounts was unnecessary. It was not until the eighteenth century that the Chancery Court similarly allowed partners to seek contribution orders against each other in respect of single partnership transactions, but Tredenham saw over half a century earlier that this was precisely the remedy needed to compel adventurers to make their due contributions to current costs (155).

After Tredenham's decrees and orders there is an exasperating gap in the records of the Vice-Warden's court until the earliest surviving volume of Vice-Warden Borlase's orders dating from 1764. In the meantime the Cornwall Convocation had enacted legislation in 1752 dealing with pursers' suits in considerable detail, and it was this legislation, as extended by decisions of the Vice-Wardens, which governed those suits for the next 100 years. What prompted Convocation to intervene will remain a mystery until private records of stannary litigation in the early eighteenth century are forthcoming. Probably some of Tredenham's successors as Vice-Wardens, being less ready to adapt the rules of equity to the special needs of the stannaries, had questioned either the capacity of the purser to sue as such to recover unpaid calls from adventurers, or the power of the court to order the sale of a defaulting adventurer's share of black tin in order to meet his arrears of calls. The enactment of 1752 met this by providing that (156)

> . . . whatever partner, or whatever executor or administrator of any deceased partner or adventurer . . . shall refuse or neglect to contribute and pay the costs and expenses of working such mines and carrying on of such adventures according to and in proportion to [his] share or part . . . in such adventure and undertaking for the space of three months after the account of the costs and expenses of carrying on the said mine has been made up by the purser or clerk and approved of and signed by the major part of the adventurers, and a copy thereof delivered to him, her or them . . . then it shall and may be lawful for . . . [the] Vice-Warden . . . on petition exhibited . . . by the purser or clerk . . . to decree and order such cost to be paid by the defendant or defendants . . . as . . . [the] Vice-Warden shall find to be justly due. And if the said defendant or defendants . . . shall refuse or neglect to pay such costs . . . by the space of one month to be computed from the time or times of such defendant or defendants being served with a copy of such decree or order, then on [a] further application . . . it shall and may be lawful for the . . . Vice-Warden . . . in the first place to order and direct the said defendant or defendants tin stuff at such mine or adventure or at the stamps being broken out of such mine or adventure, to be sold and applied in payment of the said costs and in case there is no tin stuff or not sufficient for the payment of the said costs, then it shall and may be lawful for the . . . Vice-Warden . . . to order and direct the part or share of such defendant or defendants . . . or such part thereof as he shall think fit to be sold by public outcry or survey for so much money as can be had or gotten for the same, and also to order so much of the money raised by such sale as may be sufficient to answer such costs and expenses with cost of suit to be paid into the hands of the purser or clerk for and towards the discharge of the costs of such defendant or defendants respectively and of such costs of suit as shall be awarded to be paid by him, her or them respectively, and the residue of such money (if any) to be paid over to such defendant or defendants. And if it shall happen that the part or share so intended for and offered for sale as aforesaid cannot be sold for any money whatsoever, then such share or part shall be divided, taken up and carried on by the rest of the partners and adventurers in the said mine according to and in proportion to such parts and shares as they then respectively have in the said mine and adventure. . . .

Criticisms may be made of the drafting of this prolix enactment, but the essence of the procedure it laid down is clear enough. The costs of the adventure must first be audited and approved by a meeting of adventurers; the purser must then serve a copy of the audited accounts on each adventurer; if an adventurer had not paid his share of costs within the following three months, the purser could sue him for a decree for payment; if such a decree was not complied with within one month after service of it on the adventurer, the Vice-Warden could order his share of black tin to be sold, and, if that was insufficient to meet the costs in arrear, the Vice-Warden could order the adventurer's share to be sold by public auction; if neither of these measures resulted in the costs being paid, the adventurer's share was forfeited to the other adventurers, although the enactment failed to make it clear whether the forfeiture was automatic, and if so, from what date, or whether it was necessary for the Vice-Warden to make a further decree for forfeiture at the instance of the purser or the other adventurers.

The decrees in pursers' suits made by Vice-Warden Borlase conformed strictly to the Convocation enactment of 1752, often following the wording of the enactment *verbatim*. In fact the only departure of which Borlase can be convicted is allowing the purser to retain out of the proceeds of sale of the defendant's shares in the adventure not only the costs decreed to be paid by him and the costs of the suit but also the expenses of the sale (157). Vice-Warden Thomas, Borlase's next but one successor, did not regard the enactment as limiting the courts' jurisdiction or powers in pursers' suits, and he began a number of innovations which made the proceedings fairer and more effective. In doing this he was fully justified by the history of the purser's suit, which was an equitable suit governed by the general rules of equity as well as by the Convocation enactment. Applying these equitable rules, Thomas refused to allow a purser's suit against one adventurer to proceed if he was not pursuing the other adventurers who had not paid their shares of costs equally vigorously; Thomas would also suspend the effect of a decree for payment made against an adventurer until the purser had given him such information about the company's debts and expenditure as he reasonably requested (158).

In respect of the procedural aspects of the purser's suit, Thomas expedited its three main stages—the decree for payment of the costs in arrear, the order for the sale of the defendant's tinstuff and the order for the sale of the defendant's shares—by allowing two or even all three of the stages to be combined in one decree. In 1788 he began to entertain petitions asking for a decree for payment within a given time, in default of which the defendant's tinstuff would be ordered to be sold by the same decree (159). In 1792 he allowed this to be taken a step further when, on a purser's petition alleging the defendant had no tinstuff, he made a decree for payment within a given time and on the defendant's default directed the immediate sale of his shares, the order for sale being incorporated in the decree for payment (160); after 1797 such petitions became common form. It was, of course, necessary for the purser to prove the insufficiency of the defendant's tinstuff in such cases before he could obtain an order for sale, but this could be done on the hearing of the petition even before a decree for payment had been made (161). The result of Thomas's speeding-up of the proceedings in a purser's suit was that by the first decade of the nineteenth century it had become standard practice for the purser to seek either a decree for payment or a decree for sale of the defendant's shares by his petition, instead of asking for the second as an alternative if the first proved unavailing; if the petition asked for an order for sale, this was made as a matter of course on proof that arrears of costs were unpaid, without any enquiry whether the defendant was entitled to any tinstuff from the mine, a question which it was assumed would be answered negatively, since almost all companies now paid dividends in cash instead of distributing the produce of the mine. When statute in 1836 expressly empowered the Vice-Warden to make decrees for sale instead of decrees for payment (162), Parliament merely ratified what had been the practice of Thomas and his successors during the previous thirty years.

In 1855 statute enabled adventurers to bring suits against one another for contributions in respect of the debts and expenses of the mine (163), thus extending to cost book companies the Chancery practice of sixty years' standing in relation to partnerships. By 1855 the purser's suit was so well established and so effective, however, that this alternative proceeding for collecting calls resolved on by general meetings of adventurers was not used, and the statutory provision remained a dead letter until a decision of the Court of Common Bench in 1858 cast doubt on the validity of the traditional purser's suit. In that case (164) the purser of the East Birch Tor Tin Mining Co of central Dartmoor brought an action of debt on behalf of the adventurers other than the defendants to recover calls the defendants had failed to pay. The Common Bench held quite correctly that at common law a call was not a debt; but even if it were, it was not possible for the purser to sue for it since it was not owed to him personally, and if it was a debt owed to the adventurers other than the defendants, they could not sue for it by making the purser nominal plaintiff. Unfortunately this decision cast doubt on the legality of the purser's suit in equity, although it was governed by entirely different rules, and in 1869 Parliament tried to regularise the whole matter by conferring a statutory power on the purser to sue in debt to recover unpaid calls (165). Smirke clearly saw that pursers' suits in equity were unaffected by the judgment of the Common Bench, for in his opinion on the Stannaries Bill submitted to the Duchy Council, he opposed the introduction of a power for the purser to sue in debt, because he considered the remedies afforded by the purser's suit in equity were more effective (166).

The Stannaries Act, 1869, contained no express provision with regard to pursers' suits in the traditional form apart from a general section preserving the right of a shareholder, creditor 'or other customary suitor' to bring any of the customary suits not expressly abrogated by the Act (167), but this saving clause would, of course, have been effective in keeping pursers' suits alive only if they were legally valid before the Act. Because doubts on this score persisted, it became commoner for financial adjustments between adventurers in small companies to be sought by statutory suits for an account to which all the adventurers were made parties, and after 1869 it was usual for pursers to recover unpaid calls by statutory actions in debt. That this change in practice was quite unnecessary was made manifestly clear when Vice-Warden Smirke entertained pursers' suits of the traditional kind in 1860, 1861 and 1870 (168), and when Vice-Warden Fisher made rules of procedure in respect of such suits in 1876 and 1884. Pursers' suits, like creditors' suits, were only abolished when the Vice-Warden's court itself was dissolved in 1897.

Relinquishment and forfeiture of shares

One of the distinguishing features of a cost book company was the right of any of its adventurers to relinquish or surrender his shares and to require the payment to him of the value of his shares at the date of relinquishment out of the company's assets or by his co-adventurers. The right to relinquish shares was usually expressed in the company's regulations, but it was conferred by cost book custom in any event, and existed even though not expressly mentioned in the regulations (169). In some of the decided cases the adventurer's right of relinquishment was compared to the right of a partner to terminate a partnership at any time he wished if it was not entered into for a fixed period, and the distinction was drawn that in the former case the cost book company was not dissolved but was continued by the other adventurers, whereas in the latter the other partners had to form a new partnership if they wished to continue in business together (170). This gives the misleading impression that the adventurer's right of relinquishment was a mere modification of the rules of partnership law, and that those rules governed cost book companies' shares in other respects. Historically and legally this was not so. The right to relinquish shares in an adventure was a customary right derived from times when adventurers, or at least some of them, worked in the mine personally, and because of this personal element they were not compelled to continue working with their co-adventurers longer than they wished (171). Although by the end of the eighteenth century cost book companies had become associations of investors and not of mineworkers, the personal element was perpetuated by the continued recognition of the right of relinquishment, but by this time the impersonal character of shares in a cost book company had impressed itself on the legal consequences of relinquishment, for instead of having merely a personal claim against his co-adventurers for the value of his share, a relinquishing adventurer was treated as a creditor of the company itself (172).

When relinquishing a share, the adventurer had to give notice of his wish to the purser and to tender at the same time any calls in arrear on the share (173). The notice of relinquishment could be in writing or oral (174) before 1869, when written notice was required by statute (175). A notice of relinquishment might relate to the whole or any part of an adventurer's holding of shares (176), but it seems that it was not possible for a fraction of a single share to be relinquished, even before 1869 when the rule was made statutory (175). The fact that the purser was currently suing the adventurer for unpaid calls did not prevent the latter from serving a notice of relinquishment, unless the court had already made an order for sale of his shares in the purser's suit (177). Likewise, the fact that the company was about to be wound up and that the relinquishing adventurer was a member of the committee of management did not invalidate his notice of relinquishment (178), but it was not possible for any adventurer to relinquish once the mine had ceased working or after proceedings had begun to wind up the company (173); in 1887 statute made notices of relinquishment ineffective if they were served within six weeks of the company being ordered to be wound up by the court or if it had passed a resolution for voluntary winding up (179).

When he served a notice of relinquishment on the purser, the adventurer had to tender all unpaid calls already due on his shares, but he did not have also to tender his share of the accruing costs of the current accounting period (173) unless the company's regulations so provided (180), or unless a call toward meeting future costs had already been made under the statutory power conferred in 1869 (181). Usually cost book regulations required the relinquishing adventurer to pay his share of costs up to the end of the month in which the notice was given, or up to the date of service of the notice on the purser. Calls made by cost book companies were payable immediately, unless the resolution making a call expressly deferred payment until a later date; in that case an adventurer could serve a notice of relinquishment of his shares before that date arrived, and he did not then have to pay or tender the call (182).

The valuation of relinquished shares was made by one or more persons appointed by the purser and the relinquishing shareholder, and if they did not appoint a valuer the court would make the appointment for them. The value of the shares had to be ascertained as at the date the notice of relinquishment was served (183). According to the earlier cases the valuation was to be of the adventurer's rateable share of the value of the ore, materials and machinery (184), plus debts owing to the company (185), less bad debts and debts owed by the company and the cost of bringing up its pitwork to grass (186). In other words, the relinquishing adventurer was to be paid an appropriate share of the break-up value of the mine, that is as though it were going to be closed down immediately (187), which was not necessarily so. In 1883, however, the Court of Appeal held that the mine should be valued as a going concern unless it was in fact about to close down (188), and in most cases this would have resulted in a higher value being put on the relinquishing adventurer's shares. Four years later Parliament reversed this ruling by an enigmatic direction that the valuation of the mine should be made on the assumption that all the other adventurers had relinquished their shares at the same time as the claimant (189), which presumably meant that the valuers were to assume that the company would be wound up immediately and the mine valued on a break-up basis.

Once the value of the relinquishing adventurer's shares had been ascertained, it became a debt owed to him by the other adventurers of the company from the date of his notice of relinquishment (190), but he could not demand payment until two years later (191). The continuing adventurers were jointly and individually liable for the payment of the sum due to the relinquishing adventurer (185), and he could sue all or any one or more of them for the whole sum (192), and could also sue the purser to compel him to raise the sum due out of the company's assets (193). Despite the similarity of the form of a relinquishing adventurer's suit against the purser to a customary creditor's suit, it was not considered to be a creditor's suit (194), and consequently if there was a real mining creditor's suit pending against the purser, the relinquishing adventurer could not claim to share rateably with the mine creditors in the proceeds of sale of the company's ore, materials and machinery (195).

The power of a company to forfeit the shares of an adventurer who failed to pay his share of the costs differed from the adventurer's right of relinquishment in that the initiative was taken by the company to terminate the adventurer's holding and he received no compensation for the loss of his shares. The right to forfeit, or more accurately the right of co-adventurers to petition for an order of forfeiture in respect of a defaulting adventurer's shares, was recognised in the early equity of the Vice-Warden's court (196). It was not uncommon for the regulations of the company to provide for forfeiture expressly, but the court's jurisdiction was not dependent on this. The usual practice, whether the regulations contained a forfeiture provision or not, was for the court to allow the defaulting adventurer a final fixed period within which to pay his share of costs, and if he failed to do so the initial decree provided that his share was 'to stand forfeited, to be divided and shared amongst such adventurers as have or shall pay their cost'. Even after the decree had worked a forfeiture, however, it was possible for the Vice-Warden to re-open the case if the defaulting adventurer proved that he had been prevented from paying in time by fraud or mistake, or that he would suffer exceptional hardship if the forfeiture were to stand, and in that case a further final period for payment could be allowed (197). But such late relief would not be given if the defaulting adventurer had been guilty of inexcusable delay in applying to the court, or if his failure to participate in working the mine or in paying his costs had caused serious loss to his fellow adventurers (198).

During the eighteenth century it became common form to insert a forfeiture clause in the agreement under which the company was formed or in its regulations. This was usual even if the agreement or regulations contained little else beyond such a clause and a provision that the majority opinion should prevail on matters concerning the running of the mine. Consequently, the few recorded cases in the Vice-Warden's court in which forfeiture of shares was decreed during the eighteenth century were cases where the court merely enforced a contractual clause for forfeiture, and the only novelty introduced was that in such cases the court considered it could not give discretionary relief from forfeiture to the adventurer in default (199). The fact that forfeiture decrees were made on the strength of contractual clauses and not under the court's general equitable jurisdiction encouraged the idea that such clauses in a company's regulations were essential, and in 1854 and 1858 the Chancery Court and the House of Lords respectively (200) followed two judgments of Vice-Warden Dampier (201) that gave currency to this idea by ruling that the court could not decree the forfeiture of shares for non-payment of calls unless the company's regulations expressly provided for forfeiture.

The Stannaries Act, 1869, came to the rescue of companies which had no express powers of forfeiture in their regulations by enabling all companies to serve a written notice on an adventurer in default requiring him to pay the call in arrear within a time fixed by the notice, and stating that if he failed to do so his shares would be liable to be forfeited (202). If the notice was not complied with, the company could then forfeit the shares by passing an ordinary resolution at a general meeting of which seven clear days' notice was given to the adventurers, including the adventurer in default (203). The statutory power of forfeiture did not affect such powers conferred by companies' regulations, and a company might exercise either at its option. These contractual powers of forfeiture varied considerably in detail; most of them empowered the committee of management or a general meeting to re-issue forfeited shares to new allottees and to retain the amount paid by them for the benefit of the company.

The company's power to forfeit shares for non-payment of a particular call could be waived expressly or by implication, for example by the purser registering a transfer of the shares to a purchaser (204). A waiver only took effect in respect of the call or calls in arrear when it was made, however, and if later calls on the same shares were not paid, the company had full power to exercise its right of forfeiture in respect of them (205).

The effect of a relinquishment or forfeiture before 1869, unless a cost book company's regulations otherwise provided, was that the shares in question ceased to exist and the quotas of the continuing adventurers were correspondingly enlarged. Consequently, if an adventure was divided into 128 shares and three of them were forfeited or relinquished, each remaining share became a 1/125th share. During the nineteenth century it became usual for a company's regulations to empower the committee of management or the purser with the consent of a general meeting to sell forfeited shares and sometimes relinquished shares as well, and in that case forfeiture or relinquishment obviously could not have been intended to destroy the shares. In this draftsmen of regulations followed the example of the deeds of settlement of joint stock companies, which always provided for the resale of forfeited and surrendered shares. The Stannaries Act, 1869, adopted the same pattern for all cost book companies, despite Smirke's criticism that the exercise was needless and introduced complications where there had previously been simplicity, and that the whole idea of re-issuing or reselling forfeited and relinquished shares was inconsistent with the cost book system (206). The Act provided that forfeited and relinquished shares should be credited to an 'account of forfeited shares' or 'an account of relinquished shares', and that they might be disposed of as the company (ie the committee of management or a general meeting) thought fit, including sale to existing adventurers (207). To assure purchasers of such shares that they would obtain a good title, a statutory declaration by the purser that the forfeiture or relinquishment had been properly carried out and a receipt by the purser for the price paid on the re-issue of the shares was made conclusive evidence of the validity of the forfeiture or relinquishment, and the purchaser of the shares then took them free from all calls due before the date of his purchase (208).

A consequence of the extinguishment of forfeited and relinquished shares under cost book custom was that no purser's suit lay against the former holder of the shares for unpaid calls (209), and although the former holder was not relieved of liability to creditors of the company for debts and obligations incurred before the forfeiture or relinquishment (210), he was not personally liable to creditors for future debts and obligations of the company (211). The Stannaries Act, 1869, altered the law in this connection only by enabling pursers to sue the former holders of forfeited shares for calls unpaid at the time of forfeiture by bringing actions of debt against them (212).

Transfers of shares

By cost book custom an adventurer could transfer any of his shares or a fraction of any one of his shares to whomsoever he wished (213), unless he was restricted by the regulations of the company, for example by a prohibition on the transfer of a fraction of a share, or by a power granted to the committee of management to reject the transfer. The only conditions imposed by cost book custom on this right to transfer shares freely were (1) that all calls unpaid on the shares at the date the transfer was submitted for registration in the cost book had to be paid or tendered by the transferor or transferee (214), or at least payment of such calls had to be offered by one of them if the amount of the calls was unknown (215); (2) that the transfer was not fraudulent (216), but a narrow view was taken of fraud in this connection, so that a transfer to a nominee for the transferor (217), or to a person whom the transferor paid to take his shares to avoid future liability for calls (218), was unobjectionable, and so was a transfer by an adventurer who was a member of the committee of management and who knew at the time the transfer of his shares was registered that the company was about to be wound up (219); and (3) in the case of a transfer of a fraction of a share, that the fraction was not so small as to make the collection of calls and the payment of dividends impracticable (220).

By cost book custom a transfer was effective between the transferor and transferee if made by deed under the seals of the parties, in writing signed by the transferor (221), or merely orally (222), but the regulations of companies invariably required written transfers signed by the transferor and transferee so as to preserve permanent evidence of the transaction and of the transferee's acceptance of responsibility for future calls. By 1830 the form of transfer had become fairly standardised. The instrument of transfer was signed (but not always sealed) by the transferor and transferee, and its wording closely resembled that of a transfer of shares in an incorporated or joint stock company.

A change in the form of transfer soon took place, however, in order to save stamp duty. Deeds of transfer had since 1804 been stamped at a rate dependent on the price paid as 'transfers of stock or shares in any company, society or corporation' (223), but memoranda of sale and transfer of cost book shares which were recorded in the cost book were not stamped at all, and serious doubts were entertained whether they should not bear the same stamp duty. To avoid an issue with the revenue authorities the practice arose during the late 1830s of dispensing with an instrument of transfer altogether and substituting for it either a written notice to the purser signed by the transferor and transferee that the transferor *had* transferred his shares by an instrument of transfer and that the transferee *had* agreed to accept the shares, or a written request to the purser similarly signed and authorising him to transfer the transferor's shares to the transferee in the cost book with the transferee's expressed consent. The instrument of transfer mentioned in the first form of notice was, of course, fictitious, and the object of the new practice was to achieve the desired result of getting the transferee registered in the cost book as holder of the shares without having to produce a document which might be liable to stamp duty. The attempt was successful, for in 1846 Vice-Warden Dampier (224) and in 1849 the Court of Exchequer (225) held that both a notice of transfer and a request for the registration of the transferee were effective authorities upon which the purser could act, but were not subject to stamp duty as instruments of transfer or agreements.

This set the pattern of share transfers for the remaining time that cost book companies functioned. The only addition made during the 1850s was that many companies began to issue certificates stating that they had received a notice of transfer showing the transferee to be entitled to a stated number of shares and that he was registered in the cost book in respect of those shares. These certificates of registration enabled an adventurer to show a *prima facie* title to his shares to a purchaser without resorting to the cost book in the purser's possession, and so fulfilled the same function as the share certificates of joint stock companies, which in the course of time they came to resemble in form. For convenience a blank form of notice of transfer was often endorsed on the certificate of registration issued to adventurers, and when the shares were next transferred the notice was completed and the certificate returned to the company, which replaced it by a new certificate in the name of the transferee. Whether a form of notice of transfer was endorsed on a certificate of registration or not, however, the certificate itself had to be produced before the company could be compelled to register a transfer of the shares, or at least the loss of the certificate had to be satisfactorily accounted for (226). In 1860 Parliament imposed a nominal stamp duty of 6d on notices and requests to pursers to give effect to transfers (227), but this was a small price to pay for the exemption from the duty payable on transfers of shares in joint stock companies, which from 1850 was charged at a rate of $\frac{1}{2}$ per cent on the price paid, and doubled in 1910.

The theory adopted by the Vice-Wardens and the courts at Westminster to explain the legal effect of a transfer of shares in a cost book company was that whether or not there was an instrument of transfer, the act which transferred the legal title to the shares was the entry of the transfer in the cost book by the purser (228). In some early cases the idea seems to have prevailed that it was essential for the transferee to sign the cost book so as to show his acceptance of the shares (229), but in fact this had never been necessary (230), and a later case made it clear that it was the purser's entry of the transfer in the cost book, and not any formal act of the parties, which passed the legal title (231). Nevertheless, the rule that registration passed the legal title did not mean that a transfer was effective even though the transferor and transferee had not consented to it, or even though the transferor had no title or a defective title to the shares. Consequently, where an adventurer signed an instrument of transfer of his shares and delivered it to the person expressed to be the transferee with instructions that it was not to be registered until the adventurer directed, the unauthorised registration of the transfer at the request of the person named as transferee by a purser who was unaware of the instruction did not make the person named as transferee an adventurer (232). Similarly, when an adventurer submitted to the purser an instrument of transfer of his shares to two persons and one of them refused to accept the shares, it was held that the fact that the purser had registered the transfer in the cost book did not vest the legal title to the shares in either of the intended transferees (233).

If a transferor's title to shares was defective, the fact that an unqualified transfer was entered in the cost book by the purser did not give the transferee any better title than the transferor. Consequently, in a case where, after an adventurer had executed an instrument of transfer of his shares but before it had been registered, a charging order had been made by the court against the shares, making them security for a debt owed to a personal creditor of the adventurer, it was held that the transferee, despite his ignorance of the charging order, held the shares subject to it, and could only free them by paying the debt himself (234). For the same reason it was impossible for a transferee to obtain a good title to shares by registration of a transfer if the instrument of transfer was forged, or if the instrument of transfer to a previous registered holder of the shares had been forged, or if the shares had never been issued by the company and a forged certificate of registration in respect of them had been put into circulation.

In situations where the transaction between the transferor and transferee was invalid or the title of the transferor to the shares was defective, the registration of the transferor in the cost book as the owner of the shares at the time of the transaction and the subsequent registration of the transfer to the transferee made no difference to the legal rights of the parties. Although the cost book was conclusive evidence between adventurers as to their titles to their respective shares, so that one adventurer could not challenge another's title to shares registered in his name and so seek to exclude him from dividend distributions (235), the cost book was only *prima facie* evidence of the title of the registered holder when two or more people claimed the same shares, and the validity of their respective claims was determined by the ordinary rules of property law (236). Neither the company itself nor contesting claimants to shares were bound by assertions as to the title to the shares made in the cost book or in share certificates. Cost books were not definitive records of title, and share certificates accompanied by instruments of transfer were not negotiable instruments whose acquisition by a bona fide purchaser would give him a perfect title to the shares.

One would have expected the Stannaries Act, 1869, which assimilated the law governing cost book companies to that governing joint stock companies in many respects, would have adopted the joint stock company rules in respect of share transfers intact. In fact the Act did not do so, but merely confirmed one rule of the existing customary law, namely that a company need not recognise or register a transfer of shares on which calls were in arrear (237), and altered the existing cost book custom in two other respects. The first alteration allowed companies to refuse to recognise or register transfers of fractions of shares (238), a practice permitted though not widely indulged in before the Act. This provision did not invalidate transfers of fractions of shares, and companies were at liberty after 1869 to register fractions if they saw fit and their regulations did not prohibit such transfers. The only effect of the provision was that the transferor and transferee of a fraction of a share could not compel the company to register it.

The second statutory provision, which was drafted by Smirke, was designed to widen the concept of the fraudulent transfer and to preserve the liability of the fraudulent transferor. It read (239):

> A transfer of shares made for the purpose of getting rid of the liability of a shareholder, as such, for a nominal or no consideration, or to a person without any apparent pecuniary ability to pay the reasonable expenses of working a mine, or to a person in the menial or domestic service of the transferor, shall be presumed to be a fraudulent transfer, and need not be recognised by the company, or by the court on the winding up of the company. . . .

Under this provision Vice-Warden Fisher held that a stannary company could disregard a gratuitous transfer made to the transferor's housekeeper one day before a call was made (240), or a transfer of 510 shares for £5 made to a marine corporal unconnected with Cornwall one week before a call of £127 was made on the shares (241), because in both these cases the motive for the transfer was clearly to avoid the impending call. On the other hand, where an adventurer sold his shares in the ordinary way on the Redruth Mining Share Exchange, and the purchaser found by his broker turned out to be insolvent, Fisher held that the company must treat the transfer to the purchaser as valid, for there was no evidence that the adventurer knew even the identity, let alone the financial condition, of the purchaser, and so no motive to avoid future calls could be imputed to him (242). Finally, the Court of Appeal, on appeal from Fisher in the case of the transfer to the marine corporal, ruled that since the statutory provision merely made a transfer falling within it voidable, not void, the company could exercise its statutory power to reject the transfer only within a reasonable time after discovering the transferor's motive, and in any case could not exercise the power after recognising the transfer as effective otherwise than by registering it, for example by forfeiting the shares (243).

CONCLUSION

Although cost book companies retained their distinctive features to the end, the decisions of the Vice-Wardens and of the courts at Westminster during the nineteenth century made the law governing them increasingly resemble that governing joint stock companies, the all-purpose vehicle for all kinds of business enterprises. Also the privilege of limited liability available to joint stock companies after 1856 became increasingly attractive to shareholders in mining concerns as the cost of carrying on their activities grew and personal liability for their debts and obligations became a serious burden. During the 1880s and 1890s cost book companies were mostly converted into limited liability companies registered under the Companies Act 1862, and at the turn of the century there were only three cost book companies left, West Wheal Kitty (St Agnes), East Pool and Agar (Redruth) and Levant (St Just). The first two of these became limited companies in 1911 and 1912 respectively, and Levant, the last survivor, became Levant Tin Mines, Ltd. on 1 January 1920. The cost book era was then ended.

References to this chapter are on pages 212–21.

References

CHAPTER 1

The Stannary Institutions

1 For example, *halvan* (low grade ore put aside for later smelting), related by *Oxford English Dictionary* to the word *half*, but more probably originating from the German *Halden* or *Hallen*; *knack* (to close a mine), which may originate from the Anglo-Saxon *nacian* = to strip (ie to take pitwork out of a mine with a view to abandoning it), or from the German *nageln* = to nail up (ie to close the entrance to a mine); *fathom*, from the Anglo-Saxon *faethrim* (the unit of measurement used in mining, equivalent to, but etymologically unconnected with the German *Lachter* or *Klafter*); dole, from the Anglo-Saxon *dal* = a share (ie in a mine); *skip* from *skep* = a basket or bucket (ie for raising ore); and *kibble* (a bucket for raising ore), from the Anglo-Saxon *cawl* or the German *Kübel*, but also possibly from the Cornish *kyb* = cup or bowl

2 For example, *wheal* (from *whel* = mine); *spallier* (from *spalyar* = mine-worker); *attle* (from *atal* = waste rock or rubble); *buddle*, a container for washing ore (from *budhy* = to drown); *core* (from *cors* = a working period or shift); *gunnies* (from *gonys* = a worked out mine or part of a mine)

3 Pipe Rolls, 5 and 6 Henry II (*Publications of the Pipe Roll Society*, Vol 1, 41 and Vol 2, 51)

4 Pipe Rolls, 8–12 Henry II (*Ibid*, Vol 5, 4; Vol 6, 12; Vol 7, 19; Vol 8, 79; Vol 9, 93)

5 Pipe Roll, 24 Henry II (*Ibid*, Vol 27, 16)
6 Pipe Rolls 6 and 8 Richard I and 1 John (*Ibid*, NS, Vol 5, 171 and 172; Vol 8, 6; Vol 10, 190)
7 The original charter no longer exists, but an *inspeximus* copy of it is contained in a confirmatory charter of 1251 (Charter Roll, 36 Henry III, m 18)
8 Charter Roll, 33 Edward I, m 8, Nos 40 and 41
9 Parliament Rolls, Vol 1, 164, No 50; Vol 2, 144, No 50
10 Parliament Roll (1314), Vol 1, 324, No 168
11 *Ibid* (1347), Vol 2, 190, No 64
12 *Ibid* (1376), Vol 2, 343–5
13 Carew. *Survey of Cornwall* (De Dunstanville Ed 1811), 59
14 The towns appointed by the charters for the coinage of tin were Lostwithiel, Bodmin, Liskeard, Truro and Helston for Cornwall and Tavistock, Ashburton and Chagford for Devon
15 By the end of the thirteenth century the right of feudal lords to tallage their free tenants (and miners were free men, being exempt from pleas of villeinage) was practically obsolete. The King's power to tallage otherwise than with the consent of Parliament was brought to an end in 1306 by the Statute *de tallagio non concedendo* (Statutes, 34 Edward I, stat 4, c 1)
16 In 1347 the Black Prince asserted this privilege by requiring the bailiffs of the port of Dartmouth to release six pieces of tin which they had seized from the Prince's agent for non-payment of port customs at the rate of 4d per thousandweight; the tin was being exported to Flanders to be sold on the Prince's account (Black Prince's Register [1347] fo 139 [PRO Ed, Part I, 121])
17 Charter Roll, 1 Edward III, m 12
18 Patent Roll, 5 Edward IV, part ii, m 7
19 *Ibid*, 23 Henry VII, part ii, mm 29–31
20 Pearce. *The Law and Customs of the Stannaries in the Counties of Cornwall and Devon* (1725); p xi puts it neatly: 'Henry VII (who seldom let slip any opportunity of filling his coffers) made that [the infringements of the ordinances] a pretence . . . to secure the stannaries into his own hands, but finding that it did not turn to such account as he expected was prevailed upon to accept £1,000 for all the pretended forfeitures. . . .'
21 Convocation Act (Devon), 1510, ss 12 and 13
22 *Ibid*, 1532, s 1
23 Thomas Beare in *The Bailiff of Blackmore* (printed in Pearce, *op cit*, xviii) considered that the recording of bounds was part of the custom-

ary law. He wrote at the time of Elizabeth I, and his opinion is therefore valuable because almost contemporary

24 The other commissioners were John Arundell of Tolverne, John Chamond, William Lower and John Chidley

25 The report is set out in an MS volume at the Duchy of Cornwall Office, London, 287 *et seq*

26 Convocation Act (Cornwall), 1588, ss 4 and 5

27 The bill was entitled 'An Act for settling the laws of the Stannaries of Cornwall and Devon and the encouragement of adventurers in tin and the preservation of His Majesty's revenue arising in and by the same'. See *HC Journals*, Vol 9, 418, 421 and 437

28 *HC Journals*, Vol 9, 496 and 501

29 Stannaries Bill of 1677, cl 1

30 *Ibid*, cl 2

31 *Ibid*, cl 3

32 *Ibid*, cl 5

33 *Ibid*, cl 6

34 Report of Commissioners of 1525, para 24; Beare, *op cit*

35 *Trewynnard* v *Roscarrack* (1564), 4 Coke's Institutes 229

36 Convocation Act (Cornwall), 1588, s 36; *Ibid*, 1624, s 40

37 *Black Prince's Register* (1353), fo 54 (PRO, Part 2, 51)

38 *Ibid* (1357), fo 70 (PRO, Part 2, 109)

39 *Ibid* (1357), fo 78 (PRO, Part 2, 122)

40 *Ibid* (1359), fo 98 (PRO, Part 2, 156)

41 *Ibid* (1361), fo 111 (PRO, Part 2, 178)

42 Carew, *op cit* 58

43 The record is set out in E. Smirke's *The Case of Vice* v *Thomas* (1843), 45–52

44 Convocation Act (Devon), 1510, s 16; Convocation Act (Cornwall), 1624, s 22

45 *Vavasor* v *Rowe* (1591), Tothill 157

46 *Boscawen* v *Chaplin* (1536), Sir G. Harrison. *A Report on the Laws and Jurisdiction of the Stannaries in Cornwall* (1829), Appendix Q; *Trewynnard* v *Roscarrack* (1564), 4 Coke's Institutes 229, and Harrison *op cit*, Appendix R

47 *Buesse* v *Woodcock* (1540); *Saintallyn* v *Woodcock* (1540). See *Charters etc. relating to Cornish Mines* (British Museum Add MS. 6317), 129–30

48 *Glanville* v *Courtney* (1593) *supra*

49 Convocation Act (Cornwall), 1588, s 7

50 *Ibid*, s 9

51 Harrison *op cit*, Appendix T

52 A. L. Rowse. *Tudor Cornwall* (1941), 65. The choice of venue was probably not uninfluenced by the fact that the plaintiff's son-in-law, Sir Richard Grenville, was Vice-Warden of Cornwall

53 *Langworthy* v *Scott* (1616), 3 Bulstr 183

54 *Adams* v *Hunt* (1634), Viner's Abr 36

55 Close Roll, 6 James I, part v, m 7. See also Harrison *op cit*, 48–51 and Appendices T and V

56 Convocation Act (Cornwall), 1624, ss 12 and 13

57 Close Roll, 4 Charles I, part ii, no 32.

58 Convocation Act (Cornwall), 1636, s 3

59 Stannaries Act, 1641, s 3

60 *Ibid*, s 4 (1)

61 The previous practice of the stannary courts in Cornwall was to require the defendant to enter a plea to the court's jurisdiction. This was known as a foreign plea

62 Stannaries Act, 1641, s 4 (2)

63 *Ibid*, s 4 (3) and (4)

64 *Ibid*, s 6

65 Convocation Act (Cornwall), 1686, s 20

66 *Ibid*, 1752, s 9

67 *Ibid*, s 11

68 *Ibid*, s 15

69 Hawkins Collection, Royal Institute of Cornwall Museum, Truro

70 *Incledon* v *Trehern* (1682), 3 January; *Courtney* v *Trelawny* (1682), 8 March; *Deker* v *Edwards* (1682), 20 July

71 *Stone* v *Pellow* (1683), 1 May; *Wallish* v *Ellis* (1684), 25 May; *Angwin* v *Williams* (1684), 1 July; *Cogger* v *Ellis* (1686), 23 April

72 *Hicks* v *Harris* (1684), 7 April; *Mill* v *Rogers* (1686), 1 March; *Champion* v *Treveale* (1687), 11 June

73 *Notwell* v *Jenkyn* (1683), 18 January

74 *Betty* v *Tonken* (1683), 12 May; *Borlase* v *Courts* (1685), 21 March

75 *Rogers* v *Incledon* (1686), 19 Sept

76 *Fugars* v *Hoblyn* (1682), 10 March (two weeks); *Trethewy* v *Luly* (1685), 12 December (eight weeks); *Rogers* v *Incledon* (*supra*) (one week after accounts shown to partner); *Edwards* v *Harris* (1687), 11 June (immediately after accounts shown to partner)

77 *Harry* v *Edwards* (1684), 8 April; *Wolridge* v *Hawke* (1686), 16 September

78 See Sir George Harrison, *op cit*, 140

79 *Ibid*, App F1

80 For example *Trevarthen* v *Williams* (1766), 1 January; *Basset* v *Nancarrow* (1766), 1 April; *Hornblower* v *Hall* (1766), 3 September
81 In 1785 the fees of the stewards of Blackmore and Penwith and Kerrier were £25, the steward of Tywarnhaile £17 and the steward of Foweymore nil (Harrison, *op cit*, App F1)
82 Warrants dated 6 September 1800 issued by the Lord Warden, Rear-Admiral Willett Payne (Duchy of Cornwall Office, London)
83 Warrant dated 16 February 1831 issued in the name of William IV (Duchy of Cornwall Office, London)
84 See Harrison, *op cit*, Appendix G1
85 Convocation Act (Cornwall), 1752, s 11
86 Three of the first four decrees in the earliest surviving court book of Vice-Warden Borlase are in pursers' suits, namely *Dunstone* v *Harris* (1764), 5 September; *Brown* v *Le Cheminant* (1764), 10 October; *Wills* v *Le Cheminant* (1764), 10 October
87 The Sale Particulars of the auction, which took place on 6 April 1779 at the Red Lion Hotel, Truro, are in the Gough Collection at the Bodleian Library, Oxford
88 *Simms* v *Stribling* (1789)
89 For an account of the proceedings in the two cases of *Hall* v *Vivian*, see Harrison, *op cit*, 8–16 and Appendix C
90 For an account of the pleadings in the King's Bench action, see Smirke, *The Case of Vice* v *Thomas*, 37, 38
91 *Times, The*, 16 May 1825
92 *Turner and Magor* v *Street and others* (1831), 11 February
93 Warrant dated 4 October 1834 in Letters Patent, Orders and Warrants at Duchy of Cornwall Office, London
94 Harrison, *op cit*, 16–19
95 *Ibid*, Appendix L
96 *Royal Cornwall Gazette*, 11 April 1835
97 *Ibid*, 6 June 1835
98 *Ibid*, 6 November 1835
99 See Falmouth's *A Letter to His Majesty's Commissioners for the Duchy of Cornwall*, dated 4 May 1835 (published London, June 1835)
100 See Bassett's *Remarks and Suggestions as to the Re-establishment of the Mining Courts of the Duchy of Cornwall*, dated 25 March 1836 (published London 1836)
101 The Judicial Committee had been constituted in 1833 primarily to hear appeals from the colonial courts.
102 Stannaries Courts Acts 1836, ss 1, 4, 6 and 41
103 *Ibid*, ss 26–30

104 *Ibid*, s 4
105 *Ibid*, ss 6 and 7
106 *Ibid*, s 13
107 *Ibid*, s 42
108 The major objection was that the Vice-Warden had no equity jurisdiction; the minor, that he had such a jurisdiction, but that creditors' suits were not justified by equity principles.
109 As the result of Convocation Act (Cornwall), 1752, s 16
110 Stannaries Courts Act, 1836, s 1
111 *Rogers* v *Brenton* (1847), 10 QB 26, 62–63. The court rejected the argument
112 *Harvey* v *Reed* (1859), *RCG*, 18 February
113 *Re Wheal Emily Mining Co., Cox's Case* (1863), 4 De G J & S 53, 55–6
114 *Memorandum of the Vice-Warden respecting certain defects in the jurisdiction of the Court:* dated 25 February 1854 (Duchy of Cornwall Office, London)
115 *Hansard's Parliamentary Debates* (*Third Series*), Vol 130, Col 305 (7 February 1854); *HC Journals*, Vol 109, 39
116 Stannaries Court Amendment Act, 1855, ss 3–5
117 *Ibid*, s 1
118 *Ibid*, s 32
119 *Ibid*, s 36
120 *Ibid*, s 23
121 *Procedure in the Court of the Vice-Warden of the Stannaries* (1856), Introductory Notice, x-xviii
122 See *Minutes of a meeting of persons interested in mining held on December 14 1868* (Bolitho Collection, Cornwall County Record Office, Truro). Eighteen persons attended the meeting
123 *Observations of the Vice-Warden on the Stannaries Amendment Bill:* dated 22 March 1869 (Bolitho Collection, Cornwall County Record Office, Truro)
124 Cl 36 of the Bill; s 33 of the Act
125 Cl 38 of the Bill; s 35 of the Act.
126 *Report of the Select Committee of the House of Commons on the Stannaries Act (1869) Amendment Bill*, 1887, *Minutes of Evidence* Q 4719
127 *Minute Book No 6 of Equity Causes in the Stannary Court* (Cornwall County Record Office, Truro)
128 *Winding-up Appearance Book:* January 1863 to August 1890 (*Ibid*)
129 In September 1881 there were twelve uncompleted liquidations, and in March 1894 there were three (Registrar's Accounts for Half Years ending

29 September 1881 and 25 March 1894—Duchy of Cornwall Office, London)

130 *Plaint Books Nos. 7 and 8 of the Stannary Court* (Cornwall County Record Office, Truro)

131 Letter dated January 1892 from Sir R. E. Welby of the Treasury to the Lord Warden, the Earl of Ducie, in correspondence mentioned in note 132

132 Correspondence file entitled 'Stannary Affairs', Duchy of Cornwall Office, London

133 *HL Journals*, Vol 127, 72

134 *Ibid*, Vol 128, 126

135 Stannaries Court (Abolition) Act, 1896, s 1 (1) and (2) and Order of the Lord Chancellor dated 16 December 1896 (SR and O, 1896, No 1106)

CHAPTER 2

Tin Bounding

1 See H. C. Darby and R. W. Finn. *The Domesday Geography of South West England* (1967), 248–9, 318–19 and 364

2 Charter Roll, 36 Henry III, m 18 (*inspeximus* confirmation)

3 *Ibid*, 33 Edward I, m 8

4 Pearce, *The Laws and Customs of the Stannaries of Cornwall and Devon* (1725), ii-iii

5 *Charters etc relating to Cornish Mines*, (British Museum Add MS 6317), 22

6 *Royal Commissioners' Report*, para 25

7 Convocation Act (Cornwall), 1752, s 8(1), re-enacting Convocation Act (Cornwall), 1636, s 4

8 *Charters etc relating to Cornish Mines*, 123

9 *Ibid*, 279, 281

10 *Stephen Trevanion's petition* (1357) *Black Prince's Register* 1357, fo 78, (PRO, Part 2, 122)

11 *Jenkin* v *Davie* (1539), *Charters etc*, 23–5 (a decision of Vice-Warden Godolphin)

12 *Tregurtha* v *Hale* (1766) 5 March (Vice-Warden's Court)

13 *Charters etc*, 71

14 *Ibid*, 127

15 *Royal Commissioners' Report* (1525), para 13

16 Presentation of the customs of Penwith and Kerrier (1616), Smirke *The Case of Vice* v *Thomas* (1843), 62

17 Convocation Act (Devon), 1510, s 3

18 *Ibid*, 1574, s 17
19 *Ibid*, s 20
20 *Rogers* v *Brenton* (1847), 10 QB 26, 68. The decision in *Bastard* v *Smith* (1837), 2 M & R 129, was to the same effect in respect of the tinner's claim to bring water through trenches on privately owned land in Devon for the purpose of washing tin ore
21 Thomas Beare. *The Bailiff of Blackmore* (see Pearce, *op cit*, xiii)
22 Pryce. *Mineralogia Cornubiensis* (1778), 137
23 Beare, *op cit* (see Pearce, *op cit*, xiv)
24 Convocation Act (Cornwall), 1687, s 2
25 Convocation Acts (Devon), 1532, ss 1–4 and 1574, s 36
26 Convocation Act (Devon), 1600, s 5, second part
27 Convocation Act (Cornwall), 1686, s 2
28 *Ibid*, 1752, s 8(4)
29 *Hunt* v *Allen* (1754), 20 January (Blackmore Steward's Court). The papers relating to this action are in the Godolphin Collection, Cornwall County Record Office, Truro.
30 *Rogers* v *Brenton* (1847), 10 QB 26, 50–51
31 *Ivimey* v *Stocker* (1865), 2 Dr & Sm 537
32 *Gaved* v *Martyn* (1865), 19 CBNS 732
33 Convocation Act (Cornwall) 1752, s 8(3)
34 Beare, *op cit* (printed in Pearce, *op cit*, xviii)
35 Printed in Samuel Rowe. *Perambulation of Dartmoor*, 3rd ed (1896), 308
36 *Charters etc*, 104
37 Convocation Act (Cornwall), 1588, s 15
38 Convocation Act (Devon), 1532, s 1
39 *Ibid*, s 2
40 *Ibid*, s 4
41 *Ibid*, s 15
42 Convocation Act (Devon), 1574, s 36
43 *Ibid*, 1600, s 4
44 *Ibid*, s 5, second part
45 *Ibid*, s 3
46 Pearce, *op cit*, xv; *Charters etc*, 85
47 Convocation Act (Cornwall), 1624, s 17
48 *Ibid*, 1636, s 15
49 *Charters etc*, 281, 286 and 287
50 Convocation Act (Cornwall), 1686, s 1
51 *Basset* v *Nancarroe* (1766), 16 April
52 *Hawke* v *Burgess* (1852), *RCG*, 14 May

53 *Donnithorne* v *Andrews* (1786), 6 December; *Smith* v *Williams* (1814), 11 October; *Lord de Dunstanville* v *Pascoe* (1832), 11 December
54 *Vice* v *Thomas* (1842), Smirke, *The Case of Vice* v *Thomas* (1843), 32; 4 Y & C Exch 538
55 *Spry* v *Borlase* (1837), *RCG*, 10 November
56 *Malachy* v *Hitchens* (1839), 13 August
57 *Hewett* v *Emerson* (1839), *RCG*, 16 August
58 *Clowance* v *Hoblyn* (1681), 15 November
59 *Harvey* v *Reed* (1859), *RCG*, 18 February; *Ward* v *Day* (1863), 4 B & S 337
60 Convocation Act (Devon), 1574, s 20 (see above, 76)
61 Convocation Act (Cornwall), 1686, s 2
62 *Basset* v *Basset* (1774) Amb 843
63 Carew, *op cit*, 44
64 Smirke, *op cit*, 60
65 Beare, *op cit* (printed in Pearce, *op cit*, xiv)
66 *Ibid*, xvii
67 *Charters etc*, 116
68 See Smirke, *op cit*, 59
69 Convocation Act (Cornwall), 1686, s 2
70 Convocation Act (Devon), 1532, s 1; *Ibid*, 1574, s 36
71 Beare, *op cit* (printed in Pearce, *op cit*, xvi)
72 *Charters etc*, 116
73 See Smirke, *op cit*, 59
74 Convocation Act (Cornwall), 1624, s 18
75 *Harris* v *Harris* (1682), 20 July; *Edwards* v *Emmett* (1782), 7 October
76 *Pearce* v *Borlase* (1780), 28 May
77 *Pascoe* v *Borlase* (1830), 7 December
78 *Doe d. Earl of Falmouth* v *Alderson* (1837), Smirke *op cit*, 39, 43. This case is also reported in (1837) 1 M & W 211, but the point here discussed is not dealt with in that report
79 Convocation Act (Cornwall), 1752, s 8(4)
80 Convocation Act (Devon), 1510, s 25; *Ibid*, 1533, s 10
81 *Ibid*, 1600, s 3
82 *Ibid*, 1532, s 2; *Ibid*, 1574, s 36
83 Beare, *op cit* (printed in Pearce, *op cit*, xiv)
84 Convocation Act (Cornwall), 1686, s 2
85 *Charters etc*, 116
86 Beare, *op cit* (printed in Pearce, *op cit*, xviii)
87 Convocation Act (Cornwall), 1752, s 8(4)
88 Beare, *op cit* (Pearce, *op cit*, xiv)

89 *Jenkin* v *Davie* (1539), Pearce *op cit*, 165, 166, and *Charters etc*, 153
90 Convocation Act (Devon), 1510, s 25; *Ibid*, 1533, s 10
91 *Ibid*, 1600, s 3
92 Convocation Act (Cornwall), 1636, s 5
93 *Ibid*, s 31
94 *Ibid*, 1752, s 8(3)
95 John Basset. *Origin and History of the Bounding Custom* (1839), 15
96 *Lord de Dunstanville* v *Pascoe* (1833), *RCG*, 12 January; *Thomas* v *Vice* (1838), Smirke, *op cit*, 11 (judgment of Vice-Warden Dampier), *Vice* v *Thomas* (1842) *Ibid*, 35 (judgment of the Lord Warden, Prince Albert). The Lord Warden's judgment is also reported in (1842) 4 Y & C Exch 538. *Lambe* v *Bridgman* (1843), *RCG*, 22 August; *Knight* v *Thomas* (1844), *RCG*, 30 August and 15 November (bounds unworked from 1778 to 1836); *Hawke* v *Burgess* (1852), *RCG*, 6 February (bounds unworked from 1824 to 1836)
97 *Doe d. Earl of Falmouth* v *Alderson* (1837), Smirke *op cit*, 43. The Court of Exchequer's judgment is also reported (1837) 1 M & W 211. The bounds were unworked from before 1800 until 1834
98 Basset, *op cit*, 19–23
99 *Rogers* v *Brenton* (1847), 10 QB 26. The bounds in question were unworked from 1823 to 1842. They were on land which subsequently became part of the Garlidna Mine, Wendron
100 *Ivimey* v *Stocker* (1865), 2 Dr & Sm 537 and (1866), 1 Ch App 396; *Gaved* v *Martyn* (1865), 19 CBNS 732
101 *Att Gen* v *Matthias* (1858), 4 K & J, 579, 591

CHAPTER 3
Mining Setts and Leases

1 A bargain of this kind is mentioned in the *Black Prince's Register* under 5 June 1359. The Black Prince gave notice to his 'lieges and subjects of his Duchy of Cornwall' that he had reserved the mining of Nansmorna and Tresader moors (St Columb) to Henry Trewynnard and fifteen other miners for twelve years (fo 160: PRO Ed, Part 2, 157). The fraction of ore to be rendered by the miners to the Prince was not mentioned
2 Report of the Royal Commissioners on the Stannary Laws (1525), para 25
3 Patent Rolls, 47 Henry III, part i, m 11
4 Charter Roll, 32 Edward III, m 11
5 Patent R, 31 Henry VI, part ii, m 6
6 See Indenture dated 1 February 1762 between Sir Richard Vyvyan and

James Bennetts (Vyvyan Collection, Cornwall County Record Office, Truro)

7 *Doe d Hanley* v *Wood* (1819), 2 B & Ald 724

8 *Trelawny* v *Williams* (1704), 2 Vern 483

9 *Wood* v *Leadbitter* (1845), 13 M & W 838

10 *Wallis* v *Harrison* (1838), 4 M & W 538; *Ackroyd* v *Smith* (1850), 10 CB 164

11 *Hyde* v *Graham* (1862), 1 H & C 593. The earlier decision of *Wood* v *Lake* (1751), Sayer 3, which held that the licensee could lawfully continue to exercise his licence despite revocation, was inconsistent with the later line of authority

12 *Frogley* v *Lovelace* (1859), John 353

13 *Jones* v *Earl of Tankerville*, [1909] 2 Ch 440

14 *Harker* v *Birbeck* (1764), 3 Burr 1556

15 *Hopkins* v *Robinson* (1680), 2 Leo 2; *Wickham* v *Hawker* (1840), 7 M & W 63

16 *Thomas* v *Sorrell* (1671), Vaughan 351; *Wood* v *Leadbitter* (1845), 13 M & W 838, 845

17 *Webb and Paternoster's Case* (1619), 2 Rolle 152; *Harker* v *Birkbeck* (*supra*)

18 *Trelawny* v *Williams* (1704), 2 Ver 483; *Basset* v *Basset* (1774), Amb 843

19 Statute of Frauds (1677), 29 Car II, c 3, s 1

20 *Kittow* v *Liskeard Union* (1874), LR 10 QB 7

21 *Doe d Hanley* v *Wood* (1819), 2 B & Ald 724

22 *Norway* v *Rowe* (1812), 19 Ves 144

23 *Harvey* v *Reed* (1859), *RCG*, 18 February; *Ward* v *Day* (1863), 4 B & S 337

24 *Sampson* v *Easterby* (1830), 6 Bing 644

25 *Michell* v *Carr* (1859), *RCG*, 18 February

26 *Norval* v *Pascoe* (1864), 34 LJ Ch 82

27 *Martyn* v *Williams* (1857), 1 H & N 817

28 *Watson* v *Spratley* (1854), 10 Exch 222

29 *Thomas* v *Hobler* (1861), 4 De GF & J 199; *Re Great Tregune Consols Mining Co.* (1869), *RCG*, 20 May

30 *Clavering* v *Wesley* (1735), 3 P Wms 402

31 *Wright* v *Pitt* (1870), LR 12 Eq 408

32 *Re Great Tregune Consols Mining Co.* (*supra*)

33 *Leach* v *Berriman* (1840), 29 January. The case is reported, but not on this point, in (1840) *RCG*, 1 May

34 *Clowance* v *Hoblyn* (1681), 15 November

35 Indenture dated 9 October 1804 between the Duke of Leeds of the one part and Lewis Charles Daubuz of the other part (Godolphin Collection, Cornwall County Record Office)

36 The mine comprised in the sett, Chywoon, and the adjoining Cobbernoon Mine later became part of the Leeds and St Aubyn mine

37 Stemples originally were the timber beams used to support the roofs of levels or galleries but the term later came to include the upright timbers against the sidewalls which supported the beams

38 *Duke of Bolton* v *Michell* (1781), 5 September; *Duke of Leeds* v *Borlase* (1830), 7 December

39 *St Aubyn* v *Hawke* (1830), 5 October

40 *Sampson* v *Easterby* (1829), 9 B & C 505, affirmed (1830) 6 Bing 644

41 *Michell* v *Carr* (1859), *RCG*, 18 February

42 *Re West Wheal Gorland Mining Co.* (1877), *RCG*, 18 May

43 *Wright* v *Pitt* (1870), LR 12 Eq 408

44 *Earl of Huntingdon and Lord Mountjoy's Case* (1583), 4 Leon 147

45 *Re Pendarves United Mines* (1874), *RCG*, 30 May

46 *Davis* v *Treherne* (1881), 6 App Cas 460

47 *Hext* v *Gill* (1872), 7 Ch App 699

48 *Hunt* v *Roseveor* (1766), 5 November; *Dannithorne* v *Walker* (1781), 2 October

49 *Hichens* v *Lanyon* (1782), 12 June

50 *Duke of Bolton* v *Michell* (1781), 5 September; *Poynter* v *Morcom* (1810), 14 March; *Pascoe* v *Borlase* (1830), 7 December; *Enys* v *Thomas* (1831), 4 October

51 Convocation Act (Cornwall) 1752, s 14

52 *Trelawny* v *Williams* (1704), 2 Vern 483

53 *Doe d Hanley* v *Wood* (1819), 2 B & Ald 724

54 *Thomas* v *Hobler* (1861), 4 De GF & J 199

55 *Roberts* v *Davey* (1833), 4 B & Ad 664

56 *Permeck* v *Provis* (1767), 7 January

57 *Hill* v *Barclay* (1811), 18 Ves 56

58 *Bowser* v *Colby* (1841), 1 Hare 109

59 Common Law Procedure Act, 1852 (15 & 16 Vict, c 76), ss 210–12; Law of Property Amendment Act, 1859 (22 & 23 Vict, c 35), s 4

60 Conveyancing Act, 1881 (44 & 45 Vict, c 41), s 14 (1) and (2)

61 *Ibid*, s 2 (xi)

62 *Ibid*, s 14 (8)

63 *Ibid*, s 2 (ix)

64 *Ibid*, s 14 (6)

65 This was accentuated by the fact that most of the companies were cost book companies, and therefore distributed the whole of their profits as soon as earned, so that they had no revenue reserves to fall back on
66 *Royal Cornwall Gazette*, 30 April 1886
67 Mining Leases (Cornwall and Devon) Bill, 1887, cl 1
68 *Ibid*, cl 6
69 *Ibid*, cl 7
70 *Ibid*, cl 8
71 *Ibid*, cl 5
72 *Ibid*, cl 4. The reference to 'lessors', 'lessees' and 'leases' included grantors, grantees and grants of setts and the parties to agreements for such grants and the agreements themselves (*Ibid*, cl 10)

CHAPTER 4

The Refining and Coinage of Tin

1 *Rawle* v *King* (1780), 7 April; *Edwards* v *Nicholls* (1781), 4 July
2 *Leach* v *Berryman* (1840), *RCG*, 1 May
3 Presentment of a jury of tinners of Foweymore on 30 October 1611 (printed in Smirke *The Case of Vice* v *Thomas*, 59, 61)
4 Convocation Act (Devon) 1494, ss 7 and 8; Ordinance of Prince Arthur (Cornwall), 1496, art 2 (see *Charters etc relating to Cornish Mines* (British Museum, Add MS 6317), 101); Charter of Pardon 1507, by which the tinners were pardoned '*qui non introduxerunt signa possesserum dicti stanni in dictum Scaccarium in Lostwithiel*', clearly contemplating that the owner's mark should be impressed on blocks of tin
5 *Charters etc. relating to Cornish Mines*, 242
6 *Ibid*, 47; *M.S. Volume of Stannary Law* at Duchy of Cornwall Office, 287
7 The only case in which this custom was judicially approved was *Boscawen* v *Chaplin*, decided by Vice-Warden Godolphin in 1536 on the presentment of the custom by a jury of twelve tinners and twelve merchants. Probably the bill in this case was not a smelter's bill, but a coinage bill issued by the receiver of the coinage when the tin was deposited for assessment of coinage duty. The case is set out in Sir George Harrison's *A Report on the Laws and Jurisdiction of the Stannaries in Cornwall*, Appendix Q
8 Convocation Act (Devon), 1510, s 13; Convocation Act (Cornwall), 1588, s 45

9 *Tippet* v *James* (1863), *RCG*, 13 November
10 Convocation Act (Devon), 1533, s 6
11 *Ibid*, s 3
12 Convocation Act (Cornwall), 1636, s 21, re-enacted by *Ibid*, 1686, s 16
13 *Ibid*, 1686, s 16
14 *Ibid*, 1752, s 10
15 Convocation Act (Devon), 1494, ss 6–8; Ordinances of Prince Arthur (Cornwall), 1495 or 1496, arts 1 and 2
16 Convocation Act (Devon), 1494, s 6. The Ordinances for Cornwall, art 1 were to the same effect.
17 Convocation Act (Devon), 1510, s 15
18 *Ibid*, 1494, s 9; Ordinances for Cornwall, 1495 or 1496, art 3
19 Convocation Act (Devon), 1510, s 12
20 *Ibid*, 1552, s 2
21 Good tin or soft tin was that obtained by the first smelting of ore, and because of its low viscosity was run off from the furnace into a long vat or float before it was cast in blocks. Hard tin, obtained from re-smelting the slag, was more viscous, and was therefore run off into a short float
22 Convocation Act (Devon), 1552, s 3
23 Convocation Act (Cornwall), 1588, s 47
24 *Ibid*, s 48
25 Pryce. *Mineralogia Cornubiensis*, 283 and 325
26 Convocation Act (Cornwall), 1624, s 9
27 *Ibid*, s 10
28 *Ibid*, 1636, s 10
29 *Ibid*, 1686, s 19
30 *Ibid*, 1752, s 3
31 *Ibid*, s 4
32 Convocation Act (Devon), 1510, s 13
33 Convocation Act (Cornwall), 1624, s 2
34 *Ibid*, s 3
35 *Ibid*, 1636, ss 7 and 8
36 *Ibid*, 1752, s 1
37 *Ibid*, s 10
38 *Ex. p. Concanen* (1833), *RCG*, 16 November and 14 December
39 Convocation Act (Cornwall), 1752, s 17
40 Charter R, 33 Edward I, m 8, Nos 40 and 41
41 Pat R, 2 Edward III, part i, m 28
42 State Papers (Domestic), Vol 76, 68 and Vol 77, 45
43 *Black Prince's Register*, 1357, fo 82 (PRO, Part 2, 129)

44 Patent R, 10 Eliz I (1569), part vi, no 1412. This patent directed the Midsummer coinage to be held at Liskeard on 21 and 22 June, at Lostwithiel from 23 to 25 June and at Truro and Helston on the accustomed days; the Michaelmas coinage was to be held at Helston from 28 to 30 September, at Truro from 1 to 3 October, at Liskeard on 5 and 6 October and at Lostwithiel from 7 to 9 October

45 See Convocation Act (Devon), 1510, s 4

46 *Report of the Royal Commissioners on the Laws and Customs of the Stannaries*, 1525, para 18

47 The Christmas coinage was not officially inaugurated until 1674 (Calendar of Treasury Books and Papers, 1672–5, 632), but it was held regularly for a century previously

48 Convocation Act (Cornwall), 1636, s 33

49 *Ibid*, 1686, s 29. Each coinage at Liskeard was to last for two working days, at Lostwithiel for six, at Truro for twelve, at Helston for six and at Penzance for two

50 Convocation Act (Cornwall), 1686, s 33

51 Lewis. *The Stannaries* (1908), 150–51

52 Lewis was here speaking of the period up to the sixteenth century. In later times coinages were attended only by adventurers, mine agents and smelters and their agents

53 Patent R, 33 Edward I (1304), part i, m 10; confirmed by Pat R, 9 Edward III (1335), part i, m 8 and Pat R, 16 Richard II (1393), part iii, m 4

54 Convocation Act (Cornwall), 1636, s 33

55 *Charters etc, relating to Cornish Mines*, 254

56 Convocation Act (Cornwall), 1686, s 31

57 *Boscawen* v *Chaplin* (1536)—see above, 129; *Harry* v *Edwards* (1684), 9 June

58 Convocation Act (Devon), 1510, ss 4 and 30

59 *Ibid*, 1552, s 5

60 Convocation Act (Cornwall), 1588, s 44

61 *Ibid*, 1624, s 4

62 *Ibid*, 1636, s 9

63 *Ibid*, 1686, s 17

64 *Ibid*, 1752, s 2

65 *Ibid*, 1624, s 5

66 *Royal Cornwall Gazette*, 29 March, 5 and 19 April and 24 May 1833

67 House of Commons Journal, Vol 93, 46 (23 November 1837)

68 *Hansard's Parliamentary Debates* (3rd Series), Vol 44, cols 1166–7 and 1295

69 Statutes 1 and 2 Vict, c 120
70 *Ibid*, s 1
71 *Ibid*, ss 2 and 3
72 *Ibid*, s 8

CHAPTER 5
Mining Companies

1 This was as late as the sixteenth century (Carew. *Survey of Cornwall*, De Dunstanville ed, 1811, 44)
2 The earliest reported authority for this is *Anon* (1595), Noy 55, a case in the Court of Common Bench, but the rule was much older
3 Convocation Act (Devon), 1533, s 9
4 Beare. *The Bailiff of Blackmore* (printed in Pearce. *The Law and Customs of the Stannaries of the Counties of Cornwall and Devon*, 1725, xvi)
5 Convocation Act (Devon), 1510, s 17; Convocation Acts (Cornwall), 1624, s 22 and 1636, s 19
6 Convocation Act (Cornwall), 1686, s 5
7 *Stoddard* v *Williams* (1818), 8 September and (1819), 4 May
8 Convocation Act (Cornwall), 1686, s 6
9 *Ricketts* v *Bennetts* (1847), 4 CB, 686
10 *Notwell* v *Jenkyn* (1683), 18 January
11 *Warne* v *Williams* (1687), 5 March
12 *Clements* v *Mill* (1687), 1 March
13 *Hicks* v *Harris* (1684), 7 April
14 *Tonkyn* v *Betty* (1683), 12 May
15 *Rawle* v *Usticke* (1759), reported in Harrison's *Report on the Laws and Jurisdiction of the Stannaries of Cornwall*, Appendix G1
16 *Simms* v *Stribling* (1789). The appeal papers are contained in a volume entitled *The Dartmoor Appeal*, 1787–1789, at the Duchy of Cornwall Office, London
17 *Edwards* v *Worth* (1780), 2 September; *Edwards* v *Borlase* (1783), 11 June; *Atkinson* v *Drew* (1837), *RCG*, 28 April
18 *Garland* v *Jones* (1801), 7 January; *Harvey* v *Blewett* (1813), 2 March; *Thomas* v *Wallis* (1820), 3 October; *Turner* v *Street* (1831), 1 February; *Leach* v *Berryman* (1840), *RCG*, 1 May
19 *Edwards* v *Borlase* (1783), 11 June; *Colliver* v *Tippet* (1848), *RCG* 10 May
20 Opinion of Wallis dated 24 January 1829 (set out in Harrison. *A Report on the Laws and Jurisdiction of the Stannaries of Cornwall*, App H1); *Atkinson* v *Drew* (1837), *RCG*, 28 April (see also the notebook of

Dampier's judgments between 1837 and 1840 at the Cornwall County Record Office, 8, 13 and 14)

21 *Harvey* v *Tippet* (1837), *RCG*, 3 November

22 *Vice* v *Tweedy* (1849), *RCG*, 16 February; *Watson* v *Spratley* (1854), 10 Exch 222; *Hayter* v *Tucker* (1858), 4 K & J 243

23 *Simmons* v *Pryn* (1807), 7 December; *Graves* v *Cook* (1856), 2 Jur NS 475; *Tweedy* v *Field* (1858), *RCG*, 21 May

24 *Richards* v *Simmons* (1852), *RCG*, 13 February

25 *Magor* v *Trevarton* (1850), 9 February

26 *Winn* v *Spargo* (1842), *RCG*, 26 August; *Stainsby* v *Moyle* (1842), *RCG*, 26 August

27 *Re Great Cambrian Mining Co., Richardson's Case* (1856), 4 WR 670

28 *Chester* v *Spargo* (1868), 18 LT (NS) 314

29 *Jennings* v *Broughton* (1853), 5 De M & G 126

30 *Robson* v *Earl of Devon* (1857), 3 Jur NS 576. It is questionable whether this decision was correct in the light of the later case of *Redgrave* v *Hurd* (1881), 20 Ch D 1

31 *Johnson* v *Goslett* (1856), 18 CB 728

32 *Johnson* v *Goslett* (1857), 3 CBNS 569

33 *Colliver* v *Tippet* (1848), *RCG*, 12 May

34 *Greenwood* v *Davis* (1837), *RCG*, 10 November

35 *Greenwood* v *Davis* (*supra*). Dampier's ruling on this point is set out fully in the notebook of his judgments at the Cornwall County Record Office, 31; *Colliver* v *Tippet* (*supra*)

36 Stannaries Act, 1869, s 9

37 *Ibid*, 1887, s 31, repealed by the Companies (Consolidation) Act 1908, s 286

38 *Ibid*, s 32, repealed by the Stannaries Court Abolition Act, 1896, s 5

39 *Warne* v *Tarker* (1687), 6 February; *Chaffers* v *Woolmer* (1857), 30 LT (OS), 126

40 *Thomas* v *Hosking* (1788), 1 October

41 *Harvey* v *Gundry* (1819), 2 March

42 *Vivian* v *Fegan* (1848), *RCG*, 18 February

43 Stannaries Court Amendment Act, 1855, s 22

44 *Re Condurrow Mining Co.* (1864), *RCG*, 19 August; *Re Tincroft Mining Co.* (1875), *RCG*, 27 February

45 *Re Tincroft Mining Co.* (*supra*)

46 *Re Great Wheal Vor Mining Co.* (1861), *RCG*, 23 August

47 *Re West Devon Great Consols Mine* (1884), 27 Ch D 106

48 *Atkinson* v *Drew* (1837), 24 April (set out in the notebook of Vice-Warden Dampier's judgments, 7–8)

49 *Hawken* v *Bourne* (1844), 8 M & W 703; *Gray* v *Strickland* (1855), *RCG*, 24 August

50 *Dickinson* v *Valpy* (1829), 10 B & C 128, 137 *per* Bayley, J; *Ricketts* v *Bennetts* (1847), 4 CB 686, 699 *per* Wilde, C. J.; *Newton* v *Daly* (1858), 1 F & F 26 *per* Watson, B.

51 *Harris* v *Vivian* (1780), 4 October; *Greenwood* v *Davis* (1837), *RCG*, 3 November; *Harrison* v *Stephens* (1852), *RCG*, 3 September

52 *Bennetts* v *Malachy* (1840), *RCG*, 20 November; *Re Wheal Emily Mining Co.* (1865), *RCG*, 24 February; *Re Clifford Amalgamated Mines, William's Case* (1871), *RCG*, 18 February

53 *Newton* v *Daly* (1858), 1 F & F 26

54 *Dickinson* v *Valpy* (1829), 10 B & C 128. There were alternative grounds for the decision, namely that the purser had no authority to borrow or to issue bills of exchange on the company's behalf

55 *Tredwen* v *Bourne* (1840), 6 M & W 461; *Hawken* v *Bourne* (1844), 8 M & W 703; *Re German Mining Co.* (1853) 22 LJ (NS) Eq 926

56 *Lawler* v *Kershaw* (1827), M & M 93; *Ellis* v *Schmoeck* (1829), 5 Bing 521; *Harvey* v *Kay* (1829), 9 B & C 356

57 *Elliott* v *Trevarthen* (1754), 7 October; *Blewitt* v *Gundry* (1780), 22 April; *Gluyas* v *Eady* (1784), 13 May; *Harvey* v *Blewett* (1813), 7 September

58 *Jones* v *Wills* (1780), 28 May

59 *Harvey* v *Blewett* (1813), 13 September

60 *Bennetts* v *Malachy* (1840), *RCG*, 20 November

61 *Trevarthen* v *Williams* (1766), 1 January

62 *Vivian* v *Fegan* (1848), *RCG*, 18 February

63 *Ellicott* v *Kite* (1843), *RCG*, 12 May

64 *Ward* v *Strickland* (1764), 5 September; *Keast* v *Walford* (1785), 5 December; *Busson* v *Parnall* (1804), 4 July

65 *Hornblower* v *Gundry* (1797), 5 April

66 *Leach* v *Berryman* (1840), *RCG*, 1 May

67 *Cardozo* v *Roscrow* (1848), *RCG*, 1 September

68 *Dickinson* v *Valpy* (1829), 10 B & C 128

69 *Praed* v *Gundry* (1820), 1 February

70 *Harvey* v *Hitchens* (1838), *RCG*, 27 July; *Hodge* v *Webb* (1855), *RCG*, 18 May

71 *Owen* v *Van Uster* (1850), 10 CB 318

72 *Brown* v *Byers* (1847), 16 M & W 252

73 *De Tastet* v *Southey* (1847), *RCG*, 27 August; *Tweedy* v *Field* (1858), *RCG*, 21 May

74 *Turner* v *Street* (1832), 1 May. The adventurers appealed to the Lord

Warden, but after a hearing before Samuel Croker, the Deputy Lord Warden, in June 1834, the suit was settled by a compromise between the parties (see the case of *Teague* v *Turner*: Duchy of Cornwall Office, London)

75 *Ferris* v *Thomas* (1839), *RCG*, 1 February
76 *Hawtayne* v *Bourne* (1841), 7 M & W 595
77 *Brown* v *Byers* (1847), 16 M & W 252; *Burmester* v *Norris* (1851), 6 Exch 796
78 *Ricketts* v *Bennetts* (1847), 4 CB 686
79 *Brown* v *Kidger* (1858), 3 H & N 853
80 *Re West Gwennap Consols Mining Co.* (1877), *RCG*, 11 May
81 *Re Frank Mills Mining Co.* (1881), *RCG*, 3 June
82 *Re German Mining Co., Ex p. Chippendale* (1854), 4 De G M & G 39
83 *Re Court Grange Silver Lead Mining Co., Ex. p. Sidgwick* (1856), 2 Jur NS 949
84 Stannaries Act, 1869, ss 6 and 7
85 *Ibid*, 1887, s 25
86 Convocation Act (Cornwall), 1686, s 5
87 Stannaries Act, 1869, s 5. The resolutions in question were resolutions to alter the company's regulations (s 7), to approve accounts and make calls (s 10), to forfeit shares for non-payment of calls (s 17) and to sell the company's undertaking as a going concern (s 24). The Stannaries Act, 1887, added resolutions to amalgamate mines (s 27)
88 The Stannaries Act, 1869, s 4, by implication permitted adventurers of newly formed companies to appoint proxies to vote for them at meetings. The implication may also have extended to existing companies
89 *Sharp* v *Dawes* (1876), 2 QBD 26
90 *Greenwood* v *Davies* (1837), *RCG*, 10 November; *Smith* v *Williams* (1838), *RCG*, 4 May. The judgments in these cases are more fully set out in the notebook of Vice-Warden Dampier's judgments at the Cornwall County Record Office, on 31 and 32–3, and 61 and 65 respectively
91 *Murchison* v *Richardson* (1864), *RCG*, 20 May; *Watson* v *Tom* (1866), *RCG*, 31 May; *West* v *Bigge* (1869), *RCG*, 13 May. This third case was an appeal to the Lord Warden, who was assisted by Lord Westbury and Erle, C.J.
92 *Harris* v *Vivian* (1780), 23 September; *Thomas* v *Hosking* (1788), 1 October
93 *Dymond* v *Fuller* (1860), *RCG*, 24 August
94 Stannaries Act, 1869, ss 4 and 10
95 *Ibid*, s 4
96 *Ibid*, s 7 (resolution to confirm an alteration of the regulations); and

Ibid, s 24 (resolution to see the company's undertaking as a going concern)
97 *Re Stray Park Mine* (1869), *RCG*, 13 November
98 *Re Bodmin United Mines Co.* (1857), 23 Beav 370, 382 *per* Sir J. Romilly, MR
99 *Harrison* v *Stephens* (1852), *RCG*, 3 September
100 Stannaries Act 1869, ss 6 and 7
101 *Ibid*, s 7
102 *Re East Wheal Basset Mining Co.* (1877), *RCG*, 24 August
103 *Bennetts* v *Jenkin* (1845), *RCG*, 21 November
104 *Harrison* v *Stephens* (1852), *RCG*, 3 September; *Grylls* v *Semmons* (1861), *RCG*, 15 November
105 *Clarke* v *Hart* (1854), 6 De G M & G 232 and (1858), 6 HL Cas 633
106 *Harrison* v *Stephens* (*supra*); *Re Stray Park Mine* (*supra*)
107 *Hicks* v *Rule* (1847), *RCG*, 28 August
108 *James* v *Nankivell* (1780), 5 July
109 *Thomas* v *Hosking* (1787), 31 October; *Wyatt* v *Coade* (1807), 9 November; *Polkinghorne* v *Reynolds* (1818), 17 July
110 Stannaries Act, 1869, s 11. But the resolution had to be passed separately from a resolution for a call to meet expenses and liabilities already incurred (*Grylls* v *Semmons, supra*)
111 *Ibid*, s 16
112 *Ibid*, s 24. Authorisation for such a sale could also be given by the holders of three-quarters of the company's shares in writing without holding a meeting
113 *Ibid*, s 9
114 *Ibid*, 1887, s 23
115 *Ibid*, s 25
116 *Ibid*, s 26
117 *Cook* v *Nicholls* (1780), 4 April
118 *Benbow* v *Michell* (1780), 2 August
119 *Prout* v *Richards* (1780), 4 April
120 *Knight* v *Thomas* (1844), *RCG*, 30 August
121 *Leach* v *Berryman* (1840), *RCG*, 1 May
122 *Stainsby* v *Moyle* (1842), *RCG*, 26 August
123 Convocation Act (Cornwall) 1686, s 6
124 *Winn* v *Spargo* (1842), *RCG*, 26 August; *Stainsby* v *Moyle* (*supra*)
125 *Re Wheal Ludcott and Wrey Consols Mine Co., Ex p. Jackson* (1869), 21 LT (NS) 67
126 *Sibley* v *Minton* (1858), 27 LJ Ch 53

127 *Escott* v *Gray* (1878) 47 LJ QB 606
128 Stannaries Act, 1869, s 13
129 *Re Court Grange Silver Lead Co., De Castro's Case* (1856), 2 Jur NS 1203
130 *Provess* v *Weston* (1765), 6 March; *Provis* v *Gare* (1767), 7 January; *James* v *Prout* (1780), 4 April
131 *Brokenshire* v *Bray* (1780), 10 April; *Keast* v *Walford* (1785), 6 December; *Davis* v *Swan* (1789), 10 June. In *Atkinson* v *Drew* (1837), *RCG*, 28 April, it was said that the first order for sale was made in *Warren* v *Holebrook* (1769), a decision of Vice-Warden Borlase
132 *Oxnam* v *Legge* (1780), 3 May
133 *Gluyas* v *Eady* (1784), 13 May
134 *Rawle* v *Usticke* (1759), 6 January
135 *Cock* v *Nicholls* (1780), 4 April; *Edwards* v *Nicholls* (1781), 4 July; *Daniell* v *Tyack* (1794), 3 December
136 *Prout* v *Walford* (1785), 13 December; *Honey* v *Hall* (1786), 2 August
137 *Edwards* v *Thomas* (1778), cited in *Atkinson* v *Drew* (*supra*)
138 *Garland* v *Jones* (1801), 7 January
139 Stannaries Act, 1869, s 36
140 *Hall* v *Vivian* (1823–5). The case before Vivian was *Heath* v *Hall* (1822), 1 October. For an account of *Hall* v *Vivian*, see above, 52
141 *Turner* v *Street* (1831), 1 February
142 *Atkinson* v *Drew* (1837), *RCG*, 28 April (see notebook of Dampier's judgments at the Cornwall County Record Office, 6, 7–8); *Tyacke* v *Teague* (1848), *RCG*, 18 February; *Harvey* v *Reed* (1859), *RCG*, 18 February
143 *Re Devon Kapunda Mining Co. Ltd., Truscott* v *Cook* (1861), *RCG*, 1 March
144 *Griffin* v *Bennets* (1876), *RCG*, 28 November
145 *Harper* v *Williams* (1838), 20 July (see notebook of Dampier's judgments, 67)
146 *Bennetts* v *Malachy* (1840), *RCG*, 20 November
147 *Hornblower* v *Gundry* (1797), 1 March
148 *Vivian* v *Fegan* (1848), *RCG*, 18 February
149 *Ellicott* v *Kite* (1843), *RCG*, 12 May
150 *Tonkin* v *Abbott* (1840), *RCG*, 31 January; *Cardozo* v *Roscrow* (1848), *RCG*, 1 September; *Hocking* v *Clymo* (1850), *RCG*, 10 May
151 *Harvey* v *Reed* (1859), *RCG*, 18 February
152 *Willyams* v *Thomas* (1865), *Mining Journal*, 30 September
153 *Cardozo* v *Roscrow* (*supra*)
154 *Parry* v *Bottrall* 1855), *RCG*, 24 August

155 *Hamilyan* v *Pellew* (1683), 1 May; *Mill* v *Roger* (1686), 1 March; *Warne* v *Tarker* (1687), 1 March
156 Convocation Act (Cornwall), 1752, s 11
157 *Brown* v *Le Cheminant* (1764), 10 October and 5 December
158 *Hosking* v *Thomas* (1788), 3 September; *Thomas* v *Hosking* (1788), 1 October and 5 November
159 *Thomas* v *Wallis* (1788), 3 December; *Thomas* v *Bounce* (1789), 10 June; *Pascoe* v *Perry* (1793), 2 October
160 *Phillips* v *Goodwin* (1792), 4 July
161 *Thomas* v *Borlase* (1789), 4 March; *Williams* v *De Chevalier* (1797), 3 May
162 Stannaries Courts Act, 1836, s 18
163 Stannaries Court Amendment Act, 1855, s 4
164 *Hybart* v *Parker* (1858), 4 CB (NS) 209
165 Stannaries Act, 1869, s 13
166 *Observations of Vice-Warden Smirke on the Stannaries Bill,* dated 22 March, 1869. (Duchy of Cornwall Office, London). See to the same effect W. J. Rawlings. *On the Stannary Amendment Bill of 1869 and on the Cost Book System* (Truro, 1869), 11
167 Stannaries Act, 1869, s 46
168 *Dymond* v *Fuller* (1860), *RCG*, 24 August; *Grylls* v *Semmons* (1861), *RCG*, 15 November; *Buckley* v *Carter* (1870), *RCG*, 13 August
169 *Re Prosper United Mining Co., Ex. p. Palmer* (1872), 7 Ch App 186
170 *Re Pennant and Craigwen Consolidated Lead Mining Co. Fenn's Case* (1854), 4 De G M & G 285, 293 *per* Cranworth, L.C.; *Lanyon* v *Smith* (1863), 8 LT (NS) 312, 313 *per* Blackburn, J.
171 *Harry* v *Edwards* (1684), 8 April *per* Vice-Warden Tredenham
172 *Tremayne* v *Reed* (1793), 17 April; *Vivian* v *Simmons* (1797), 3 May
173 *Re Pennant and Craigwen Mining Co., Fenn's Case* (*supra*); *Re Prosper United Mining Co. Ex. p. Palmer* (1872), 7 Ch App 286
174 *Northey* v *Johnson* (1852), 19 LT (OS) 104
175 Stannaries Act, 1869, s 22
176 *Viner* v *Noell* (1863), *RCG*, 20 February
177 *Williams* v *Edwards* (1791), 4 April. This was a decision of the Lord Warden, Viscount Lewisham, on appeal from Vice-Warden Thomas. The papers in the appeal proceedings are at the Duchy of Cornwall Office, London
178 *Re Kilbricken Mines Co., Libri's Case* (1857), 30 LT (OS) 185
179 Stannaries Act, 1887, s 22
180 *Re Cuddra Mine, Tate* v *Hitchens* (1873), *RCG*, 31 May
181 Stannaries Act, 1869, s 11

182 *Re Mixon Copper Mining Co., Edward's Case* (1860), 1 LT (NS) 399
183 *Re Prosper United Mining Co., Ex p. Palmer* (1872), 7 Ch App 286
184 *Harry* v *Edwards* (1684), 8 April; *Tremayne* v *Reed* (1793), 17 April
185 *Provis* v *Harvey* (1822), 23 July
186 *Bowden* v *Williams* (1795), 14 October
187 *Re Cuddra Mine, Tate* v *Hitchens* (*supra*)
188 *Re Frank Mills Mining Co.* (1883), 23 Ch D 52
189 Stannaries Act, 1887, s 21
190 *Provis* v *Harvey* (*supra*); *Harvey* v *Vivian* (1824), 6 January; *Re Prosper United Mining Co., Ex. p. Palmer* (*supra*)
191 *Re Prosper United Mining Co., Ex. p. Palmer* (*supra*); *Re Treleigh Wood Mining Co.* (1877), *RCG*, 30 November
192 *Tremayne* v *Reed* (*supra*); *Provis* v *Harvey* (*supra*); *Harvey* v *Vivian* (*supra*)
193 *Badwen* v *Williams* (*supra*); *Vivian* v *Simmons* (1797), 3 May; *Daubuz* v *Warren* (1828), 3 October
194 *Cardozo* v *Roscow* (1848), *RCG*, 29 August
195 *Harvey* v *Mitchell* (1856), *RCG*, 15 February
196 *Fugars* v *Hoblyn* (1682), 10 March; *Biggs* v *Hayman* (1685), 10 March; *Rogers* v *Incledon* (1686), 12 October; *Edwards* v *Harris* (1687), 11 June
197 *Trethewey* v *Luly* (1685), 12 December
198 *Matthew* v *Sawle* (1672), 29 July
199 *Bennett* v *Libby* (1795), 14 October
200 *Hart* v *Clarke* (1854), 6 De G M & G 232, affirmed on appeal *sub nom* *Clarke* v *Hart* (1858) 6 HL Cas 633
201 *Smith* v *Williams* (1838), *RCG*, 4 May; *Bennetts* v *Jenkin* (1846), *RCG*, 4 September. For a fuller account of Dampier's judgment in *Smith* v *Williams* see the notebook of his judgments between 1837 and 1840 at the Cornwall County Record Office, 61, 66
202 Stannaries Act, 1869, s 16
203 *Ibid*, s 17
204 *Paddon* v *Pentecost* (1848), *RCG*, 25 August
205 *Watson* v *Tom* (1866), *RCG*, 31 May
206 *Observations of Vice-Warden Smirke on the Stannaries Bill* dated 22 March, 1869 (Duchy of Cornwall Office, London)
207 Stannaries Act, 1869, ss 18 and 21
208 *Ibid*, ss 19 and 23
209 *Buckley* v *Carter* (1870), *RCG*, 13 August
210 *Lanyon* v *Smith* (1863), 8 LT (NS) 312; *Harvey* v *Clough* (1863), 8 LT (NS) 324

211 *Northey* v *Johnson* (1852), 19 LT (OS) 104; *Lanyon* v *Smith* (*supra*); *Viner* v *Noell* (1863), *RCG*, 20 February
212 Stannaries Act, 1869, ss 13 and 20
213 *Harvey* v *Jeffery* (1837), 15 July (Vice-Warden Dampier's judgment is set out at p 57 of the notebook of his judgments between 1837 and 1840 at the Cornwall County Record Office); *Harvey* v *Tippet* (1837), *RCG*, 10 November
214 *Simmons* v *Vivian* (1820), 27 June; *Boase* v *Phillips* (1846), *RCG*, 20 November. The company could not refuse registration of a transfer because other debts owed to it by the transferor were unpaid—*Bruton* v *Hodge* (1847), *RCG*, 19 November
215 *Harvey* v *Tippet* (1837), *RCG*, 10 November; *Watson* v *Eales* (1857), 23 Beav 294 and (1856) 26 LJ Eq 361
216 *Smith* v *Williams* (1838), *RCG*, 5 May; *Re Pennant and Craigwen Mining Co., Fenn's Case* (1854), 4 De G M & G 285, 296
217 *Angove* v *Thomas* (1806), 1 January; *Re Wheal Emily Mining Co., Cox's Case* (1863), 4 De G J & S 53; *Bryant* v *Nicholls and Tonkin* (1884), *RCG*, 29 February
218 *Re Hafod Lead Mining Co., Slater's Case* (1866), 35 Beav 391
219 *Re Kilbricken Mines Co., Libri's Case* (1857), 30 LT (OS) 185
220 *Harvey* v *Jeffery* (*supra*)
221 *Landeryon* v *Williams* (1835), *RCG*, 2 September
222 *Northey* v *Johnson* (1852), 19 LT (OS) 104
223 The duty was first imposed by the Stamp Act 1804, Schedule A, and was increased by the Stamp Act 1815, Schedule, Part I. The duty went up in steps from £1 when the purchase price did not exceed £50, to £3 when it did not exceed £500, to £9 when it did not exceed £1,000, and to £12 when it did not exceed £2,000
224 *Michell* v *Chipman* (1846), *RCG*, 15 May
225 *Toll* v *Lee* (1849), 4 Exch 230
226 *Re East Wheal Martha Mining Co.* (1863), 33 Beav 119, 121
227 Stamp Act, 1860, s 11 and Schedule: Cost Book Mines. The imposition was re-enacted in 1870 and 1891 and was belatedly abolished in 1949
228 *Michell* v *Chipman* (1846), *RCG*, 28 August; *Toll* v *Lee* (1849), 4 Exch 230; *Landeryon* v *Williams* (1853), *RCG*, 2 September; *Nicholls* v *Rosewarne* (1859), 6 CB (NS) 480; *Re Wrysgan Slate Quarry Co., Ex. p. Humby* (1859), 28 LJ Ch 875; *Bryant* v *Nicholls and Tonkin* (1884), *RCG*, 29 February
229 *Harvey* v *Kay* (1829), 9 B & C 356
230 *Benbow* v *Michell* (1780), 23 September; *Williams* v *Benbow* (1781), 3 January

231 *Richards* v *Cleave* (1849), *RCG*, 24 August
232 *Thomas* v *Clark* (1856), 18 CB 662
233 *Vice* v *Fleming* (1827), 1 Y & J 227
234 *Nicholls* v *Rosewarne* (1859), 6 CB (NS) 480
235 *Curling* v *Flight* (1847), 6 Hare 41
236 *Basset* v *Reynolds* (1846), *RCG*, 4 September, affirmed on appeal to the Lord Warden (1847), *RCG*, 3 September
237 Stannaries Act, 1869, s 14
238 *Ibid*, s 15
239 *Ibid*, s 35
240 *Re Wheal Unity Consols* (1870), *RCG*, 19 November
241 *Re Wheal Unity Wood Mining Co.* (1879), *RCG*, 22 August
242 *Re Great South Work Mining Co.* (1879), *RCG*, 30 May
243 *Re Wheal Unity Wood Mining Co., Chynoweth's Case* (1880), 15 Ch D 13

Appendix

LORD WARDENS OF THE STANNARIES OF CORNWALL AND DEVON

	Date of Appointment
William de Wrotham	20 November 1197
William de Putot (Cornwall)	8 September 1220
John fitz Richard and Stephen de Croy (Cornwall)	24 November 1220
Waleran Teutonicus (Devon)	8 February 1221
Richard de Langeford (Devon)	2 January 1234
Adam Wymer (Devon)	27 January 1253
Ralph de Oddiscumb (Devon)	9 February 1262
Hugh Peverel (Devon)	8 December 1264
Walter de Aylesbury (Cornwall)	1289
Thomas de la Hyde (Cornwall)	1306
John de Bedewynde (Cornwall)	1312
Thomas Lercedekne (Cornwall)	1314
Henry de Wylyngton (Cornwall)	1318
Simon Belde and Gilbert de la Forde (Devon)	12 July 1321
Thomas de Shirygg (Devon)	1328
Richard Caleware (Devon)	28 February 1328
William de Montacute (Devon)	8 June 1330
Thomas West (Cornwall)	4 March 1337
Sir Edmund de Kendale (Cornwall)	1346
Bartholomew de Burghersh (Devon)	1350
Sir John Dabernon (Cornwall)	1350
Robert de Elford (Cornwall)	1357
Sir John Dabernon (Cornwall)	1359
Bartholomew de Burghersh, the Younger	1361
John de Skirbec (Cornwall)	1366
John Cary (Devon)	1375

Sir John de Kentwode (Cornwall)	26 August 1378
Richard Ruyhale (Devon)	13 September 1385
Richard Breton (Cornwall)	1 April 1386
John de Coplestone (Devon)	15 March 1388
Sir Philip de Courtenay (Cornwall)	13 November 1388
Warin Waldegrave (Devon)	25 June 1389
John Colshull (Cornwall)	24 February 1392
Richard Chelmswyke (Cornwall)	26 February 1397
John Wynter (Cornwall)	29 September 1399
John de Waterton (Devon)	29 September 1399
Sir John Arundell (Cornwall)	8 December 1400
John Willecotes (Devon)	2 April 1413
John Coplestone and Thomas Congreve (Devon)	24 November 1422
Lewis Johan (Devon)	10 February 1423
Philip Courtenay (Cornwall)	18 February 1430
Sir John Bonevile (Cornwall)	8 November 1437
Ralph Babthorp (Cornwall)	31 December 1439
Thomas Courtenay, Earl of Devon (Cornwall)	7 May 1441
William de la Pole, Marquis of Suffolk	22 October 1442
John Trevelyan (Cornwall)	30 October 1442
Thomas Courtenay, Earl of Devon (Cornwall)	7 May 1444
John Trevelyan (Devon)	30 October 1446
Sir William Bonevile (Cornwall)	8 March 1452
Thomas Clemens (Cornwall)	1 May 1461
Sir Humphrey Stafford (Cornwall)	15 June 1461
Roger Dynham (Devon)	18 July 1461
John Dynham (Devon)	17 October 1469
Sir John Stafford (Cornwall)	7 November 1469
Walter Courtenay (Devon)	20 September 1485
Sir John Haleweyll (Cornwall)	12 October 1486
Robert Willoughby de Broke	9 December 1502
Sir Henry Marney	18 May 1509
Henry Courtenay, Marquis of Exeter	27 May 1523
Sir John Russell	4 July 1539
Edward Seymour, Duke of Somerset	1548
John Russell, Earl of Bedford	1552
Sir Edward Hastings	4 April 1555
Francis Russell, Earl of Bedford	13 April 1572
Sir Walter Raleigh	10 September 1584
William Herbert, Earl of Pembroke	27 January 1603
Philip Herbert, Earl of Pembroke and Montgomery	30 August 1630
John Grenville, Earl of Bath	22 June 1660
Charles Bodville, Earl of Radnor	24 January 1701
John Granville (later Baron Granville)	19 June 1701
Francis Godolphin, Earl Godolphin	7 May 1705
Hugh Boscawen, Viscount Falmouth	27 April 1708
Col John Schutz	6 December 1734
Thomas Pitt	6 May 1742
James Waldegrave, Earl Waldegrave	23 August 1751
Humphrey Morice	29 July 1763

George Legge, Viscount Lewisham (later Earl of Dartmouth)	13 November 1783
Sir John Morshead	6 April 1798
Rear-Admiral Sir John Willett Payne	30 April 1800
Thomas Tyrwhitt	18 November 1803
Francis Charles Seymour, Earl of Yarmouth (later Marquis of Hertford)	25 July 1812
Albert, Prince of Saxe-Coburg and Gotha	16 April 1842
Henry Pelham, Duke of Newcastle	6 February 1862
Edward Berkeley, Baron Portman	20 January 1865
Henry John Reynolds, Earl of Ducie	19 December 1888
Alexander Hugh Bruce, Baron Balfour of Burleigh	27 March 1908
Charles John Robert Hepburn-Stuart-Forbes-Trefusis, Baron Clinton	22 October 1921
William Robartes, Earl of Radnor	5 May 1933
Geoffrey Noel Waldegrave, Earl Waldegrave	2 July 1965

VICE-WARDENS OF THE STANNARIES OF CORNWALL

Sir William Godolphin	c 1529
William Beare	c 1540
Sir Thomas Smith	1548
Sir William Godolphin	1554
Sir Richard Grenville	1578
William Carnsew	1580
Sir Francis Godolphin	1586
Christopher Harris	1591
William Coryton	1603
John Mohun, Baron Mohun	1627
William Coryton	1630
John Trefusis	1641
William Scawen	1660
Sir John Trelawney	1678
Sir Joseph Tredenham	1681
John Waddon	1689
Hugh Tonkin	1701
Sir Richard Vyvyan	1702
Walter Moyle	1708
John Gregor	1711
Thomas Hearle	1723
John Hearle	1740
Christopher Hawkins	1744
Francis Gregor	1747
John Hearle	1751
Rev Walter Borlase, LLD	15 November 1756
Henry Rosewarne	17 May 1776
John Thomas	23 August 1783
John Vivian	19 March 1817
John Wallis	11 December 1826

John Lucius Dampier	7 August 1834
Edward Smirke	2 July 1853
Herbert William Fisher	1 October 1870

VICE-WARDENS OF THE STANNARIES OF DEVON

John Sapcote	c 1490
Sir Thomas Deneys	c 1510
Sir Philip Champernown	1532
Sir John Charles	1551
Sir Nicholas Slanning	c 1688
Samuel Rolls	c 1704
William Bickford	1763
Warwick Hele Tonkin	26 November 1784
Richard Gurney	25 November 1812
John Parry	16 February 1818
John Farnham Cock	2 June 1824
John Wallis	26 November 1826
Thomas Commins	19 January 1827
John Lucius Dampier	14 December 1850
Edward Smirke	2 July 1853
Herbert William Fisher	1 October 1870

Index